Studies in Global Justice

Volume 20

In today's world, national borders seem irrelevant when it comes to international crime and terrorism. Likewise, human rights, migration, climate change, poverty, inequality, democracy, development, trade, bioethics, hunger, war and peace are all issues of global rather than national justice. The fact that mass demonstrations are organized whenever the world's governments and politicians gather to discuss such major international issues is testimony to a widespread appeal for justice around the world.

Discussions of global justice are not limited to the fields of political philosophy and political theory. In fact, research concerning global justice quite often requires an interdisciplinary approach. It involves aspects of ethics, law, human rights, international relations, sociology, economics, public health, and ecology.

Studies in Global Justice takes up that interdisciplinary perspective. The series brings together outstanding monographs and anthologies that deal with both basic normative theorizing and its institutional applications. The volumes in the series discuss such aspects of global justice as the scope of social justice, the moral significance of borders, global inequality and poverty, the justification and content of human rights, the aims and methods of development, global environmental justice, global bioethics, the global institutional order and the justice of intervention and war.

Volumes in this series will prove of great relevance to researchers, educators and students, as well as politicians, policymakers and government officials.

More information about this series at http://www.springer.com/series/6958

Christodoulos Kaoutzanis

The UN Security Council and International Criminal Tribunals: Procedure Matters

Springer

Christodoulos Kaoutzanis
Stamford, CT, USA

ISSN 1871-0409 ISSN 1871-1456 (electronic)
Studies in Global Justice
ISBN 978-3-030-23776-9 ISBN 978-3-030-23777-6 (eBook)
https://doi.org/10.1007/978-3-030-23777-6

This Springer imprint is published by the registered company Springer Nature Switzerland AG.
The registered company address is: Gewerbestrasse 11, 6330 Cham, Switzerland

In memory of my grandparents,
Christodoulos Kaoutzanis
Thaleia Kaoutzani
Dimitrios Protopapas
Lydia Protopapa

Preface

Since the end of the Cold War, the United Nations Security Council ("UNSC") has a leading role in investigating atrocities. Yet, the UNSC has only authorized the investigation of atrocities committed in 11 out of the 92 states that have experienced atrocities during this period. This book examines the reasons behind this disparity. To do so, this book examines how past studies on atrocities investigations do not account for the work of the UNSC in this field and how past studies on the UNSC cannot explain its actions on atrocities investigations. Instead, by relying on historical records and interviews with participants in the UNSC's deliberations on atrocities, this book argues that the UNSC's decisions on which atrocities to investigate are committee projects, which can only be understood through the prism of the UNSC's decision-making process. Because of the constraints imposed by the UNSC process, an atrocities investigation will take place only after (i) a diplomat brings specific atrocities to the attention of the UNSC, (ii) an independent commission of inquiry supports the creation of an atrocities investigation, and (iii) the UNSC members agree with the text of the authorizing resolution. This book examines the decisions behind each of these three steps and highlights how the decision-making process guides and influences the UNSC's actions. By doing so, it provides an explanation on the UNSC's disparate record vis-à-vis atrocities.

Stamford, CT, USA Christodoulos Kaoutzanis

Acknowledgments

This book has benefited from the assistance and guidance of many individuals. Most of all, it benefitted from the constant attention of Professor Michael W. Doyle, University Professor at Columbia University, who nurtured its argument when it was only an idea, challenged its findings when these were only preliminary, and strongly supported the book as a finished product. He also guided me during the publication process. Beyond this book, Professor Doyle's thinking and analysis have had a profound influence on me.

This book has also benefitted from the attention of Professor Petros C. Mavroidis, the Edwin B. Parker Professor of Foreign and Comparative Law at Columbia Law School. Professor Mavroidis read every draft I gave him and challenged multiple assumptions of my work. Among his countless jokes, I learned an immense amount from his questions and observations, and the book has a much more coherent argument because of him.

This book improved due to the pointed questions and debates with a number of other academics at Columbia University. Professor Matthew C. Waxman brought a sense of pragmatism and practicality to an often theoretical discussion, which improved the focus of my research and the findings of the book. Professor Jack L. Snyder and Professor Johannes Urpelainen engaged with, and advanced, the substance of this work as members of my Ph.D. dissertation committee. Similarly, Professor Andrew J. Nathan provided guidance in the early stages of the research, always providing incisive and helpful comments. In 2014, while conducting the research for this book, I presented the materials on the role of diplomats that ended up forming Chap. 5 at the International Studies Association Annual Convention in Toronto, where Naazneen Barma, Associate Professor of the National Security Affairs at the Naval Postgraduate School in Monterey, California, served as discussant and gave me valuable constructive feedback.

This book has also benefitted from a number of anonymous reviewers, who provided constructive comments on all parts of the manuscript. It has also received the detailed attention of the Springer team, including Neil Olivier, Executive Editor; Deen Chatterjee, Series Editor; and Diana Nijenhuijzen, Assistant Editor.

Beyond the academic setting, while writing this book, I received the encouragement of several family members. My father, Marios Kaoutzanis; my mother, Photini Kaoutzani; my sister, Lydia Kaoutzani; and my brother, Dimitrios Kaoutzanis were always there to support and cheer. My father-in-law, Michael Courtney, also read a draft and, together with my mother-in-law, Vivian Courtney, encouraged me along the way.

In particular, my father, Marios Kaoutzanis, has always been the biggest supporter of this book. He read a number of drafts of this work and made several hundred stylistic edits and suggestions in order to ensure that this book is correct in substance and appearance. He also constantly encouraged me to keep working on the book, even at times when I had doubts. Without his help, this project likely would not have reached this final form.

My wife, Jocelyn Courtney Kaoutzanis, has had an immeasurable influence on this book, one that would require a book of its own to document. She served as sounding board, research assistant, editor, timekeeper, and talisman. Together with our daughter, Fotini Josefina, she also provided me emotional support to get this book over the finish line. In the final stages of this book, she also gave birth to our son Mikhael Glafkos. While she may deny it, this is her product as much as its mine.

I am grateful for all.

Contents

About the Author

Christodoulos Kaoutzanis, a native of Nicosia, Cyprus, holds a Ph.D. degree from the Department of Political Science, Columbia University. He graduated magna cum laudae from Georgetown School of Foreign Service, Washington D.C. He also earned a J.D. degree at Columbia Law School, where he was a Harlan Fisk Stone Scholar and a James Kent Scholar, and an LL.M. cum laudae from the University of Amsterdam in International Criminal Law. His academic focus is placed on the intersection of international law and international relations, with a focus on the reactions of the United Nations Security Council to mass atrocities. His publications also examine issues of international criminal justice. He speaks Greek, English and French.

Abbreviations

AFRC	Armed Forces Revolutionary Council, paramilitary group in Sierra Leone's civil war
CDF	Civil Defense Forces, paramilitary group in Sierra Leone's civil war
DfID	Department for International Development, United Kingdom
E10	Elected ten member states of the United Nations Security Council
ECCC	Extraordinary Chambers in the Courts of Cambodia
ECOMOG	Economic Community of West African States Monitoring Group
ECOWAS	Economic Community of West African States
IAEA	International Atomic Energy Agency
ILC	United Nations International Law Commission
ICC	International Criminal Court
ICTR	International Criminal Tribunal for Rwanda
ICTY	International Tribunal for the Prosecution of Persons Responsible for Serious Violations of International Humanitarian Law Committed in the Territory of the Former Yugoslavia since 1991
NATO	North Atlantic Treaty Organization
NPRC	National Provisional Revolutionary Council, junta in Sierra Leone
NGO	Nongovernmental Organization
OLA	United Nations Office of Legal Affairs
P5	Permanent five member states of the United Nations Security Council
RPF	Rwandan Patriotic Front, Tutsi paramilitary group in Rwanda's civil war
RUF	Revolutionary United Front, paramilitary group in Sierra Leone's civil war
SCSL	Special Court for Sierra Leone
UK	United Kingdom
UN	United Nations
UNFICYP	United Nations Peacekeeping Force in Cyprus
UNMSIL	United Nations Mission in Sierra Leone
UNSC	United Nations Security Council
USA	United States of America
WHO	World Health Organization

List of Maps and Graphs

List of Tables

Chapter 1
Introduction

> *Over a month ago the United States proposed to the United Kingdom, Soviet Russia and France a specific plan, in writing, that these four powers join in a protocol establishing an International Military Tribunal, defining the jurisdiction and powers of the tribunal, naming the categories of acts declared to be crimes, and describing those individuals and organizations to be placed on trial. Negotiation of such an agreement between the four powers is not yet completed.*
>
> *Justice Robert Jackson, Report to the President on Atrocities and War Crimes, June 7, 1945.*
> (Jackson 1945)

Abstract The Introduction presents the main question of this book, namely why the 15 members of the UNSC decide to investigate some atrocities, but fail to do so for others, and then offers an overview of this book's argument that the UNSC three step decision-making process matters. The Introduction also presents the research sources used to develop this argument and presents the structure of the subsequent chapters. It concludes by defining some core terms.

On July 14, 2008, the Prosecutor of the International Criminal Court ('ICC'), Luis Moreno-Ocampo, requested from the judges of the ICC's Pre-Trial Chamber the issuance of an arrest warrant for President of Sudan, Omar al Bashir. Moreno-Ocampo explained that "there are reasonable grounds to believe that Omar Hassan Ahmad Al Bashir…bears criminal responsibility under the Rome Statute for the crime of genocide…for crimes against humanity…and for war crimes."[1] From a legal perspective, Moreno-Ocampo's presentation of evidence and law convinced the judges. They issued the arrest warrant against Bashir. But, since Sudan is not a

[1] Public Redacted Version of the Prosecutor's Application under Article 58, ICC-02/05 (July 14, 2008).

C. Kaoutzanis, *The UN Security Council and International Criminal Tribunals: Procedure Matters*, Studies in Global Justice 20,
https://doi.org/10.1007/978-3-030-23777-6_1

party to the Rome Statute (i.e. Sudan is not a member of the ICC), how did Moreno-Ocampo have the power to prosecute Bashir? How could the ICC pierce Sudan's sovereignty by authorizing an investigation into the actions of its government and targeting its head of state? The answer to these questions lies in United Nations Security Council ('UNSC') Resolution 1593,[2] whereby the members of the UNSC created the international atrocities investigation into Darfur.[3] The goal of this book is to clarify the political dynamics in international affairs behind such UNSC decisions.

Judicial investigations take place for only a small number of atrocities, creating a peculiar situation for international politics. Victims of overlooked atrocities justifiably complain that their perpetrators should also face justice. Those alleged perpetrators under investigation, perhaps also justifiably, complain that they should not be tried and punished for acts that routinely go unpunished. The world is rife with such examples. The RUF atrocities in Sierra Leone became the focus of an international criminal tribunal, while nothing happened for the RUF atrocities in neighboring Liberia and Guinea. The ICC is investigating the atrocities committed by the Qaddafi regime in Libya, but it is not doing so for the worse atrocities committed by the Assad regime in Syria. The politics of international justice for atrocities are such that these disparities often appear within the same country and at the same time. In Rwanda, for example, the ICTR has not investigated crimes committed by Tutsis against Hutus, but has focused on those committed by Hutus against Tutsis. In Cambodia, while Khmer Rouge leaders are on trial for crimes they committed between 1975 and 1979, the temporal span of the international investigation has been restricted to exclude crimes committed by the Khmer Rouge before their rise to power in 1975 and after their fall in 1979.

While such disparities relating to issues of international criminal justice abound, this book focuses on the actions of the UNSC and its decisions to initiate international criminal investigations in the post-Cold War period. As illustrated in Map 1.1 below, out of the 92 states that have experienced atrocities since the end of the Cold War, the UNSC has authorized the creation of international atrocities investigations in only five instances, which cover only 11 states. The limited number of atrocities that the UNSC has investigated is even more puzzling as some of the five investigations authorized by the UNSC target atrocities that are very similar to other atrocities that have not received an investigation. For example, the UNSC created an atrocities investigation for the Hutu-Tutsi atrocities committed in Rwanda in 1994, but not for the Hutu-Tutsi atrocities committed in neighboring Burundi from 1993 until 2005. Similarly, the UNSC created an investigation into the suppression of the Arab Spring in Libya by Colonel Qaddafi, but not for similar or worse atrocities arising out of the suppression of the Arab Spring in other countries (e.g. Syria, Egypt, Bahrain). So, *why do the 15 members of the UNSC decide to investigate some atrocities, but fail to do so for others*? This is the question this book will answer.

---

[2] S/RES/1593 (2005).

[3] Darfur is a region in the western part of Sudan.

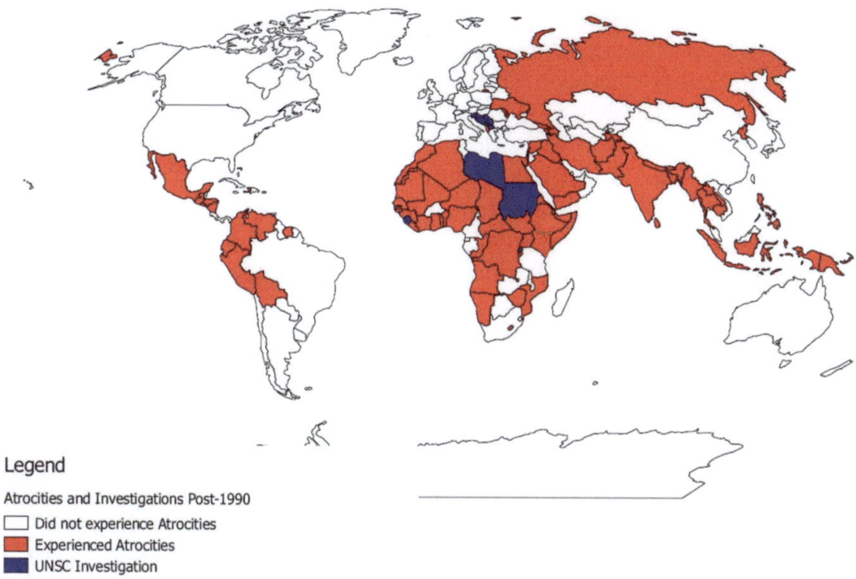

Map 1.1 States with atrocities and UNSC investigations post-1990

Ultimately, when trying to understand these apparent differences, all participants in international justice, whether perpetrators, victims, defendants, prosecutors, or even presidents who have been indicted by the ICC realize that, behind the UNSC's decision to create an international atrocities investigation, 'it's all politics.' Previous examinations of the politics behind international atrocities investigations present three broad categories of answers for why the UNSC creates such investigations. On the one hand, past analyses of atrocities investigations identify four explanations for which a state would not support an atrocities investigation. On the other hand, other analyses set forth four different explanations for why a state would support a decision to investigate atrocities. Beyond these two categories of studies, analyses of decision-making at the UNSC, which focus on issues such as sanctions, peacekeeping and military intervention, provide a number of legal and political explanations into why the UNSC so rarely decides to investigate the commission of atrocities.

Despite their breadth, the past analyses do not account for the coordination and cooperation problems faced by UNSC members and therefore fall short of providing a satisfactory explanation on the UNSC's decisions to create international atrocities investigations. To fill this gap, this book asserts that the UNSC's decisions to authorize atrocities investigations are best explained by examining decision-making within the UNSC. More specifically, this book locates the answer to the question posed above (i.e. why the UNSC decided to investigate certain atrocities but not others?) in the UNSC's procedures of operation, which allow the UNSC members to coordinate and cooperate within the UNSC.

The UNSC decision-making procedure involves three steps, as the UNSC (i) comes to hear about certain events, (ii) evaluates its responses to these events and

(iii) formulates its decisions. Successful completion of each of these three steps is necessary for a UNSC decision to authorize an atrocities investigation. As a result, the main argument of this book is that the UNSC decided to investigate only certain atrocities because the UNSC's 15 members were able to successfully complete each of the three steps in the UNSC's decision-making process only for those certain atrocities. To develop this argument, this book examines each of these three steps, and identifies the elements that are central to the successful completion of each step, namely (i) the work of a patron diplomat in the first step, (ii) the support from a commission of inquiry in the second step and (iii) the UNSC's reliance on precedent in the third step.

To conduct this examination, the research for this book focused on the historical record of the UNSC's activity, which was supplemented by numerous interviews with participants at the UNSC's deliberations on atrocities investigations. The interviews shed considerable light on the nuances of the behind-the-scenes negotiations at the UNSC. Beyond this, however, the interviews also challenged some assumptions of the literature on the UNSC. The participants in the interviews found it impossible to identify a few factors that trigger the UNSC's decision to create international atrocities investigations. To the contrary, across all interviews, the constant theme was that all factors matter and no two situations with atrocities are ever similar. In the eyes of the participants, therefore, it was hard, if not impossible, to identify a clear causal mechanism for the UNSC's work and to answer the question of this book in a few words.

Additionally, the participants at these interviews were quick to highlight that the decision-making procedures at the UNSC are of central importance in understanding the UNSC's decisions. The majority view among those interviewed was that, while procedural steps are not sufficient to lead to the final outcome, they are necessary. Both of the above observations clash with long-held assumptions of the previous academic research on the UNSC, which has emphasized the existence of identifiable causal pathways and the role of power politics, not procedure, in the work of the UNSC. The clash becomes particularly noteworthy as, apart from the active role that the participants of the interviews had in the decisions of the UNSC, most participants also had (perhaps surprisingly) a good understanding of the academic writings on the work of the UNSC.

Even though this book as a whole relies of the historical records and the interviews, the various chapters use these sources in different ways. Methodologically, the use of the historical case studies is a contested point in political science,[4] with those in one extreme arguing for detailed case studies exceeding in number the tested explanations,[5] while those on the other extreme relying on one detailed case study for all explanations.[6] Because of the thorough data collected through the his-

[4] For an overview, see McKeown (1999).

[5] E.g. King et al. (1994).

[6] E.g. Eckstein (1975) (the 'crucial case-study').

torical records and the interviews, the chapters of this book use, in turn, all possible approaches. Chapter 5 examines how diplomats are central to bringing up atrocities at the UNSC through three case studies. Chapter 6 presents one case study for all the explanations on why the UNSC members use third-parties before deciding. Finally, Chapter 7 presents a series of five short case studies to examine why diplomats rely on precedent at the UNSC.

The argument and findings of this book present important lessons for the study of international affairs. To start, this book presents a few lessons for the greater field of international relations. In line with the institutionalist literature, this book confirms that a state's power within an institution is an important explanatory variable in international relations. While more traditional writings assert that states prioritize power in the absolute or vis-à-vis other states, the research of this book suggests that states are also concerned about their power within an international organization. New Zealand, not a very powerful state by any measure, was able to convince the members of the UNSC to create the ICTR. And, while the veto at the UNSC preserves a central role for the more traditional notion of power, its use does not reflect a policy of constant emphasis on absolute or relative power. The United States, for example, chose not to veto the referral of the Darfur investigation to the ICC, because a veto would have undermined its position, and made it more difficult to accomplish other goals, within the UNSC.

Additionally, this book underscores why studies of international organizations should consider the procedural elements of international organizations. In the past, a few significant studies have examined various characteristics of international organizations, such as their precision, delegation and organization.[7] However, these studies overlook the fact that the procedure of international organizations with similar levels of such characteristics may affect their operations in significantly different manners. For example, the European Union ('EU') and the World Trade Organization ('WTO') both increasingly delegate tasks to judicial bodies. In both cases, a judicial body can determine if a member state of that international organization has violated the policies and rules of the organization. Yet, the procedure for bringing a case to these judicial bodies is significantly different and each procedure leads to substantially divergent results. In the EU, for example, any individual citizen of an EU member state can file a complaint against a member state and can claim retroactive damages. At the WTO, only a member state can file a complaint and such complaint can only seek prospective compensation. These two procedural differences between potential plaintiffs and type of compensation are sufficient to substantially differentiate the role of the EU court from that of the WTO and to render the common category of 'high delegation to judicial body' practically meaningless.

Finally, the present book emphasizes the role of evolution in international relations. Many past studies present discrete historical facts. Yet, international affairs are constantly in flux. Moreover, the UNSC's decisions on atrocities investigations

[7] Abbott and Snidal (2000).

in 2005 were certainly influenced by its decisions in 1994. A few participants in the interviews for this book, for example, emphasized that their actions on a certain topic were influenced by their past policy on the topic, their past decisions on a similar topic, their future goals, or ongoing events. An analysis that focuses on a narrow set of historic events is thus likely to miss this larger context. Through the prism of the UNSC's decision making procedures, this book allows for the observation of these moving pieces in a coherent framework, with the goal of capturing the greater evolution of international affairs with regards to atrocities investigations rather than making an argument that only applies to a few specific case studies.

The rest of this book is organized in seven chapters. Chapter 2 presents the facts. It identifies the atrocities committed in the post-Cold War era and the role of the UNSC in international affairs. Chapter 3 presents how previous analyses answer the question of this book, and explains how these answers do not adequately explain the UNSC's decisions on atrocities. Then, Chap. 4 develops the argument of this book, namely that the UNSC's procedure shapes the outcome of its deliberations on international atrocities investigations. The subsequent three chapters examine in turn the three necessary steps for the creation of an atrocities investigation by the UNSC. Chapter 5 thus considers the role of a patron diplomat at the UNSC in initiating the debate on the role of an atrocities investigation. Chapter 6 turns to the role that an independent third-party has in the deliberations of the UNSC members over the creation of an atrocities investigation. Chapter 7 presents the UNSC's decisions relating to the drafting of the final resolutions. Finally, the Conclusion summarizes the argument and presents some general observations on the UNSC.

Before proceeding further, however, it is important to define the phrase 'authorize an international atrocities investigation,' which is used throughout this book. The term atrocity, despite its clarity in colloquial use, is "unclarified and infuriatingly obscure" for use in political science or the law.[8] Past attempts to arrive at a precise definition have been largely unsuccessful.[9] At the Nuremberg tribunal, after the end of World War II, an atrocity was described as an act "in evident contradiction to all human morality and every international usage of warfare."[10] Grappling with the vagueness of this term, the United Nations International Law Commission later adopted an expansive definition.[11] Nevertheless, as the term remains unwieldy for any precise application, it has never been used by the various international

[8] Osiel (1998).

[9] This obscurity appears to be a rather ancient problem. In the Justinian code, for example, an atrocity included all acts that were legally inexcusable even when carried out under formal orders – see Digest of Justinian, Law 157, tit. XVII, Lib. L.

[10] War Crimes Reports 7 (1947) 27, 41–42.

[11] Report of the International Law Commission on the work of its Forty-Third Session, U.N. GAOR, 46th Sess., Supp. No. 10, at 198, U.N. Doc. A/46/10 (1991) (defining atrocities "as acts of inhumanity, cruelty or barbarity directed against the life, dignity or physical or mental integrity of persons [in particular wilful killing, torture, mutilation, biological experiments, taking of hostages, compelling a protected person to serve in the forces of a hostile Power, unjustifiable delay in the repatriation of prisoners of war after the cessation of active hostilities, deportation or transfer of the civilian population and collective punishment];").

criminal tribunals. The latter, rather than going after atrocities, have targeted the more precisely defined crimes of genocide, crimes against humanity and war crimes. For the purposes, therefore, of this analysis, an atrocity is a reference to any act that could amount to genocide, crimes against humanity, and war crimes. In line with previous such uses of this term,[12] it is used as reference to all of the acts that could qualify as violations of international humanitarian law, international criminal law, and laws and customs of war.

The second term used throughout this book is 'investigation.' As defined by the jurisprudence of the ICC, an investigation "signif[ies] the taking of steps directed at ascertaining whether [individuals] are responsible for that conduct, for instance by interviewing witnesses or suspects, collecting documentary evidence, or carrying out forensic analyses.[13] Once authorized by the appropriate political authority, investigations are carried out by legal bodies. For international atrocities, as discussed in Chap. 2, investigations may be authorized by the UNSC, the state connected to the atrocities or, in certain specified instances, by the judges of the ICC. Once an atrocities investigation has been authorized, the investigation is carried out by the prosecutor of an international criminal tribunal or the prosecutor of the ICC, as applicable. While the concept of an investigation of a crime is closely related to that of a criminal trial, there is an important conceptual distinction between the two processes. Once an investigation into an atrocity crime has been authorized—a political decision—there are many non-political considerations that can prevent or compel the creation and/or success of the subsequent trial. For example, when the prosecutor of the ICTY investigated the practice of extrajudicial killings in Bosnia, the prosecutor examined hundreds of mass graves throughout the countryside. Yet, ultimately, she decided to indict only certain individuals and presented only a small subset of the evidence from the mass graves at these trials. A prosecutor's rationales for his or her primary initial decisions (namely, who to accuse and with what evidence) can vary and often are not political (e.g. lack of proper evidence or trial time management).[14] But, the decision of the UNSC to authorize the investigation of the atrocity crimes committed in Bosnia was, at its core, a political decision, which the rest of this book will focus on explaining.

Finally, this book uses the term "authorize" an atrocities investigation to portray the UNSC's decision to either (a) establish an *ad hoc* international criminal tribunal, such as the ICTY and the ICTR, or (b) refer a situation to the prosecutor of the ICC, such as the referrals of Darfur and Libya. As subsequently discussed in Chap. 2, there are practical differences between the two decisions. Also, in light of the ICC's existence, it is unlikely that the UNSC will agree to create another *ad hoc* tribunal,

---

[12] E.g. Scheffer (2013).

[13] ICC, Appeals Chamber, The Prosecutor v. Francis Kirimi Muthaura, Uhuru Muigai Kenyatta and Mohammed Hussein Ali, 30 August 2011, ICC-01/09-02/11-274, paras. 1 and 40; ICC, Pre-Trial Chamber I, The Prosecutor v. Saif al-Islam Gaddafi and Abdullah al-Senussi, 11 October 2013, ICC-01/11-01/11, para. 66.

[14] For the same reasons, this book does not examine the *proprio motu* investigations commenced by the ICC's Prosecutor. *See more* below.

as such tribunals have high financial and political costs that would not be required by a referral to the ICC. Yet, since the underlying decision at the UNSC is the same, namely to target atrocities through an international criminal investigation, this book refers to both actions as an authorization of an investigation.

References

Books and Articles

Abbott, Kenneth, and Duncan Snidal. 2000. Hard and Soft Law in International Governance. *International Organization* 54.03: 421–456.

Digest of Justinian, Law 157, tit. XVII, Lib. L. 1985. ed. Theodore Mommsen and Paul Krueger, Trans. A. Watson. University of Pennsylvania Press.

Eckstein, Harry. 1975. Case Study and Theory in Political Science. In *Handbook of Political Science*, Political Science: Scope and Theory, ed. Fred I. Greenstein and Nelson W. Polsby, vol. 1. Reading: Addison-Wesley.

King, Gary, Robert O. Keohane, and Sidney Verba. 1994. *Designing Social Inquiry: Scientific Inference in Qualitative Research.* Princeton: Princeton University Press.

McKeown, Timothy J. 1999. Case Studies and the Statistical Worldview: Review of King. *International Organization* 53: 161–190.

Osiel, Mark J. 1998. Obeying Orders: Atrocity, Military Discipline, and the Law of War. *California Law Review*: 939–1129.

Scheffer, David. 2013. *All the Missing Souls: A Personal History of the War Crimes Tribunals.* Princeton: Princeton University Press.

Court Documents

International Criminal Court

Appeals Chamber, The Prosecutor v. Francis Kirimi Muthaura, Uhuru Muigai Kenyatta and Mohammed Hussein Ali, "Judgment on the appeal of the Republic of Kenya against the decision of Pre-Trial Chamber II of 30 May 2011 entitled 'Decision on the Application by the Government of Kenya Challenging the Admissibility of the Case Pursuant to Article 19(2)(b) of the Statute'," ICC-01/09-02/11-274 (August 30, 2011).

Pre-Trial Chamber I, The Prosecutor v. Saif al-Islam Gaddafi and Abdullah al-Senussi, "Decision on the admissibility of the case against Abdullah Al-Senussi", ICC-01/11-01/11 (October 11, 2011).

Public Redacted Version of the Prosecutor's Application under Article 58, International Criminal Court, ICC-02/05 (July 14, 2008).

Government Documents

Justice Jackson's Report to the President on Atrocities and War Crimes (June 7, 1945), accessible at http://avalon.law.yale.edu/imt/imt_jack01.asp.

War Crimes Reports 7 (1947) 27.

UN Documents

Reports

A/46/10, Report of the International Law Commission on the work of its Forty-Third Session, U.N. GAOR, 46th Sess., Supp. No. 10 (1991).

Resolutions

S/RES/1593, Sudan (March 19, 2005).

Chapter 2
The Facts: Atrocities Investigations and the UN Security Council

3 November 2013
Nairobi, Kenya

Dear Mr. President,

I attach a letter expressing the opposition of the victims in the Kenyatta case at the International Criminal Court to any resolution by the Security Council to suspend the prosecution of that case.

On behalf of those victims, I would be grateful if you could bring this letter urgently to the attention of the members of the Security Council.

Please accept, Mr. President, the assurances of my highest consideration.

Fergal Gaynor
Legal Representative of Victims
The Prosecutor v. Uhuru Muigai Kenyatta, International Criminal Court.
(Gaynor 2013)

Abstract This chapter sets the stage by presenting the facts relating to both atrocities investigations and the UNSC. To do so, it presents where atrocities have taken place in the post-Cold War era, and then evaluates how domestic and international atrocities investigations have been created in response to these atrocities. It proceeds to document the role of the UNSC in international affairs and the important role the UNSC's procedural rules have in its decision-making process.

In the post-Cold War era, conflicts—both international and civil—continue to plague the world. Similarly, repressive states and dictatorial regimes continue to suppress, often violently, their own populations. As a result, even though the Cold War ended, atrocities continue to take place.

C. Kaoutzanis, *The UN Security Council and International Criminal Tribunals: Procedure Matters*, Studies in Global Justice 20,
https://doi.org/10.1007/978-3-030-23777-6_2

At the same time, and continuing since the end of World War II, the UNSC has been the primary institution for maintaining peace and stability in the international system. Since 1993, unshackled from the East-West divide of the Cold War, the UNSC has responded to several atrocities through the creation of international investigations, leading to the questions behind this book.

This chapter provides an introduction to the subsequent analysis of the UNSC's decisions on atrocities. Its goal is to present the existing facts relating to both atrocities investigations and the UNSC, in an effort to create the setting for the subsequent analysis. To do so, Sect. 2.1 presents where atrocities have taken place in the post-Cold War era. Sections 2.2 and 2.3 evaluate how other domestic and international atrocities investigations have been created in response to these atrocities, indicating that the UNSC is one of many actors in this field. In Sect. 2.4, the Chapter turns its attention to the role of the UNSC in international affairs. Section 2.5 explains how the UNSC operates and specifies the extensive role of its procedural rules. Finally, Sect. 2.6 concludes the presentation of this Chapter.

2.1 The Location of Atrocities

It is hard to know where, when and which atrocities have taken place. Many atrocities remain unreported. Perpetrators seldom talk about their acts. Victims of violence often prefer not to report the events, causing bias in any count of atrocities.[1] In Darfur, for example, after conducting interviews and surveys of Darfuri refugees, the Atrocities Documentation Team of the U.S. Department of State, which was organized by the U.S. government to catalogue the crimes committed in Darfur,[2] was able to get some sense of the scale of the atrocities that had been committed in the region. It concluded that 67% of refugees had witnessed a killing and 16% had witnessed or experienced rape. It clarified its findings, however, by noting that "it is very likely that rapes are underreported because of the social stigma attached to acknowledging such violations of female members of one's family."[3]

Additionally, it is hard to document even those atrocities that get reported, i.e. those for which someone is willing to speak out. For example, how can a research team away from the conflict zone know, with reasonable certainty, that a death, rape or kidnapping occurred in a remote village? In the case of Darfur again, the Atrocities Documentation Team noted how "the data may actually undercount the extent of atrocities because mass attacks often leave few survivors."[4] This uncertainty introduces additional bias in the count of atrocities.

[1] Such bias is the result of Type II errors (i.e. false negatives).

[2] For an overview of the work of the Atrocities Documentation Team, see Documenting Atrocities in Darfur (2004); Totten and Markusen (2006).

[3] Documenting Atrocities in Darfur (2004).

[4] Documenting Atrocities in Darfur (2004).

Such difficulties are hard to overcome even with an abundance of resources. In Cambodia, for example, the Documentation Center for Cambodia, with a significant budget, permanent staff and the cooperation of Yale University's Cambodian Genocide Project and—at least sometimes—of the Cambodian government, spent 10 years to identify 19,733 mass burial pits and 196 prisons that operated during the Khmer Rouge regime (1975–1979). Even though it has created a map of the killing fields,[5] the Documentation Center has yet to complete its task of reconstructing the historical records.

In addition to these practical difficulties, any attempt to quantify atrocities overlooks their qualitative nature. In other words, not all atrocities should be counted as equals. The murder of ten random local civilians is unlikely to have the same effect on a conflict with, for example, the killing of ten local leaders. One could even argue that the mere kidnapping of the ten local leaders could have a greater impact on a local community and a conflict than the murder of ten random civilians. In reality, countless suicide bombings in Pakistan over recent years have resulted in hundreds of casualties in the aggregate, yet have not had the same effect on the peace and security of Pakistan as the 2007 killing of Prime Minister Benazir Bhutto or the 2014 massacre of 132 schoolchildren in Peshawar. A quantification measure, however, would treat all these atrocities equally and would omit important qualities of the underlying facts.

Creating a dataset of atrocities appears to be an impossible task. Yet, some past studies have tried to identify the commission of atrocities by relying on proxy measures. A few datasets that count the number of deaths in conflict are often used as proxies for the presence of atrocities. Jo and Simmons, for example, in their attempt to determine the deterring effect of the ICC on atrocities, rely on the dataset of one-sided violence by Eck and Hultman.[6] Similarly, Valentino, Huth and Balch-Lindsay, in their effort to examine why guerillas resort to violence against noncombatants, rely on the Correlates of War Project and construct a count of mass killings.[7]

A few other studies have constructed more complicated proxies for atrocities, by moving beyond the measure of deaths in conflict. Mullins, for example, examines all civil and international conflicts from 1945 until 2008 and, borrowing techniques from domestic criminology, estimates the number of atrocity victims.[8] In Mullins' count, for example, the atrocities committed in Angola's civil war, which ranged from 1974 until 2002, led to approximately 1,500,000 victims. In a similarly nuanced count of atrocities,[9] Harff created a dataset that categorizes atrocities committed from 1955 until 2012 by magnitude of death (on a 0–5 scale) and the type of

---

[5] The map of the Khmer Rouge killing fields is accessible here http://www.d.dccam.org/Projects/Maps/MappingKillingField.htm.

[6] Jo and Simmons (2016).

[7] Valentino et al. (2004).

[8] Mullins (2010).

[9] Harff (2003).

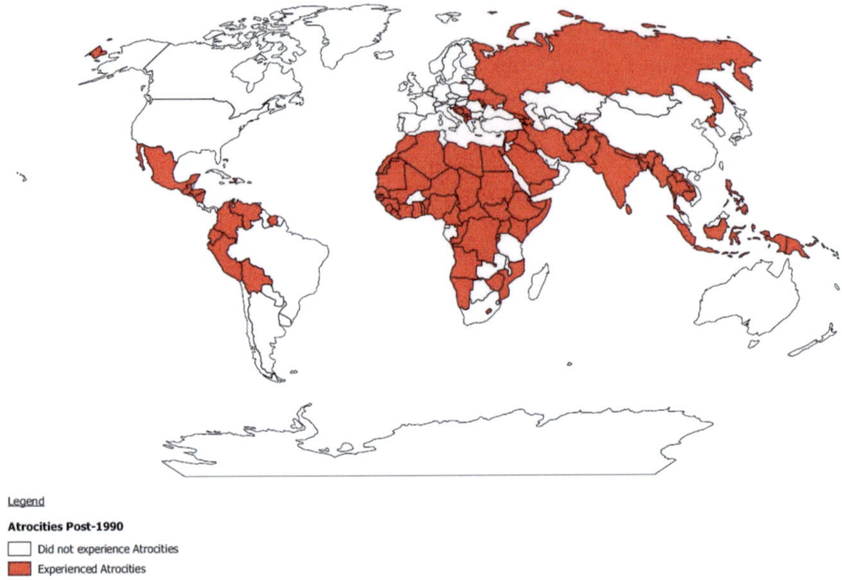

Map 2.1 States with atrocities post-1990

violence (ethnical, revolutionary, regime change and general).[10] According to this scale, Angola's civil war was a regime change war that averaged at 2.96 on the magnitude of death scale.[11]

A different route in documenting atrocities is to avoid numerical references. Stanton, for example, constructed an eight-step model to describe the escalation of mass killings. The steps are, in increasing order: classification, symbolization, dehumanization, organization, polarization, preparation, extermination and denial.[12] Stanton applied this eight-step model to all conflicts since 1945 and created a list of countries that have erupted or are likely to erupt into genocidal violence.[13] In Stanton's model, Angola's civil war was a, step five, polarized conflict.

By relying on "the best available measure to assess" where atrocities have taken place in the post-Cold War era,[14] these studies risk presenting biased estimates of atrocities. But, even though the magnitude of victimization may be under- or over-reported, the above studies are helpful in laying out the geographical span of atrocities. As portrayed in Map 2.1 and listed in Table 2.1, the above datasets, when

[10] Harpff's 0–5 scale of magnitude of death is (code – number of deaths): 0 < 300; 0.5 = 300 – 1000; 1.0 = 1000 – 2000; 1.5 = 2000 – 4000; 2.0 = 4000 – 8000; 2.5 = 8000 – 16,000; 3.0 = 16,000 – 32,000; 3.5 = 32,000 – 64,000; 4.0 = 64,000 – 128,000; 4.5 = 128,000 – 256,000; 5.0 > 256,000.

[11] The dataset can be accessed at http://www.gpanet.org/content/genocides-and-politicides-events-1955-2002.

[12] The description of each step can be found at http://www.genocidewatch.org/aboutgenocide/8stagesofgenocide.html.

[13] The dataset can be accessed at http://www.gpanet.org/content/genocides-politicides-and-other-mass-murder-1945-stages-2008.

[14] Jo and Simmons (2016).

Table 2.1 Countries with atrocities since 1990

1. Afghanistan	32. Gambia	63. Niger
2. Albania	33. Georgia	64. Nigeria
3. Algeria	34. Ghana	65. North Korea
4. Angola	35. Guatemala	66. Pakistan
5. Armenia	36. Guinea	67. Palestine[a]
6. Azerbaijan	37. Guinea-Bissau	68. Papua New Guinea
7. Bangladesh	38. Haiti	69. Peru
8. Benin	39. Honduras	70. Philippines
9. Bhutan	40. India	71. Russia
10. Bolivia	41. Indonesia	72. Rwanda
11. Bosnia	42. Iran	73. Saudi Arabia
12. Burma	43. Iraq	74. Senegal
13. Burundi	44. Israel	75. Serbia
14. Cambodia	45. Kenya	76. Sierra Leone
15. Cameroon	46. Kosovo[b]	77. Slovenia
16. Central African Republic	47. Kuwait	78. Somalia
17. Chad	48. Laos	79. South Sudan
18. Colombia	49. Lebanon	80. Sri Lanka
19. Comoros	50. Lesotho	81. Sudan
20. Congo	51. Liberia	82. Suriname
21. Cote d'Ivoire	52. Libya	83. Syria
22. Croatia	53. Mali	84. Tajikistan
23. Djibouti	54. Mauritania	85. Thailand
24. Democratic Republic of the Congo	55. Mexico	86. Togo
25. East Timor	56. Moldova	87. Uganda
26. Ecuador	57. Montenegro	88. Ukraine
27. Egypt	58. Morocco	89. Venezuela
28. El Salvador	59. Mozambique	90. Western Sahara
29. Eritrea	60. Namibia	91. Yemen
30. Ethiopia	61. Nepal	92. Zimbabwe
31. FYROM	62. Nicaragua	

[a]As of the writing of this book, Palestine has been recognized as a state by 136 of the 193 UN member states. In 2012, Palestine was granted the status of non-member observer state by the UN General-Assembly. But, Palestine has not been recognized as a state by the UNSC or the UN. Among the P5, France, the United Kingdom and the United States do not recognize Palestine as a state. Yet, several initiatives relating to atrocities investigations (such as the ICC's preliminary examination into the situation in Palestine, which started in 2015) have treated Palestine as if it were a state.

[b]As of the writing of this book, Kosovo has been recognized as a state by 111 out of the 193 UN member states. But, Kosovo has not been recognized as a state by the UNSC or the UN. Among the P5, Russia and China do not recognize Kosovo as a state. Yet, several initiatives relating to atrocities investigations (such as the Kosovo War and Ethics Crimes Court established by the United Nations Interim Administration Mission in Kosovo) have treated Kosovo as if it were a state.

combined, identify that 92 states have experienced atrocities in the post-Cold War era. While this list may be incomplete, precisely for the reasons mentioned above, historical records, reports from human rights NGOs, the U.S. State Department and the EU Commission confirm that these 92 countries have experienced atrocities since 1990. Since atrocities investigations require the prior commission of atrocities, the map below identifies where atrocities investigations are likely to arise and provides a useful starting point for the subsequent analysis.

The UNSC is not the only institution to consider an investigation into atrocities. To the contrary, both domestic judicial bodies and other international actors are often active in responding to atrocities. The next two Sections examine their work.

2.2 Domestic Judicial Responses to Atrocities

By the end of the Cold War, the global human rights movement had advanced its determination to instill justice mechanisms in the aftermath of atrocities. In what started as reactions to the Greek and Argentine juntas,[15] states were gradually using domestic judicial tools to examine their pasts. Trials of former strongmen became emblematic of the movement for human rights accountability. In 1999, victim groups and human rights organizations succeeded in convincing the Spanish and U.K. authorities to examine the actions of former Chilean dictator Augusto Pinochet. Similarly, in 2000, the authorities in Senegal were persuaded to investigate the brutal crimes committed by former Chadian President Hissène Habré. As the movement for accountability grew stronger, more states started examining their past.[16] In Central America, Guatemala decided to investigate the actions of its military and political leaders during its civil war. In Eastern Europe, Romania prosecuted the commander of a communist-era labor camp.[17]

A few states appeared eager to support the "justice cascade" even for atrocities committed outside their borders.[18] To do so, these states empowered their criminal justice systems with extra-territorial jurisdiction. In these instances, a state may prosecute domestically citizens of foreign countries who are accused of perpetrating atrocities in foreign countries. While laws granting such extraterritorial jurisdiction have substantive legal differences,[19] they have been responsible for a few notable atrocities investigations. Belgian courts, most famously, have investigated, prosecuted and convicted Rwandan nuns for helping Hutu genocidaires. A U.S. District Court in Florida convicted Chucky Taylor, the son of Liberian dictator Charles Taylor, because of Chucky's actions in the Liberian civil war. Equally well-known, Spain's prosecutors have investigated and attempted to prosecute Pinochet for his

[15] See Sikkink (2011).

[16] See Ratner et al. (2009).

[17] Gillet, The Guardian (September 24, 2014).

[18] Sikkink (2011).

[19] See e.g. Randall (1987); Macedo (2006).

actions in Chile, and have investigated, prosecuted and convicted Argentine military officers for the disappearance of Spanish citizens in Argentina.

The "justice cascade," however, did not proceed uninterrupted. Some states that had experienced atrocities chose to prioritize arriving at the truth surrounding their atrocities rather than justice. The best-known example of this approach to atrocities comes from South Africa, where at the end of apartheid a Truth and Reconciliation Commission was set up "to enable South Africans to come to terms with their past on a morally accepted basis and to advance the cause of reconciliation."[20] In some form, such commissions were also created in various other countries.[21] The work and results of many of these commissions is a highly contested topic, as they are often created in an effort to stem criticism of inaction rather than to produce any substantive results.[22] For this book, however, it is important to note that such truth commissions are often organized together with criminal investigations. In the most famous example of such co-existence, in Argentina, the report of the National Commission on the Disappearance of Persons (Comisión Nacional sobre la Desaparición de Personas) paved the way for the Trial of the Juntas.

States, furthermore, interested in conducting a legal investigation for atrocities committed on their territory may face logistical problems. In such cases, states often resort to community-based initiatives for achieving justice and reconciliation. After the genocide in Rwanda, for example, it was impossible for the government of Rwanda to investigate and prosecute the actions of each genocidaire. Not only did the country not have the necessary infrastructure in place for such investigations, but such investigations were also believed to be counterproductive for peace as they would alienate Hutus and cripple the local economy, since multitudes of genocidaires would probably end up in jail. As a result, Rwanda instituted *gaçaça* proceedings, which are traditional community based initiatives, aimed at exposing the truth, empowering victims, achieving closure and punishment. Similar proposals for community-based investigations have occurred more recently in northern Uganda. There, Acholi leaders, in their effort to deal with the Lord's Resistance Army, insisted on relying on traditional dispute resolution mechanisms rather than the Ugandan courts or the ICC.

Similar to truth commissions, such community-based initiatives often go hand-in-hand with criminal investigations. In Rwanda, for example, while local communities conducted *gaçaça* procedures, the state of Rwanda organized its own domestic investigations and trials in Rwandan courts. Despite the existence of the state and local involvement in Rwanda, the international community, through the ICTR conducted another parallel investigation. To understand how the latter came about, the

[20] Omar (1995) (Minister of Justice of South Africa).

[21] This list includes: Argentina, Brazil, Canada, Colombia, Chile, Czech Republic, Ecuador, El Salvador, Fiji, Ghana, Guatemala, Haiti, Kenya, Liberia, Morocco, Panama, Paraguay, Peru, Poland, Philippines, Sierra Leone, Solomon Islands, South Korea, East Timor, Uganda, and Ukraine.

[22] See e.g. Hayner (2001).

next Section presents how international actors become involved in atrocities investigations.

2.3 The International Judicial Responses to Atrocities

Apart from domestic atrocities investigations, the international community has also developed three tools for the investigation of atrocities, namely the creation of international criminal investigations at the request of: (a) the UNSC, (b) the state that had experienced atrocities, or (c) for state-parties to the Rome Statute, the ICC's prosecutor.

With the end of the Cold War, the UNSC turned its attention to regional conflicts and their attendant consequences. In the mid-1990s, with the P5 cooperating in unprecedented ways, the UNSC expanded its activities in an effort to stop conflict. With this mindset, the UNSC created international criminal tribunals with the task of investigating the atrocities committed in the former Yugoslavia (1993) and Rwanda (1994). As Chap. 6 describes, the UNSC also seriously debated the creation of a similar international criminal tribunal for atrocities committed in Burundi (1993–1996). The creation, however, of the International Tribunal for the former Yugoslavia ('ICTY') and the International Criminal Tribunal for Rwanda ('ICTR') meant that the UNSC had to deal with the management of international criminal justice. Among other things, funds had to be raised, evidence collected, witnesses protected, and judges selected. As all of these decisions fell on the UNSC members, by the late 1990s, the UNSC underwent a period of 'tribunal fatigue.' As a result, the UNSC was skeptical when faced with establishing another complete international criminal tribunal for the atrocities committed in Sierra Leone (2000). It instead decided to delegate the daily management of the Special Court for Sierra Leone ('SCSL') to the United Nations Secretary-General (the 'Secretary-General') and the government of Sierra Leone, thereby creating the first hybrid international criminal tribunal.

While the UNSC was experiencing 'tribunal fatigue,' a different use of international atrocities investigations begun in 1997. As part of a coalition government, attempting to transition to peace after more than 20 years of civil war, the co-Prime Ministers of Cambodia, Prince Norodom Ranariddh and Hun Sen, sent a letter to the Secretary-General of the United Nations asking "the assistance of the United Nations and the international community in bringing to justice those persons responsible for the genocide and crimes against humanity during the rule of the Khmer Rouge from 1975 to 1979."[23] The positive response of the UN led to the creation of the Extraordinary Chambers in the Courts of Cambodia ('ECCC'), a hybrid domestic and international court, which has investigated, prosecuted and convicted some, and is investigating other, high-level Khmer Rouge leaders. Since the Cambodian request, several other states have also sought international assistance with investiga-

[23] S/1997/488 (June 24, 1997).

tions into crimes committed on their territory. Sierra Leone, for example, asked for such assistance in 2000, in the midst of the UNSC's deliberations on the creation of the SCSL.

By the mid-1990s, supporters of international justice—both states and NGOs—had been working towards the creation of a permanent international criminal court. Initially, the idea was proposed by Prime Minister A.N.R. Robinson of Trinidad and Tobago, who suggested to the General Assembly in 1989 that the UN create an international court to counter the illegal drug trade. Soon thereafter, the UN General Assembly tasked the United Nations International Law Commission ('ILC'), a group of international legal experts, with the drafting of a statute for a permanent international criminal court. Gradually, with the creation of the ICTY in 1993 and the ICTR in 1994, the focus of the ILC's work shifted from drugs to atrocities. Then, from 1996 to 1998, six drafting sessions were held in New York on the creation of a statute for an international criminal court, with the participation of NGOs and state delegations. These sessions paved the way for a full debate on a draft statute in Rome, in July 1998. After a heated conference, the Rome Statute for the creation of the ICC was ratified on July 17, 1998. The ICC became operational on July 1, 2002, after 60 states ratified the Rome Statute.

Article 13 of the Rome Statute details how the ICC may investigate atrocities. First, following the logic of the request of the Cambodian co-Prime Ministers mentioned above, Article 13 allows any state to request the assistance of the ICC in the investigation of an atrocity committed on its territory. Since the ICC became operational in 2002, Uganda asked the ICC for such assistance in 2003, the Democratic Republic of the Congo in 2004, the Central African Republic in 2004, Ivory Coast in 2010, Mali in 2012, Comoros in 2013, and Ukraine in 2014.

Second, following in the footsteps of the ICTY and the ICTR, Article 13 of the Rome Statute invites the UNSC to refer atrocities investigations to the ICC. The UNSC has referred two investigations to that court, namely the Darfur genocide in 2005 and the Qaddafi atrocities in Libya in 2011.

Finally, Article 13 also enables the ICC's prosecutor to investigate atrocities committed in state-parties to the court on the prosecutor's own volition.[24] So far, these *proprio motu* investigations have been initiated for atrocities committed in Kenya in 2010, the Central African Republic in 2014, Georgia in 2016 and Burundi in 2017. Such investigations are supposed to be based on the prosecutor's assessment of specific legal factors,[25] even though political calculations may also affect them.[26] Despite the small sample of such investigations, the fear of a full *proprio motu* investigation has led many state-parties to the ICC to reform their domestic criminal law system. The most important such reforms are rumored to have occurred in Colombia, where a preliminary investigation by the ICC Prosecutor is still on-

[24] Article XX of the Rome Statute.

[25] See the factors enumerated at Office of the Prosecutor, Policy Paper on the Interests of Justice (2007).

[26] For a cogent and non-conspiratorial analysis of such factors, see Bosco (2014).

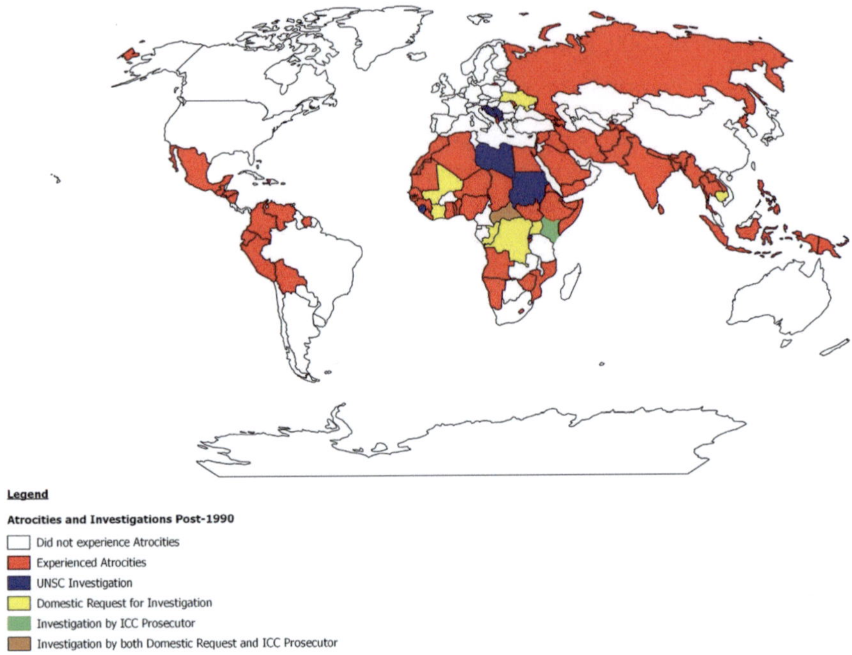

Map 2.2 States with atrocities and all investigations post-1990

Table 2.2 Who authorizes international atrocities investigations

United Nations Security Council	Domestic requests	ICC prosecutor
1. The former Yugoslavia,	1. Cambodia,	1. Kenya,
2. Rwanda,	2. Uganda,	2. Central African Republic (2014),
3. Sierra Leone,	3. Central African Republic (2004),	3. Georgia, and
4. Sudan, and	4. Democratic Republic of the Congo,	4. Burundi
5. Libya	5. Ivory Coast,	
	6. Mali,	
	7. Comoros, and	
	8. Ukraine	

going, but due to the changes made by the local government appears unlikely to result in a full-fledged atrocities investigation.[27]

So far, the three uses of international atrocities investigations have led to the creation of the investigations depicted on Map 2.2 and categorized in Table 2.2.

[27] Interview: 17.

2.4 The UNSC Within International Affairs

The UN Charter lays out the details of the UNSC's power and operations. First, Article 23 clarifies that the UNSC is composed of two-tiers of states.[28] In the first rank are the five permanent members of China, France, Russia, the United Kingdom, and the United States of America (the "P5"). The second tier is composed of ten non-permanent members (the "E10"). These latter states hold a UNSC seat for a 2-year rotation, with half of the seats contested every year. These states are elected to the UNSC through the General Assembly. As the UN Charter calls for an "equitable geographical distribution"[29] for the non-permanent members of the UNSC, each of the five regional groups (i.e. Africa, Asia-Pacific, Eastern Europe, Latin America and Caribbean, and Western Europe and Others) elects a representative to the UNSC each year. An Arab state is also always elected as a non-permanent member of the UNSC, alternatively from the African or Asian-Pacific regional group.

The voting system of the UNSC is set out in Article 27. To approve any substantive (as opposed to procedural) decision, such as the creation of an atrocities investigation, the UN Charter requires that two elements be satisfied[30]:

1. Nine out of the 15 members of the UNSC vote in favor of the decision; and
2. "[T]he concurrent votes of the permanent members."

The obvious result of the requirement for a "concurrent vote" is the conferral of a veto to the P5. Through the process of backwards induction, the veto is a central element to the operation of the UNSC, one that affects all other elements of its functioning. In practice, the reach of the veto is such as to predetermine the agenda and content of the debates at the UNSC. It is, for example, unreasonable to expect that the UNSC will debate the situation in Tibet or Chechnya, as China or Russia are (reasonably) expected to veto any action on these respective issues.

The text of the UN Charter does not clarify how the requirement for a "concurrent vote" would deal with the practice of abstentions. This ambiguity seems to have triggered more academic commentary[31] than concern from the UNSC's member states, which continued to abstain. It was, finally, resolved in 1970, when the International Court of Justice in the *Namibia* case clarified that abstentions should be counted as concurrent votes under Article 27.[32] As a result, Article 27 now provides that the UNSC can decide (i) without counting abstentions, after (ii) nine positive votes and (iii) no veto from the P5.

The UN Charter also establishes the primacy of the UNSC on issues of peace and security. The leadership role of the UNSC on such matters is set out in Chapter VII

[28] UN Charter, Article 23.

[29] UN Charter, Article 23(1).

[30] UN Charter, Article 27.

[31] See e.g. Stavropoulos (1967); Liang (1950); Gross (1968); McDougal and Gardner (1951).

[32] ICJ, Namibia Advisory Opinion (1970).

of the UN Charter,[33] according to which the UNSC "shall determine the existence of any threat to the peace, breach of the peace, or act of aggression"[34] and shall decide on actions against this threat. Most importantly, the actions of the UNSC may also include "such action by air, sea, or land forces as may be necessary to maintain or restore international peace and security."[35] While the UNSC cannot restrict any state from exercising its right of self-defense,[36] the text of the UN Charter clearly allows the UNSC ample flexibility to determine both the existence of a threat to international peace and security and the method of dealing with this threat.

The UN Charter did not only place the UNSC at the leading institutional position within the UN on issues of war and peace. It also placed the UNSC in the leading position of such issues in international affairs at large. Legally, the position of the UNSC in international affairs depends on the supremacy clause of the UN Charter.[37] The latter mandates that the UN system enjoys primacy over any other regional or international system or multilateral or bilateral treaty in international affairs. As a result, the UNSC sits at the very top on issues of war and peace in international affairs.

In this leading role, the UNSC has arguably big shoes to fill. It was given unprecedented powers to take any necessary action. Yet, deciding on such actions presupposes a common understanding among the members of the UNSC, and particularly among the P5, as to what constitutes a "threat to the peace, breach of the peace, or act of aggression."[38] With no clear criteria on this point, the need to make such determinations guaranteed that Roosevelt's vision of the "Four Policemen" would continue to govern the international system, as the P5 would prioritize their own preferences in arriving at common decisions at the UNSC.

The preferences of the P5 thus became a defining characteristic of the UNSC's work. Because of this defining factor, the United States and Soviet vetoes acted as gating items to the UNSC's involvement in the most important security issues during the Cold War. The wars in Korea and Vietnam, several civil wars in Africa and Central America, the Middle Eastern conflicts, the invasions of Grenada and Afghanistan and the division of Europe were among the obvious threats to peace and security that were never resolved at the UNSC because the preferences of the two great superpowers clashed. Yet, when both superpowers considered a situation as a threat to peace, the UNSC would take significant far-reaching actions. For example, it authorized peacekeeping missions in Zaire and Cyprus, brokered peace agreements in the Middle East and imposed sanctions against South Rhodesia.[39]

After the end of the Cold War, without the U.S.-Soviet split, it has been easier for the P5 to arrive at a common conclusion over threats to international peace and

---

[33] UN Charter, Articles 39–51.

[34] UN Charter, Article 39.

[35] UN Charter, Article 42.

[36] UN Charter, Article 51.

[37] UN Charter, Article 103.

[38] UN Charter, Article 39.

[39] Bosco (2009).

security. As a result, the UNSC has taken actions more frequently than in the past.[40] Peacekeeping missions, diplomatic initiatives, sanctions and criminal tribunals have all been agreed upon for situations that would have likely prompted a P5 veto during the Cold War (e.g. those imposed on the former Yugoslavia). Additionally, in their analysis of peace and security, the focus of the P5 has shifted from international conflict to civil wars and failed states. The increased cooperation, however, has not changed the reality that the preferences of the P5 remain paramount in defining and targeting threats to international peace and security. As witnessed, for example, in the UNSC's actions on the ongoing conflict in Syria, the preferences of the P5 remain crucial.

Because of the importance that the P5 preferences play in the work of the UNSC, a constant debate exists about the success of the UNSC on issues of war and peace. Since the creation of the UNSC, deaths in conflict have decreased, nuclear war has not materialized, superpower conflicts have been neither direct nor global and, in some instances, significant threats to peace and security have been dealt with through the actions of the UNSC. Yet, the UNSC may not be responsible for any of the above. State preferences may operate independently of the UNSC. But, even those who assert that the UNSC has had a minimal role in maintaining international peace and security acknowledge that the UNSC enjoys unparalleled prestige and symbolism in international affairs.[41] Because of these secondary roles, considering the actions of the UNSC is unavoidable when examining issues of peace and security.

Understanding, however, UNSC decisions requires more than merely looking at its voting rules and acknowledging the role of the P5's preferences. Similar to any institution, the UNSC follows a set of rules that control the debate and the outcome of its deliberations. In an effort to better appreciate how the UNSC arrives at its decisions, the next Section turns to these rules.

2.5 How the UNSC Operates

The UN Charter, apart from endowing the UNSC with the responsibility for the maintenance of international peace and security, and setting its voting rules, also gave the UNSC the power to "adopt its own rules of procedure…."[42] Subsequently, in 1946, when the UNSC held its initial meetings at Church House in London, it agreed to adopt its Provisional Rules of Procedure (the "Rules"). The Rules, which have been amended seven times since 1946, determine the method through which the UNSC acts. For example, Rule 18 determines that each UNSC member shall

[40] Up to the end of 1990, in its first 46 years, the UNSC passed 683 resolutions, which leads to an average of 14.9 resolutions per year. In the following 28 years, the UNSC has passed 1,768 resolutions, for an average of 63.1 resolutions per year.

[41] See e.g. Bolton (2007).

[42] UN Charter, Article 30.

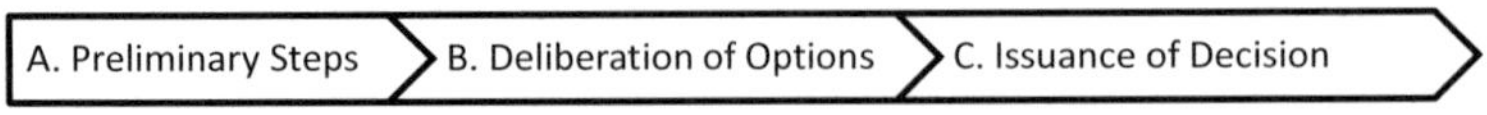

Graph 2.1 UNSC procedures

hold the Presidency of the UNSC for one calendar month, in alphabetical order, according to the member state's English name. While this is a ceremonial position with no substantive benefits, it entails significant procedural responsibilities. The coverage of the Rules is broad enough to detail the most important elements of the UNSC's work, such as the types of meetings available, the procedure for setting the agenda for each meeting, the procedure for each decision, and the role of the UN Secretariat at the UNSC. In brief, the Rules control the decision-making procedures of the UNSC.

Chronologically, the order of the UNSC's work follows Graph 2.1. The UNSC is first made aware of an event or situation that threatens the international peace and security through some form of communication. According to the Rules, such communications can come in the form of letters from either state members, other organs of the United Nations system (e.g. ECOSOC, IAEA), or the Secretary-General.[43] The letters from the Secretary-General often consist of reports or statements on specific issues that the UNSC, in prior resolutions, had asked the Secretary-General to undertake.[44] Finally, the UNSC sometimes also sends some of its representatives on missions, the results of which are also reported to the UNSC in the form of a letter.[45]

All forms of communication that are addressed to the UNSC must be placed on the UNSC's agenda by the Secretary-General. The agenda is public and is adopted at the beginning of every UNSC meeting. The President of the UNSC calls a meeting of the UNSC, with each meeting focusing on a distinct topic. Sometimes multiple meetings are called in a single day.

Once a meeting has been called and the agenda has been adopted, the UNSC members decide what type of meeting will be held. There is a presumption in the Rules that a public hearing will be held on all matters,[46] but any state can request the President of the UNSC to change the meeting to a private meeting.[47] During private meetings, notes are taken, but only a single copy is kept with the Secretary-General.[48] As a result, the public most often cannot find the opinions voiced or the reasoning behind the decisions taken during such private meetings.

---

[43] Rules, Chapter II.

[44] See e.g. S/2012/894, Report of the Secretary-General on the Situation in Mali, 29 November 2012.

[45] See e.g. S/1994/1039, Report of the UNSC Mission to Burundi on 13 and 14 August 1994, 9 September 1994.

[46] Rules, Chapter IX.

[47] Rules, Chapter I.

[48] Rules, Chapter I.

The deliberations on a specific topic signal the beginning of the main decision-making phase at the UNSC, during which the UNSC members engage in, mostly private, conversations to decide on the best response for a specific issue. Procedurally, at this stage, and even though it is not required by the Rules, the UNSC members routinely seek the recommendation of a third-party (e.g. the Secretary-General, the sanctions committee, a fact-finding mission). Such third-parties range from the Secretary-General and the subsidiaries bodies created by the UNSC to fact-finding missions and commissions of inquiry. In 2013, for example, the UNSC sought the opinion of the Secretary-General relating to the conflict in Mali.[49] In another example, the UNSC mission to Burundi offered suggestions to the UNSC members on the diplomatic and peacekeeping roles the UNSC could play vis-à-vis that conflict. The International Commission of Inquiry on Darfur also provided the UNSC with a list of crimes that took place.

After the UNSC has received the recommendations of these third-parties, it decides what actions it will take on a specific topic. Over the years, the UNSC has become very innovative. Despite their diversity, for analytical purposes, the actions of the UNSC can be divided into the following categories:[50]

1. taking no decision;
2. calling for a solution;
3. proposing diplomacy;
4. sending humanitarian aid;
5. creating an investigation;
6. imposing sanctions; [51]
7. sending peacekeepers; or
8. authorizing military force.

The above ranking places the categories of UNSC action in order of intrusiveness, with military action being the greatest burden on a targeted state's sovereignty.[52]

After they have come to an agreement over the preferred course of action, the UNSC members translate their understanding into a document, resulting in two subsequent political decisions. First, the UNSC members have to decide which legal tool they will use as the conduit for their decision. The UNSC can call for a solution and propose a diplomatic plan of action (categories 2 and 3) through a Presidential

[49] S/Res/2100 (2013).

[50] For a slightly different catalogue of the UNSC's actions, see Luck (2006).

[51] This category is not limited to economic sanctions but any measure against specified individuals. As such, it captures the UNSC's decisions that target terrorism, including the creation of domestic anti-terrorism legislation.

[52] There is a debate on the significance of the UNSC's anti-terrorism resolutions, which dictate what measures all states must take to internally prevent and suppress terrorism. Some argue that the resolutions appear legislative in substance and exceed the legal scope of prior UNSC decisions. *See e.g.* Talmon (2005); Szasz (2002); Alvarez (2003). While recognizing the merit of these arguments, this book follows the traditional ranking of UNSC actions, in which military intervention ranks as more intrusive than obligations to combat terrorism.

Statement. The UNSC can also take any step (categories 2–8) through a Resolution. However, a Resolution specifying that it is drafted under Chapter VII carries more legal power than one that does not make any mention of this Chapter. Admittedly, there are many different types of threats to international peace and security, some of which cannot be addressed with certain categories of actions described above. For example, Iran's nuclear program cannot be solved through an international atrocities investigation, while Somalia's civil war and famine cannot be effectively addressed through sanctions. As a result, not all options may be available for all situations.

Second, the UNSC members have to overcome drafting difficulties. Should, for example, a resolution authorize "all necessary means" or should it inform its target that it "will face serious consequences?"[53] While the second option remains vague, some have argued that it includes the use of force as an available option.[54] The first one, however, specifically allows the use of force. The choice between such formulations is a political decision that the UNSC members have to make before issuing their decision. Interestingly, even though it is not required by the Charter or the Rules, the UNSC routinely, and across all topic areas, resorts to its own precedent during the drafting phase.

For UNSC decisions that have been taken under Resolutions, the public record also includes statements that any UNSC member state volunteered at the time a Resolution was adopted. While sometimes these statements are elusive, they often help explain the reasons behind the decision.

Apart from examining the Rules that guide the decision-making process, it is important to emphasize that the UNSC members have some other unusual ways of controlling the content of the agenda and the deliberations. Instead of waiting for a topic to appear in the agenda, a member of the UNSC can propose that the UNSC meet in informal consultations or that its members engage in an informal dialogue. Some members of the UNSC can even organize an "Arria meeting," in which only other interested states will be invited to attend.[55] Through these unofficial paths, the members of the UNSC can agree off the record to a solution to a certain topic, then place that topic on the agenda and deal with it officially, even though the course of action is already determined.[56] It is for this reason that the public records for some UNSC Resolutions note that the topic and the proposed Resolution are placed on the agenda "in light of prior consultations."[57] As a result, the member states can determine the content of the deliberations.

---

[53] Compare, for example, Resolution 1973 (2011) with Resolution 1441 (2002).

[54] For a detailed overview of such arguments, see Peter Goldsmith's memo to Tony Blair (March 7, 2003).

[55] Rules, Chapter I.

[56] In doing so, the UNSC members are combining Steps A and B, and even Step C.

[57] See e.g. S/PV.5153, UNSC 5153 Meeting (March 29, 2005) (relating to the vote of Resolution 1593 (2005)).

Table 2.3 UNSC procedure and options

A. Preliminary steps	B. Deliberation of options	C. Issuance of decision
Information from:	No decision,	Type of tool:
States,	Call for solution,	Presidential statement,
UN organs,	Propose diplomacy,	Non-chapter VII Resolution, or
Secretary-General, or	Sending of humanitarian aid,	Chapter VII resolution.
UNSC missions.	Create legal investigations,	Drafting decisions:
Agenda:	Impose sanctions,	Reliance on precedent.
Organized by SG, and	Send peacekeepers, or	
Adopted at start of meeting.	Authorize military force.	

In practice, the use of the closed consultations has resulted in the lack of public deliberation by the UNSC. Most of the time, after the deliberations and the voting has already taken place, the UNSC members read prepared statements in public. In very few instances the UNSC will hold public debates, in which any UN member state can express its views. When these debates lead to a UNSC Resolution, the Resolution deals with the broadest topics.[58] Despite the presumption of a public hearing, through the use of non-public consultations, in practice, most important decisions are made behind closed doors.

The steps identified in Table 2.3 present the decision-making process at the UNSC, which is, both by design and in practice, cumbersome. Within each of its three steps, there are several political decisions that the UNSC members have to agree on. The rest of this book focuses on to these decisions.

2.6 Conclusion

This Chapter has presented the contextual facts for answering the question of this book. It started by specifying the locus of atrocities since the end of the Cold War, and explaining how some of these atrocities have been the targets of investigations created by domestic states or by international actors, including the UNSC. It then shifted its attention to the UNSC, and described its role within international affairs and its decision-making procedures. The following Chapter builds on this context to present the answers put forth by existing analyses to the question of this book.

[58] E.g. S/PV.4213, UNSC 4213 Meeting (October 31, 2000) (debating the issue of women and peace and security).

References

Books and Articles

Alvarez, Jose E. 2003. Hegemonic international law revisited. *American Journal of International Law* 97.1: 962.

Bolton, John. 2007. *Surrender is not an option, defending America at the United Nations and abroad*. New York: Threshold Editions.

Bosco, David. 2009. *Five to rule them all: The UN security council and the making of the modern world*. Oxford University Press.

———. 2014. *Rough justice: The international criminal Court's Battle to fix the world, one prosecution at a time*. Oxford University Press.

Gross, Leo. 1968. Voting in the security council: Abstention in the post-1965 amendment phase and its impact on article 25 of the charter. *American Journal of International Law*: 315–334.

Harff, Barbara. February 2003. No lessons learned from the holocaust? Assessing risks of genocide and political mass murder since 1955. *American Political Science Review* 97 (1): 57–73.

Hayner, Priscilla B. 2001. *Unspeakable truths: Confronting state terror and atrocity*. Psychology Press.

Jo, Hyeran, and Beth A. Simmons. 2016. Can the International Criminal Court Deter Atrocity? *International Organization* 70: 443.

Liang, Yuen-Li. 1950. Abstention and absence of a permanent member in relation to the voting procedure in the security council. *American Journal of International Law*: 694–708.

Luck, Edward C.U.N. 2006. *Security council: Practice and promise*. Routledge.

Macedo, Stephen, ed. 2006. *Universal Jurisdiction: National Courts and the Prosecution of Serious Crimes Under International Law*. Philadelphia: University of Pennsylvania Press.

McDougal, Myres S., and Richard N. Gardner. 1951. The veto and the charter: An interpretation for survival. *Yale Law Journal*: 258–292.

Mullins, Christopher. 2010. Conflict Victimization and Post-Conflict Justice, 1945–2008. In The Pursuit of International Criminal Justice: A World Study on Conflicts, Victimization, and Post-conflict Justice, Vol. 1, ed. M. Cherif Bassiouni. Intersentia, Antwerp.

Randall, Kenneth C. 1987. Universal Jurisdiction Under International Law. *Texas Law Review* 66: 785.

Ratner, Steven, Jason Abrams, and James Bischoff. 2009. *Accountability for Human Rights Atrocities in International Law: Beyond the Nuremberg Legacy*. 3rd ed. Oxford: Oxford University Press.

Sikkink, Kathryn. 2011. *The Justice Cascade: How Human Rights Prosecutions Are Changing World Politics*, The Norton Series in World Politics. New York: WW Norton & Company.

Stavropoulos, Constantin A. 1967. The practice of voluntary abstentions by permanent members of the security council under article 27, paragraph 3, of the charter of the United Nations. *American Journal of International Law*: 737–752.

Szasz, Paul C. 2002. The security council starts legislating. *American Journal of International Law*: 901–905.

Talmon, Stefan. 2005. The security council as world legislature. *American Journal of International Law*: 175–193.

Totten, Samuel, and Eric Markusen, eds. 2006. *Genocide in Darfur: Investigating the Atrocities In The Sudan*. New York: Routledge.

Valentino, Benjamin, Paul Huth, and Dylan Balch-Lindsay. 2004. 'Draining the sea': mass killing and guerrilla warfare. *International Organization* 58.02: 375–407.

News Sources

The Guardian

Gillet, Kit, *Romania Confronts Communist Past in Trial of Prison Camp Chief*. The Guardian (September 24, 2014).

Court Documents

International Criminal Court

Gaynor, Fergal, Letter on Behalf of Victims of Kenyatta Case (November 3, 2013), accessible at http://www.iccnow.org/documents/Letter to UNSC from the Victims Lawyer in the Kenyatta case.pdf.

Government Documents

Documenting Atrocities in Darfur, State Publication 11182, Released by the Bureau of Democracy, Human Rights, and Labor and the Bureau of Intelligence and Research (September 2004). available at http://2001-2009.state.gov/g/drl/rls/36028.htm.

Omar, Dullah, Minister of Justice of South Africa, Introduction to the Truth and Reconciliation Commission (1995). available at http://www.justice.gov.za/trc/legal/justice.htm.

Chapter 3
The Existing Explanations

The case of Darfur highlights a number of UN realities. Even Security Council agreements about issues such as the need to put an end to atrocities and to hold those responsible for them accountable at law translate into action only with enormous effort and luck.

Nicholas Rostow, General Counsel and Senior Policy Adviser to the U.S. Permanent Representative to the United Nations, 2001–2005.
Rostow (2010)

Abstract This Chapter looks at prior writings on atrocity investigations and the UNSC with the goal of identifying the reasons for which the UNSC creates international atrocities investigations. In doing so, this Chapter identifies a group of reasons according to which a member of the UNSC would not support an atrocities investigation, and a separate group of explanations for why UNSC members would create such an investigation. It further presents how past studies have understood the UNSC's work in areas beyond atrocities investigations. Throughout its analysis, this Chapter identifies how the prior writings on the UNSC do not adequately respond to the question posed in this book.

This book aims to explain why the UNSC has authorized atrocities investigations in only 11 of the 92 states that have experienced atrocities since 1990. The previous Chapter presented the facts relating to these atrocities, including how both domestic states and international actors have responded to them by creating atrocities investigations. It also presented the UNSC and its decision-making procedures.

Taking all of these elements together, one wonders how exactly the UNSC members arrive at a decision over atrocity investigations. As explained in detail below, past studies provide a number of explanations for the UNSC's actions in this field. The explanations can be grouped into two large families. Some studies explain why

C. Kaoutzanis, *The UN Security Council and International Criminal Tribunals: Procedure Matters*, Studies in Global Justice 20,
https://doi.org/10.1007/978-3-030-23777-6_3

a member of the UNSC would not support an atrocities investigation, thereby diminishing the likelihood that the UNSC as a whole would come to a decision to authorize an atrocities investigation. These studies are presented in Sect. 3.1. As documented in Sect. 3.2, an equally important set of studies documents the incentives UNSC members have to create such an investigation. While both families contain helpful explanations for the UNSC's actions on atrocities investigations, these explanations do not satisfactorily account for the vast majority of such actions. They also do not explain how UNSC members coordinate to aggregate their preferences into a single outcome.

With the goal of finding a more comprehensive framework for explaining the UNSC's actions on atrocities investigations, Sect. 3.3 examines how past studies have understood the UNSC to work in areas beyond atrocities investigations. The findings are, unfortunately, equally not satisfying in responding to the question posed in this book. The legal writings on the work of the UNSC, while full with important details on the work of the UNSC, do not focus on the political considerations of the UNSC members, which ultimately guide each member's actions at the UNSC. To the contrary, the political science writings focus on the incentives of the UNSC members, yet reach conclusions that are hard to generalize beyond their specific case studies and do not recognize the role that the UNSC's procedure plays in coordinating UNSC members with divergent (and perhaps clashing) preferences towards a single common decision.

This Chapter concludes by summarizing the prior works on the UNSC and demonstrating that there is no satisfactory theoretical framework for understanding the work of the UNSC as a collective decision-making body on atrocities investigations. In doing so, this Chapter lays the ground for the presentation of this book's argument in the following Chapter.

3.1 Atrocities Investigations Are Sidelined

As a UNSC decision requires an affirmative vote of 9 member states and lack of veto from any of the P5, an atrocities investigation will only materialize if it has significant support among the UNSC members. A strong preference against an investigation by any of the P5 or by a significant number of UNSC members signals the doom of an investigation.

Over the past 20 years, since the creation of the ICTY, a significant number of reasons have been proposed for which a UNSC member will not support an atrocities investigation.[1] While most of these reasons have been presented as side-arguments in larger works, and while many of them are case-specific (e.g. Russia will never allow an atrocities investigation in Georgia), this Section presents them in an organized manner to elicit the characteristics of possible opposition to an

[1] See e.g. Bass (2000); Bosco (2009); Zahar and Sluiter (2008); Scheffer (1999); Schabas (2004); Funk and Fake (2009); Black and Williams (2010).

investigation within the UNSC. The collective presentation of these arguments is also supported by their common premise, namely that some other interest, value or priority trumps an atrocities investigation.

3.1.1 *The Four Categories of Reasons Against an Atrocities Investigation*

The reasons for which a state shall oppose an atrocities investigation can be grouped into four broad categories: *complicity, war tactics, alliance* and *ideology*. These four categories of arguments identify the causes and the causal mechanisms behind the rejection of international atrocities investigations. Among others, they answer the following questions: (i) who opposes an investigation, (ii) under what circumstances, (iii) for what goal and (iv) for which atrocities. While the four categories present concise and coherent answers to these four questions, they are not exclusive explanations for the opposition to any single atrocities investigation. In reality, factors from each of the four categories overlap when it comes to opposing an investigation. For purposes of intellectual clarity, however, it is important to examine each category in turn.

3.1.1.1 Complicity

A frequent contention in the human rights community is that states that have directly committed, or are complicit in the commission of, atrocities will oppose an investigation into these atrocities. In such instances, a state does not want to expose its own conduct to international and domestic criticism, as such conduct violates international and domestic laws and contradicts strong normative expectations.[2] Additionally, atrocities investigations can have personal repercussions for state leaders, who can be jailed for participating in, orchestrating, or not prosecuting the perpetrators of, the crimes. Concerned with self-preservation, the government hinders an investigation.

Historically, there have been several important examples of such behavior. As Bass documents, the United Kingdom was exploring the prosecution of Ottoman officials in its custody for crimes committed against the Armenians. Such prosecutions were opposed, however, by the Ataturk government, which managed in 1921 to exchange those officials for a small group of British prisoners.[3]

More recently, the same hostility towards atrocities investigations has been exhibited by a number of African countries (e.g. Kenya, Uganda), with Burundi providing the most vivid illustration of this argument. Burundi experienced a return

[2] E.g. Bosco (2014) (US in Afghanistan); Prunier (2005) (US hesitant to empower ICC due to Iraq).

[3] Bass (2000, p. 138).

to violence in late April 2015, after President Nkurunziza announced he would seek a third term.[4] One of the main participants in the ensuing violence was the government of Burundi, which frequently deployed its military and police forces, as well as the Imbonerakure, a government-allied youth group. In the course of these events, the government has been accused of summary executions, imprisonments, torture, rapes and other sexual violence, and enforced disappearances. In response to allegations of such crimes, the prosecutor of the ICC launched a preliminary examination into the situation in Burundi in April 2016.[5] As the atrocities continued, the UN Human Rights Council also resolved to create a commission of inquiry into the human rights abuses in Burundi in September 2016.[6]

In response to the ICC's preliminary examination, on October 12, 2016, 94 of the 110 parliamentarians in Burundi voted in favor of withdrawing from the ICC. The legislation was signed by President Nkurunziza on October 18, 2016 and the government of Burundi presented its letter of intent to withdraw from the ICC to the UN Secretary-General on October 27, 2016. The reaction of most international actors mirrored the statements of Elise Kepper, associate director of international justice at Human Right Watch, who associated the withdrawal with the "allegations of ongoing abuse in the country since President Pierre Nkrunziza's controversial bid for a third term last year."[7] These reactions were not entirely dispelled when the foreign minister of Burundi, Alain Aimé Nyamitwe, retorted "[w]e believe that it is too much fabrication to say that the government of Burundi has withdrawn from the ICC because it was accused of crimes against humanity."[8]

3.1.1.2 War Tactics

A second argument against an atrocities investigation comes from states participating in a war or other armed hostilities, whether or not they were involved in atrocities. The goal of the war should be victory and peace; to which justice is set in opposition.[9] This line of reasoning suggests that a warring state does not want an investigation into its military actions, tactics and outcomes out of two concerns. First, the government does not want an atrocities investigation that would publicize its fighting methods, allowing its adversaries an opportunity to look into its capacities and tactics. Second, the government wants to avoid being second-guessed about its tactical decisions. According to this argument, hostility to atrocities investiga-

[4] For the 1994 violence, see Chap. 6.

[5] Statement of the Prosecutor of the International Criminal Court, Fatou Bensouda, on opening a Preliminary Examination into the situation in Burundi (April 25, 2016), available at https://www.icc-cpi.int/Pages/item.aspx?name=otp-stat-25-04-2016.

[6] A/HRC/RES/33/24, Situation of human rights in Burundi (October 5, 2016).

[7] Butty, VOA News (October 27, 2016).

[8] Nechepurenko, Ivan and Nick Cumming-Bruce, New York Times (November 16, 2016).

[9] Bass (2004) (presenting the case against this dichotomy).

tions should increase with the escalation in military action and the importance of the target.

In the past, NATO had to deal with exactly such concerns in the aftermath of the Kosovo bombing campaign. Following the 1998 military campaign into Kosovo, the ICTY Prosecutor Louise Arbour received requests to investigate the actions of NATO in the aerial bombings. In her last months in office, during the Spring of 1999, Arbour notified all NATO countries of the preliminary investigation that she was conducting, but did not indicate that she would investigate their actions.[10] In June 2000, her successor, Prosecutor Del Ponte found insufficient evidence to open a proper investigation into the NATO crimes.[11] In the meanwhile, however, NATO countries were concerned about the prosecutor's ability to expose their military actions. This concern was manifested at that time in Sierra Leone, where the UK foreign minister did not want to risk that a prosecutor would investigate the actions of UK troops,[12] even though these troops were never accused of committing any atrocities.

Critics of this argument point out that several governments that have participated in wars have actually supported atrocities investigations into those wars. For example, the government of the Democratic Republic of the Congo referred the situation in the eastern part of the country to the ICC in 2004. More recently, in 2012, the government of Mali did the same for war crimes in three northern regions and incidents occurring in the south, in Bamako and Sévaré. Such examples indicate that war alone is not a good enough reason to oppose an atrocities investigation. Instead, critics argue that such opposition is better explained by participation or complicity in crimes, as explained by the *complicity* category above. Yet, such criticism ignores the fact that many governments, while legally in control of their country, have no control of the participants in the war. In its referral to the ICC, for example, the Democratic Republic of the Congo was more concerned with marginalizing rebel factions and rising warlords, rather than protecting the exposure of its military conduct during the war.[13] As a result, such governments are not concerned with the possibility of revealing their military actions, tactics and outcomes. They are more concerned with targeting their opponents, a stance that is discussed in Sect. 3.2 under the *victorious* category.

3.1.1.3 Alliance

A third line of reasoning suggests that a state will not support an investigation into the actions of one of its allies. States rely on their allies to deal with some of their most significant concerns in international affairs. Supporting an atrocities investigation into an ally is seen as an affront to the spirit of cooperation expected among

[10] Scheffer (2013, p. 292).

[11] Prosecutor's Press Release (June 13, 2000).

[12] Scheffer (2013, p. 331).

[13] Burke-White (2005).

allies.[14] It is also seen as a risk to the stability of the alliance, as an investigation may target leaders on whom the alliance depends,[15] may incentivize defections towards other partners[16] and may impede third areas of cooperation.[17]

There are several well-known examples in international affairs of a state consistently opposing an atrocities investigation into the actions of an ally. China's shielding of the Sri Lankan government, Russia's intervention on behalf of former Soviet states and the United States' constant support for Israel are cases in which the strength of an alliance prohibits any discussion at the UNSC of an investigation into atrocities committed in these areas.

Beyond the moment of an investigation's creation, the alliance category expects that a state with power will continue to oppose an atrocities investigation into one of its allies even after the investigation has been created. In the mid-1990s, after the initial post-Cold War euphoria subsided, Russia became increasingly hostile towards the ICTY and, particularly, its investigations of Serbian actions. Through its seat at the UNSC, Russia delayed the appointment of new judges, argued against increases in the ICTY's budget and softened any pressure exerted by the UNSC on Belgrade relating to the ICTY. It is suspected that similar opposition exists by Russia on the ICC's examination of the situation in Georgia, by the United States on the ICC's examination of the situation in Palestine, and by France on the ICC's investigations in Cote d'Ivoire.[18]

Despite its apparent strengths, the alliance argument sometimes borders on the conspiratorial, as its claimants seem to believe that any state connection will outweigh an interest in an atrocities investigation. Apart from ignoring the incentives states have to support an investigation (presented in Sect. 3.2 below), such arguments over-extend the value of an alliance. A well-known case of such over-extension comes from China's relation with Sudan. The governments of Beijing and Khartoum had important economic ties in the early 2000s. In Sudan, China found a source to satisfy its growing energy needs. In turn, Khartoum found a no-questions-asked development partner in Beijing. When China opposed the UNSC's referral of the situation in Darfur to the ICC's prosecutor, supporters of the alliance category saw proof that the Sino-Sudanese economic cooperation was the reason behind

[14] Myers, The New York Times (1997) (arguing that US officials limited their public criticism of Kabila's opposition to investigation due to alliance considerations).

[15] Barltrop (2011), Prunier (2005) (France protected Idris Deby of Chad in Darfur events); Caplan in Totten and Markussen (2006) (US protected relationship with Sudanese intelligence chief Slaha Abdullah Gosh); Kabbah (2010) (expressing criticism on the prosecution of CDF leader Chief Higa Norman); Ku and Nzelibe (2006).

[16] Taylor in Black and Williams (2010); Brosché and Rothbart (2012) (presenting China's interest to avoid jeopardizing its access to Sudanese oil).

[17] Stedjan and Thomas-Jensen, in Black and Williams (2010), Prunier (2005) (arguing the US in Darfur was concerned about jeopardizing counter-terrorism relationships with the government of Sudan); Barltrop (2011) (China worried about sanctions against Sudan that would harm Sudan-China trade).

[18] Bosco (2014).

Beijing's opposition to an atrocities investigation.[19] While there may be some truth to this argument, it fails to explain how China turned its opposition into an abstention vote in 2005 thereby allowing the authorization of the investigation of atrocities committed in Darfur, while continuing to grow its economic ties with Sudan.

3.1.1.4 Ideology

Beyond the three above arguments, some states are consistently opposed to atrocities investigations for matters of principle. This principled opposition views atrocities investigations as a tool of expanding Western values at the expense of the core international legal concept of state sovereignty. States, the argument goes, should retain the prerogative to both fight wars and to judge whether their actions in such wars remain within the boundaries of international criminal law. Side-stepping this construct risks unravelling the foundational principle of sovereignty, upon which the international system of equal states is created.

At the UNSC, the most consistent reminder of such a principled stance comes from China and Russia.[20] The Chinese position was eloquently put forth in diplomatic language at the time the UNSC voted to create the ICTR. In abstaining, the Chinese argued that:

> At present people still have doubts and worries about the way in which an international tribunal is established by a Security Council resolution under Chapter VII of the United Nations Charter, and careful studies are still being carried out. In principle, China is not in favour of invoking at will Chapter VII of the Charter to establish an international tribunal through the adoption of a Security Council resolution. That position, which we stated in the Council last year during the deliberations on the establishment of an International Tribunal for the Former Yugoslavia, remains unchanged.[21]

The strength of this argument, however, waned with the rise of the concept of the Responsibility to Protect in the late 1990s.[22] Sovereignty is no longer seen as the only bedrock principle of the international system.[23] As Chapter VII was invoked to respond militarily to on-going internal wars, its applicability to a more restricted atrocities investigation became less contested.

Beyond reasons of legal theory, the appeal of the principled opposition to atrocities investigation was also undercut by the fact that its main supporters were those on the receiving end of atrocities investigations. In the past 25 years, one of the most vigorous manifestations of a principled opposition to atrocities investigation came

---

[19] Barltrop (2011) (China worried about sanctions against Sudan that would harm Sudan-China trade); Brosché and Rothbart (2012) (presenting China's interest to avoid jeopardizing its access to Sudanese oil).

[20] Black and Williams (2010) (arguing China, Russia and have a preference for a pluralist stance, which they contrast to the solidarity approach); Châtaignier (2005) (noting that Russia "sans surprise" supported a domestic tribunal in Sierra Leone).

[21] S/PV.3453 (November 8, 1994).

[22] For the effects of the Responsibility to Protect on sovereignty, see e.g. Serrano and Weiss (2014).

[23] Doyle (2015).

from Slobodan Milosevic, from the docket in The Hague. Milosevic considered the ICTY both illegal and illegitimate.[24] In his view, presented in his opening statement at his trial at the ICTY,[25] Milosevic maintained that:

> [t]here is a fundamental historical fact that one should proceed from when seeking to understand what happened and which led to everything that happened in the territory of Yugoslavia from 1991 until the present day, and that is the violent destruction of a European state, Yugoslavia… It is not only that a state was destroyed. The United Nations system was destroyed. Also the corpus of principles upon which the world civilisation was based has been destroyed.

Milosevic went on to also directly criticize the ICTY:

> I will not dwell on the lack of the legal basis for the establishment of this Tribunal. I would just like to recall that the source of judicial power can only come from international treaties and not resolutions, as stated by the UN Secretary-General himself in a statement to the Security Council on May 3rd, 1993. However, you owe a response to the international community of where does the right of the Security Council come to suspend legal treaties? We have the legal the Geneva Conventions from 1949 as well as Additional Protocols to punish war crimes which place the responsibility for a trial of such cases on national courts. An international court can have authority only if it was created by a lege artis act and if it is of a general nature. This Tribunal lacks both elements. The act of the establishment of this Tribunal is of an individual nature. It's a political nature.

In later years, similar arguments have been voiced by several African leaders who found themselves, or are afraid to find themselves, in the cross-hairs of an atrocities investigation. Initially, such claims of principled opposition surfaced after the ICC issued summonses to appear against six prominent Kenyan politicians in March 2011. More recently, the principled opposition to atrocities investigations led Burundi, Gambia and South Africa to withdraw from the ICC in late 2016 – early 2017. The African Union leaders agreed to follow suit. Gambia and South Africa subsequently reversed their decisions to withdraw and the government of Burundi is suspected of committing atrocities, indicating that a principled opposition to atrocities may be more a matter of self-interest than principle. Yet, the idea that the ICC is a neo-colonial institution has picked up strength to such a degree that it has spurred rigorous academic debates[26] and has led to repeated public questioning of the ICC's prosecutor Fatou Bensouda on the targeting of the investigations.[27] This debate is unlikely to fade soon.

---

[24] Sadat (2002).

[25] Prosecutor v. Slodoban Milosevic, Defence Opening Statement (2004, p. 32174).

[26] See e.g. the excellent articles by several invited experts on the question *Is the International Criminal Court (ICC) targeting Africa inappropriately?*, found at http://iccforum.com/africa, hosted by the ICC Forum, a legal journal and world-wide discussion forum on issues facing the Prosecutor of the International Criminal Court, which is run by the UCLA School of Law's Human Rights Project in a partnership with the Office of the Prosecutor of the International Criminal Court.

[27] See e.g. Oladimeji (2016) (reporting on statements made in April 2016 by Prosecutor Bensouda at the African Bar Leaders Conference).

3.1.2 Limits of the Four Categories

When taken together, the four categories highlight important reasons for which a UNSC member would oppose atrocities investigations. In brief, atrocities that (i) were committed by a UNSC member, (ii) took place in a war that involved a UNSC member or (iii) implicate an ally of a UNSC member are not likely to receive an atrocities investigation. Additionally, some UNSC members may be categorically opposed to an investigation as a matter of principle.

The biggest strength of these arguments lies in their simplicity. Everyone accepts that states will act towards self-preservation, protect their military methods, desire friendships and act on the basis of their ideology. And, similar to most simple things, these arguments are often correct. The most notorious case of the applicability of these arguments at the UNSC is the case of Syria.

Since the earliest massacres in Syria, in late 2011, there have been repeated attempts at the UNSC to refer the atrocities to the ICC. The main state behind an ICC referral has been France. A strong supporter of the ICC, France has also been represented at the UN by a team that includes former-ICC employees.[28] For the first stage of their efforts, the French were supported by the United Kingdom and a number of non-permanent members of the UNSC. Outside the UNSC, the idea of an atrocities investigation into Syria received strong support from 57 other states, under the leadership of Switzerland, which, on January 13, 2013, authored a letter to the UNSC calling for a referral.[29]

These initial French attempts were, however, mired with problems. First, some commentators thought that an outright referral would be misplaced. For example, Moreno-Ocampo, the former ICC Prosecutor, argued that, to stop the killings, the UNSC should use the ICC as the sword of Damocles.[30] An immediate referral could lead to more violence. The threat of a referral would be more likely to deter atrocities and stem the war. Additionally, the French actions and the Swiss letter failed to corral the support of some states that strongly supported the ICC. Guatemala—a non-permanent member of the UNSC at the time—and a vocal supporter of international criminal law was perhaps the most surprising absence. For these states, another referral that lacked provisions on financing of the investigation and cooperation with the ICC was—again like the referrals of Darfur and Libya—doomed to fail.[31] Then, the proposal for an ICC referral also faced the hurdles of Russia and China, which had been opposed to any action on Syria. In private consultations with the other P5, Russia clarified its intent to use its veto against such a resolution.[32]

---

[28] E.g. One of the French legal advisers at the UN was former advisor to ICC Prosecutor Moreno-Ocampo.

[29] S/2014/361 (May 19, 2014).

[30] Moreno-Ocampo (2013).

[31] Interview: 20.

[32] Interviews: 10, 13, 14, 20.

Before, however, even reaching a Russian veto, the ICC referral faced the opposition of the United States.

The U.S. government supported the use of a justice mechanism for Syria. But, it did not think that this mechanism should be the ICC.[33] Afraid that any ICC investigation in Syria could look into the status of the Golan Heights, the United States was skeptical about authorizing an investigation that could implicate Israel.[34] Additionally, many in the Obama administration were not convinced that an international court could be of any help. Having seen the constant failures of the Darfur and Libya investigations, as well as the inability of the Special Tribunal for Lebanon to arrest any of those charged by its prosecutor, the United States preferred to support a Syrian justice mechanism as part of a future domestic transitional justice system. A court, together with a truth and reconciliation commission similar to those set up in Sierra Leone would provide the best option for U.S. preferences.[35]

Admittedly, the United States was not alone in its suggestion of a domestic judicial mechanism. Guatemala's negative reaction to another ICC referral reflected some of the same concerns.[36] Additionally, a few influential individuals in the field of human rights supported the regionalization of the justice mechanism. The Middle East, as a geographical region, could be better served with a permanent human rights court rather than a one-off ICC referral.[37]

The position of the United States, however, changed significantly over the ensuing months. In January and February 2014, talks among the Syrian parties and the international community ended with little success. At the UNSC, Russia was holding out for the Assad regime's survival. After months of debate, in February 2014, Russia accepted an innocuous UNSC resolution for humanitarian aid.[38] Then, in the beginning of April 2014, the Ukrainian crisis became the focal point of the relationship between the United States and Russia, which had continued to stray in the course of the prior years.

At approximately the same time, the French rejuvenated their efforts for an ICC referral on Syria. On April 3, 2014, France circulated to the UNSC members a report on the atrocities perpetrated by the Assad regime, which included 55,000 photos from Assad's secret prisons provided by a defector code-named Caesar.[39] The chilling report was accompanied by an interview with France's ambassador to

---

[33] Interview: 14.

[34] Interview: 20.

[35] Interview: 14.

[36] Interview: 20.

[37] The New York Times (April 4, 2012).

[38] S/RES/2139 (2014).

[39] France, Press Release (April 15, 2014).

the UN regarding the need for accountability.[40] The French initiative was welcomed by various states. Again under Swiss leadership, on May 21, 2014, 58 countries co-sponsored the French resolution.[41] By the time France submitted the resolution to the UNSC for a vote, on May 22, 2014, 64 states were listed as co-sponsors.[42] Satisfied with all the provisions,[43] the United States was among them. When draft resolution S/2014/348 was put to the UNSC for a vote, it was quickly vetoed by Russia and China, who remained opposed to any intervention in Syria.

Since the Russian and Chinese vetoes, the prospect of an atrocities investigation in Syria has shifted away from the UNSC. In late December 2016, the UN General Assembly adopted a resolution drafted by Lichtenstein for the UN to create the International, Impartial and Independent Mechanism to:

> collect, consolidate, preserve and analyse evidence of violations of international humanitarian law and human rights violations and abuses and to prepare files in order to facilitate and expedite fair and independent criminal proceedings, in accordance with international law standards, in national, regional or international courts or tribunals that have or may in the future have jurisdiction over these crimes, in accordance with international law;[44]

In the meanwhile, the UN Human Rights Council's Independent International Commission of Inquiry on the Syrian Arab Republic, which was created in August 2011, continues to conduct investigations and publicize its findings. It has highlighted numerous incidents of atrocities, including the genocide of the Yazidis.[45] It has also repeatedly called for accountability.[46] The void created by the UNSC's inaction has also been filled with NGOs, such as the Commission for International Justice and Accountability and the Syria Justice and Accountability Center,[47] which attempt to preserve evidence of atrocities and galvanize support for an atrocities investigation.

For purposes of this Chapter, the events in Syria highlight how all four factors have led some of the UNSC member states to oppose an atrocities investigation. Both Russia and the US had military reasons to oppose an investigation, as they have combat forces in that war. Russia has also been accused on perpetrating war crimes in Syria, which would be exposed in an investigation. Additionally, for Russia, the Assad regime is a strong ally. The US is also hesitant to authorize an

---

[40] The New York Times (April 4, 2014).

[41] S/2014/361 (May 19, 2014).

[42] S/2014/348 (May 22, 2014).

[43] The New York Times (May 21, 2014).

[44] A/RES/71/248 (January 11, 2017).

[45] A/HRC/32/CRP.2 (June 15, 2016).

[46] See e.g. Office of the High Commissioner for Human Rights, *Too long a wait for peace and justice – Commission on Inquiry* (July 1, 2016) (available at http://www.ohchr.org/EN/NewsEvents/Pages/Syriapeacejusticecannotwait.aspx).

[47] See https://syriaaccountability.org/about/; See also Taub, The New Yorker (April 18, 2016).

Table 3.1 Countries with Atrocities since 1990 in which the UNSC members have reasons not to investigate

1. Afghanistan	11. Moldova
2. Armenia	12. North Korea
3. Azerbaijan	13. Pakistan
4. Angola	14. Palestine[a]
5. Colombia	15. Russia
6. Egypt	16. Saudi Arabia
7. Iran	17. Syria
8. Iraq	18. Tajikistan
9. Israel	19. Ukraine
10. Mexico	

[a]As of the writing of this book, Palestine has been recognized as a state by 136 of the 193 UN member states. In 2012, Palestine was granted the status of non-member observer state by the UN General-Assembly. But, Palestine has not been recognized as a state by the UNSC or the UN. Among the P5, France, the United Kingdom and the United States do not recognize Palestine as a state. Yet, several initiatives relating to atrocities investigations (such as the ICC's preliminary examination into the situation in Palestine, which started in 2015) have treated Palestine as if it were a state.

investigation that could implicate the Golan Heights due to its alliance to Israel. For China, there as an ideological opposition to an investigation, due to its support of state rights. Guatemala also opposed a referral because of a principled belief that a proper international atrocities investigation required broader parameters and more committed material support.

While the example of Syria illustrates how considerations of complicity, war, alliance and principle may lead states away from atrocities investigations, the effect of these considerations on the work of the UNSC is more limited than one would expect. For most of the 92 states that have experienced atrocities in the post-Cold War era, none of these factors is visibly at play. As a result, while these categories may account for the lack of an atrocities investigation by the UNSC in atrocities committed in countries, such as Egypt, Israel, Moldova, North Korea, Syria and Tajikistan, they do not explain the UNSC's actions in a host of other countries, such as Angola, Bangladesh, Burundi, Chad, and Sierra Leone. Overall, as presented in Table 3.1 above, the four categories explain the UNSC decision not to create an atrocities investigation into 19 of the 92 states with atrocities. To explain the UNSC's actions in the remaining 73 cases, the next Section presents the literature on the incentives states have to create an atrocities investigation.

3.2 Atrocities Investigations to the Forefront

The creation of an atrocities investigation, whether domestic or international, involves a significant political decision. Not only will the investigation require material support, but there are reasonable fears that it may upset the political balance of power within a state, exacerbate the conflict and prolong, rather than end, the atrocities. Despite these fears, however, the previous Chapter documented how investigations have been taking place with increasing frequency.

3.2.1 The Four Categories of Reasons in Favor of an Atrocities Investigation

Several analyses have looked into the reasons why atrocities investigations are created. These analyses can be grouped in one of four ideal categories, namely the *victorious*, *idealist*, *identity* and *liberal* categories. These four categories identify the causes and the causal mechanisms behind the creation of international atrocities investigations. Accordingly, they answer, among others, the following questions: (i) who creates the investigation, (ii) under what circumstances, (iii) for what goal and (iv) for which atrocities. While the four categories present concise and coherent answers to these four questions, they are not exclusive explanations for the creation of any single atrocities investigation. In reality, and similar to the four categories presented in Sect. 3.1 above, factors from each of the four categories overlap when it comes to supporting an investigation. For purposes of intellectual clarity, however, it is important to examine each category in turn.

3.2.1.1 The Victorious Category

The victorious category for the creation of atrocities investigations is rooted in the teachings of the realist school of political science. Under this category, political leaders, craving for power, use an atrocities investigation to target the losers of a political conflict. Whether following a successful international war or domestic regime change, the victorious leaders use atrocities investigations as a method to solidify their grip on power and ostracize the losers from the political community. These leaders are thus more interested in getting rid of a political opponent than in the details of an investigation. The creation of atrocities investigations in these circumstances is more likely to take place when the victors are not powerful enough to forgo dealing with the losers, but nonetheless confident that the investigation will not decrease their grip on power. In such situations, atrocities investigations will be created with the clear mandate of bolstering those who are already the most powerful.

Historically, such use of atrocities investigations has been frequent. At the end of World War I, the victorious allies, as part of the Versailles Peace Treaty, aimed to put the German Kaiser Wilhelm I on trial for his role in beginning and then continuing the Great War. While the victorious allies were able to extract important concessions and payments from the losing Germans, they remained worried that the Kaiser could act as a polarizing figure, one who would reignite the feuds leading to World War I. To avoid such a scenario, the victorious allies sought to prosecute the Kaiser, which they only gave up on when the Kaiser found refuge in the Netherlands, as a guest of the Dutch royal family, thereby removing himself from the political life in Germany and the continent. At that point, the desire for an investigation into his actions gradually waned.

Later on, such uses of investigations became abundant in Europe. Hitler, for example, following his writings in Mein Kampf, created the Volksgerichtshof (People's Court) that targeted the enemies of the Aryan race.[48] Similarly, the Soviets used investigations in order to target weaker political opponents. Having perfected this system of political targeting in the domestic arena with the Moscow trials of 1936–1938, the Soviets supported investigations as a way to consolidate power and to undermine weaker opponents in the states of the Eastern bloc.[49] Decades later, Huntington and Elster each documented how similar goals led the countries of Eastern Europe to hold transitional justice trials after the fall of the Soviet Union.[50] In all of the above examples, the ruling regime targeted its weaker political opponents by instituting criminal investigations, which in turn allowed the new regime to consolidate power.

The most recent clear manifestation of the victorious category comes from the creation of an atrocities investigation in the Ivory Coast. Following the civil war and the ouster of Laurent Gbagbo from the presidency, the government of his successor, Alessandre Ouattara, was quick to seek the assistance of the ICC in investigating atrocities committed during the Gbagbo era. As the victorious category would predict, the creators of the investigation were not entirely in control of the country, as they were propped up by UN forces and by France, which had intervened militarily. The Gbagbo side, which had lost the civil war, still had some political power, mainly in the predominantly Christian south of the country. By asking the ICC to investigate the local atrocities, the new Ouattara regime ensured that Gbagbo, his wife Simone Gbagbo, and his strongman, Charles Blé Goudé, were imprisoned at The Hague. This both physically impeded them and politically discredited them, precluding them from claims to power. Due to these facts, it is no surprise that pro-Gbagbo supporters consider the ICC investigations to function as a biased form of "victor's justice."[51]

3.2.1.2 The Idealist Category

The idealist category for the creation of international atrocities investigations has its roots in the constructivist school of political science.[52] Leaders can use atrocities investigations to restore the normative framework of a society. In such cases, the

---

[48] Bass (2000).

[49] E.g. the 1952 trial Rudolph Slansky in Czechoslovakia, who was the General Secretary of the Communist Party of Czechoslovakia and was purged by Stalin after Joseph Tito broke away from the U.S.S.R. After an 8 day trial, Slansky was sentenced to death and executed by public hanging.

[50] Huntington (1991); Elster (1998).

[51] BBC, November 30, 2011.

[52] For similar arguments for the power of the norm of justice, see Scheffer (2013); Orentlicher (1991); Meron (1998); Sikkink (2011).

targets of investigations are not ordinary criminals, but those responsible for breaking the moral fabric of society and violating its foundational norms. Leaders are interested in the process of the investigation, as it helps with the healing that a post-conflict society has to undergo in order to overcome the trauma of the atrocities and deal with its past. In such instances, the creators of the investigation focus on the potential catharsis for the social group—both victims and perpetrators—rather than mere punishment or attribution of guilt.

Historically, the most famous case study for this category arose at the end of World War II. The allies arrested the remaining leaders of the Nazi party and put them on trial. The process for the creation of the Nuremberg tribunals was initiated by the United States a few years before the end of World War II. Within the Roosevelt administration, there had been two opposing camps. Henry Morgenthau Jr., the Treasury Secretary and a close friend to President Roosevelt, tried to convince the Roosevelt administration to summarily execute the captured Nazi leadership. On the other side, Henry Stimson, Secretary of War, as part of his strategy to avoid reducing Germany to rubble, argued in favor of a trial for the Nazi leadership. Stimson, a Republican politician from New York, is most remembered for his decision to use two atomic bombs against Japan. For Germany, however, Stimson believed that a criminal investigation would help restore the normative boundaries that had been shattered by the Nazi ideals. The tribunal was thus created by the "massed angered forces of common humanity,"[53] not a single state. Its goal was not only to punish the Nazis but also to "bring our law in balance within the universal moral judgment of mankind." Its result was to create a standard for judging aggressive war, a prerequisite to "mak[ing] onward to a world of law and peace."[54] As a result, when commenting on these preferences during his opening statements at the Nuremberg trial, U.S. Supreme Court Justice Robert Jackson, in his capacity as one of the four prosecutors at Nuremberg, considered the allies' decision to create the court as "one of the most significant tributes that Power ever paid to Reason."[55]

After Nuremberg, the idealist category was most recently manifested through the creation of the Special Court for Sierra Leone. While Chap. 5 presents the facts behind the creation of that court in more detail, at this point it is worth noting that the court was partly created because President Kabbah of Sierra Leone asked the United Nations for assistance in dealing with the RUF leaders. Kabbah's decision to seek such a court may also fall under the victorious category, as the court offered a means of ridding the country of, and diminishing the influence of, the RUF leaders. In part, however, Kabbah's decision was based on a need to restore the foundational norms of the Sierra Leonean society. Even though the chant "Di Wah Dohn-Dohn" signaled the end of hostilities, the fabric of the Sierra Leonean society had been torn apart, with hundreds of thousands of atrocities victims, including tens of thousands

[53] Stimson and Bundy (1948, p. 588).

[54] Stimson and Bundy (1948, p. 589–591).

[55] Nuremberg Opening Statement, Chief U.S. Prosecutor (1945).

suffering from amputations of the hands, arms, feet or legs, living side by side with thousands of former rebels, many of whom had been mere children when they committed the atrocities. An atrocities investigation was one of the mechanisms that would allow the Sierra Leoneans, in President Kabbah's words, to "deal effectively with the trauma, the emotional pain resulting from that bitter conflict."[56]

3.2.1.3 The Identity Category

The identity category for the creation of international atrocities investigations has its roots in the ethnographic studies of political science. Under this category, those who seek to reaffirm their own identity, particularly if they perceive their identity to be under threat, initiate atrocities investigations. An investigation is thus a means to nourish, strengthen and better define the imaginary community of people who initiate the investigation. Similar to the construction of nationalist movements, the target of the investigation is the "other," defined both as the threat to, but also in contrast to, the initiators' own community.

The most famous manifestation of the identity category is the Eichmann trial of 1961. Israel, yearning to find and punish the Nazis who planned and carried out the Holocaust, tracked down Adolph Eichmann in Argentina, kidnapped him and brought him to Jerusalem and then put him on trial. Eichmann was unrepentant, the evidence (with his own hand-writing) conclusive. A death sentence was handed down, and following his execution, Hannah Arendt ignited a debate on criminal responsibility that continues to this day.[57] For purposes of this book, however, it is important to note that Israel, first, decided to find Eichmann and, then, decided to kidnap and prosecute him, rather than merely killing him in Argentina. This is somewhat counterintuitive. As Bass notes, "if one wants to get rid of undesirables, using the trappings of a domestic courtroom is a distinctly awkward way to do so."[58] Grappling with the reasons behind the trial, Arendt consistently refers to the larger goals of the Israeli state, which under the leadership of Prime Minister Ben-Gurion was not as interested in Eichmann as it was in highlighting the suffering of the Jewish populations during World War II.[59] The clearest statements of such goals were offered by Ben-Gurion himself. In reacting to Argentina's protests regarding the kidnapping of Eichmann from its territory, Ben-Gurion said "…I am certain that only a very few persons in the world would fail to understand the profound motivation and supreme moral justification of the details of his capture." Due to this "profound motivation," the "trial of Adolf Eichmann illustrates the inescapable link between justice and identity politics."[60]

---

[56] Kabbah (2010, p. 176).

[57] Arendt (1963).

[58] Bass (2000, p. 6).

[59] Arendt (1963).

[60] Sanders (2015).

Following the Eichmann case, the identity category for the creation of atrocity trials is also manifest in the trials of the juntas in Argentina and in Chile, and in the trials of high-level Nazi collaborationists in France. In the 1980s, France prosecuted Maurice Papon, Klaus Barbie, and Paul Touvier, as part of a larger attempt to address the role the country played during World War II. These three trials highlighted how the actions of these members of the Vichy regime were incompatible with the national identity of modern France. Papon's trial was "a particular vivid example… of France's…passionate involvement with its past."[61] Far from an ordinary criminal trial in a domestic court, it was attended over its course by 146 accredited journalists and 1413 scholars, and "was attendant with the expectation that [it] would yield lessons of a … symbolic nature for French society as a whole."[62] The yearned-for symbolism was aptly summarized by Prime Minister Jospin's statement that "Vichy was the negation of France"[63] and by President's Chirac conclusion that "[t]here is also France, one certain idea of France, correct, generous, loyal to its traditions, to its ethos. That France was never at Vichy."[64] The France that was at Vichy, i.e. Papon, Barbie and Touvier, was now in the docket.

3.2.1.4 The Liberal Category

The liberal category for the creation of international atrocities investigations developed from liberalism, which is one of several second-image theories of political science. The category predicts that state governments create atrocities investigations to further their own domestic preferences. In creating an atrocities investigation, the government is trying to satisfy its supporters, whether the electoral public in a democracy or the backers of a dictator, with the ulterior motive of staying in power. In this process, the government also takes into consideration pressure from NGOs, activists and civil society. Atrocities investigations are thus expected to focus on those atrocities that target, or are condemned by, such groups.

Bass offers the most thorough application of this category to atrocities investigations. Bass argues that international atrocities trials are initiated when liberal states take up the cause of international justice. Liberal states, imbued with judicial frameworks and a preference for the rule of law, are more likely to choose an investigation as a response to atrocities than non-liberal states. Yet, Bass argues, because they prioritize their own domestic political preferences, liberal states are more likely to resort to trials when (i) doing so poses no risk to their own soldiers, (ii) the atrocities targeted their own citizens, (iii) public opinion—rather than only political elites—is

[61] Bracher (1999).

[62] Wood (1999).

[63] Le Monde, October 23, 1997.

[64] "[I]l y a aussi la France, une certaine idée de la France, droite, généreuse, fidèle à ses traditions, à son génie. Cette France n'a jamais été à Vichy." Speech at the memorial for the Vel d'Hiv Roundup (July 16, 1995).

outraged at the atrocities, and (iv) NGOs shame liberal states into action and provide legal expertise.

Bass documents how the interplay of these factors led to Napoleon's banishment to Saint Helena (rather than his trial by the restored Bourbons), the allies support for the trial of Kaiser Wilhelm I at the end of World War I, the creation of the Nuremberg trials and the UNSC's decision to create the ICTY.[65] Through his analysis, Bass illustrates that the electoral public of western liberal democracies holds important power in influencing the creation of atrocities investigations, as the governments of these states react to public pressure.

Bass' argument, however, also points to an important shortcoming of the liberal category, namely that atrocities investigations created for domestic political preferences are prone to face significant limitations. After the Armenian genocide, for example, the "British public and much of its elite were outraged."[66] Such was the push for justice that the United Kingdom arrested some high-ranking members of the Ottoman government and put them on trial. Gradually, however, the interest shifted towards "punishing crimes against Britons than crimes against Armenians."[67] When Ataturk held a small group of Britons as prisoners in 1921, the U.K. government exchanged them with the alleged atrocity perpetrators, thereby ending any prospect for an atrocities investigation. In the words of the Foreign Office, the need for a trial was "outweighed by necessity of obtaining release of our prisoners."[68] The desire for an investigation dropped with the shift in the focus of the U.K. public.

3.2.2 Limits of the Four Categories

The four categories described above are seldom used exclusively in the creation of an atrocities investigation. Collectively, these four categories stand for the proposition that an atrocities investigation is likely to be created when a state (i) wants to target specific opponents, (ii) feels a strong normative demand for justice, (iii) wants to strengthen its identity, and (iv) is liberal, gripped by a principled idea, and wants to target crimes committed against its soldiers without risking the lives of its troops. Blending elements from all four of these categories, Rudolph argues that a combination of real-politik with domestic interests, bureaucratic prerogatives and idealism play an important role in the creation of such investigations.[69] He also documents how these various factors have influenced the creation of the ICTY and the ICTR,

[65] However, Bass does not explain why the non-western and non-liberal UNSC members, such as Russia and China supported the creation of the ICTY.

[66] Bass (2000, p. 106).

[67] Bass (2000, p. 138).

[68] FO 371/6504/E10662, 27 September 1921, quoted in Bass (2000, p. 142).

[69] Rudolph (2001).

as well as the ECCC and the ICC. The historical literature on the creation of tribunals also highlights the co-existence of these factors.[70]

Despite the potential overlap in practice, the four existing categories clarify why a state would decide to prosecute atrocities domestically or would ask the international community for help in prosecuting atrocities committed on its territory. Perhaps the government in a state wants to target its political opponents (e.g. the victorious category in Cambodia in 1997). It is equally likely that the government has a normative commitment to the idea of justice (e.g. the idealist category in Ukraine in 2014). Alternatively, the state may want to reestablish its image domestically and in the international community as a law-abiding state (e.g. the identity category in the Democratic Republic of the Congo in 2003). Finally, liberal governments, not facing any material risk, may be seeking justice as a means of satisfying domestic demands for accountability (e.g. the liberal category in Kenya in 2011).

In practice, however, the explanatory power of the four categories is significant restricted, as variables beyond each of the categories interfere with their application to a number of atrocities. Historically, there are several instances of atrocities that, despite having all the elements necessary for the manifestation of one of the four categories, never received an atrocities investigation. Haiti, for example, is a good candidate for victor's justice, as a number of times political leaders took power away from atrocity perpetrators (e.g. Jean-Bertrand Aristide over Jean-Claude Duvalier (also known as Baby Doc) and later Jean-Bertrand Aristide over a military dictatorship). Yet, no atrocities investigation has taken place. Similarly, the elements of the idealist category were present in both El Salvador and Guatemala after the end of their respective civil wars. Still, neither country decided to repair its social fabric through the use of investigations. Further, all of the elements of the identity category were manifest in Indonesia following the end of the Suharto era in 1998, as Indonesia began a democratization effort and an attempt to reconcile with its past. But, no atrocities investigation was created. Finally, the liberal category should have meant an investigation for Liberia, where a democratically elected government with an active civil society has developed after a long brutal civil war. Again, despite the category's predictions, there is no investigation.

Furthermore, these explanations focus on the role of state preferences in the creation of atrocities investigations. *None of these explanations, however, accounts for the post-Cold War uses of international atrocities investigations by the UNSC.* Admittedly, the preferences of some members of the UNSC vis-à-vis certain atrocities may fit within one of the four present categories. But, contrary to using a veto that is a solitary act, the UNSC members have to overcome a cooperation problem before authorizing the creation of an international atrocities investigation. Yet, these categories are state-centric. They do not explain how the motives of individual states align at the UNSC. For two reasons, the need for international cooperation in creating an atrocities investigation by the UNSC cannot be explained by such state-centric categories.

---

[70] Scharf (1997); Bassiouni (1996).

First, the 15 member states of the UNSC may have independently determined that an investigation is necessary for some atrocities. To arrive at a common decision on the creation of an atrocities investigation, the members of the UNSC have to aggregate their independent determinations into a single decision. This presupposes the existence of a method by which the members of the UNSC reveal their true preferences to each other. The four state-centric categories do not explain how the preferences of the UNSC members are revealed and aggregated. In practice, these two steps can have significant consequences on the likelihood that an investigation is initiated. In the case of Sierra Leone, for example, the United States spent months trying to ascertain if the United Kingdom supported an investigation.

Additionally, if only a few UNSC members have preferences in favor of an international atrocities investigation, the current state-centric categories do not explain why the other UNSC members go along. In the presence of uncertainty over the actions and the preferences of other states, undecided or opposing states have little incentive to change their views and support an investigation. There is a constant concern that the benefits of an atrocities investigation will not be uniformly distributed across all UNSC members. It was, for example, reasonable for Russia to view the investigation of Qadaffi's action in Libya with suspicion, as the investigation was coupled with an effort for regime change, which could be detrimental to Russia's greater political preferences. Yet, Russia somehow overcame its hesitations. The state-centric view of the four current categories restricts them from explaining how that happens.

Beyond their inability to account for the coordination problems faced by the members of the UNSC, the four categories do not explain the obvious disparities in the UNSC's decisions on atrocities, i.e. why the UNSC would investigate certain atrocities over others. As demonstrated in Map 1.1, factors that are not accounted for by these four categories seem to sway the UNSC towards or away from an investigation in otherwise identical atrocities.

A well-known example helps clarify how these four categories do not account for the actions of the UNSC. In May 1994, following the Rwandan genocide, some UNSC member states independently desired to create an international investigation. As the liberal category suggests, the public outrage in the United States pushed the Clinton administration to support an investigation.[71] In line with the victorious category, the Tutsi regime in Rwanda, which had a seat on the UNSC at the time, wanted an investigation into the atrocities perpetrated by the losing Hutus.[72] Reflecting the idealist category, New Zealand, the Czech Republic and Argentina, supported an investigation because of their belief in the norm of justice.[73] While the existing categories explain why each of these states had a preference for the creation of an investigation, they do not explain how these divergent preferences were revealed and aggregated into the creation of the ICTR. In essence, why and how did China, France, Russia, the United Kingdom, Nigeria, Djibouti,

[71] Scheffer (2013).

[72] Akhavan (1996).

[73] Keating (2004); Kovanda (2010).

Oman, Pakistan, Argentina and Spain also come to support the creation of the ICTR? These questions become especially hard to answer in the case of France, for example, which had been a supporter of the prior Hutu regime in Rwanda, even intervening to stop the advance of the Tutsi RPF with Operation Turquoise in May 1994. Furthermore, assuming that the 15 members of the UNSC considered the atrocities in Rwanda as ripe for justice, why did they find the mirror atrocities in Burundi not to be so suited?

In brief, the four current categories of atrocities investigations cannot explain the UNSC's decisions to create atrocities investigations, because they do not recognize the significance of the cooperation and coordination problems faced by the UNSC members. With the goal of finding a suitable answer to the question of this book, the next Section shifts its attention to past analyses of the UNSC's work. It concludes, however, that these analyses provide equally unsatisfactory answers to the present question, thereby leaving room for the introduction of an alternative explanation in Chap. 4.

3.3 Past Analyses of the UNSC's Actions

Since past writings on atrocities investigations do not provide a satisfactory answer to the work of the UNSC on atrocities investigation, this Section turns its attention to previous analyses of the UNSC. Unsurprisingly, the UNSC has attracted much scholarly attention in the past. Writings from both legal academics and political scientists have attempted to untangle the UNSC's complicated decision-making procedures. In an effort to ascertain if they provide a satisfactory response to the question of this book, this Section presents these analyses on the UNSC's operations and explains their strengths and weaknesses.

3.3.1 The Legal Literature

The legal literature on the UNSC is enormous in volume. In the early years of the UNSC's operations, the writings of legal scholars aimed to grapple with the nature and scope of the UNSC's actions. Schachter, for example, investigated the UNSC's power to authorize peacekeeping missions[74] and its growth vis-à-vis the power of UN General Assembly.[75] Jessup examined various proposals through which the UNSC could improve its dispute settlement and fact-finding functions.[76] Arangio-Ruiz looked into the role of the UNSC on the development of the law on peaceful

[74] Schachter (1968).

[75] Schachter (1964).

[76] Jessup (1970).

settlement of international disputes.[77] Cançado Trinidade analyzed the interplay between domestic jurisdiction of UN member states and the UNSC.[78]

Having attained a valuable understanding of how the UNSC works, the focus of legal authors has more recently turned to the UNSC's powers in dealing with current issues of international affairs. Following the Lockerbie case, for example, which was brought by Libya against the United States at the International Court of Justice challenging the UNSC's sanctions against Libya, Alvarez investigated if and how the actions of the UNSC can be judged, and if the UNSC can serve as both executive and judiciary within the UN system.[79] Similarly, when faced with regimes that target their own citizens, Evans suggested that the UNSC could understand threats to peace and security as to include the responsibility to protect.[80] On the issue of terrorism, for example, Szasz noted that the UNSC has shifted to a legislative approach.[81] Franck, further, examined the future of the UNSC following its 2003 breakdown over Iraq.[82]

On the issue of atrocities investigations, the legal literature again presents a detailed explanation on the powers of the UNSC to create such investigations. Schabas, for example, documents how the UNSC has the legal power to create independent investigations, refer cases to the ICC, and defer ICC prosecutions.[83] Werle also presents how the UNSC created the ICTY and the ICTR.[84] In contrast, Zahar and Sluiter take a critical stance on the power of the UNSC to authorize international atrocities investigations.[85]

The legal analyses, a small sample of which has been described above, provide significant insights into the workings of the UNSC. These writings elaborate on the interpretations of the UN Charter and the interplay of the UNSC with other bodies of international affairs. Additionally, they explain the UNSC's power to reinterpret the UN Charter in response to new threats to peace and security. The latter is a necessary prerequisite in the UNSC's decision to create international atrocities investigations, since these were not expressly mentioned in the UN Charter and were not used in the first 40 years of the UNSC's existence. By clarifying the legal basis behind the UNSC's decisions to authorize the creation of international atrocities investigations, the legal literature demystifies much of the work of the UNSC.

Despite its important contributions, the legal literature does not take into account the political preferences of the members of the UNSC. In dealing with terrorism, for example, the legal literature reveals that the UNSC legislates and focuses on the problems behind such legislative acts. Yet, it does not examine why the UNSC

[77] Arangio-Ruiz (1979).

[78] Cançado-Trindade (1976).

[79] Alvarez (1996).

[80] Evans (2009).

[81] Szasz (2002).

[82] Franck (2003).

[83] Schabas (2004).

[84] Werle (2005).

[85] Zahar and Sluiter (2008).

members decided to start legislating and how the decision to start legislating affects future votes at the UNSC on terrorism and other issues. In turning, however, a blind eye to the divergent incentives for cooperation between states, the legal literature cannot explain how the UNSC members make decisions at the UNSC. The reader is left to believe that decisions just happen, without appreciating the complicated machinations through which they take place. Additionally, while the legal analyses document the evolution of the UNSC's actions, they cannot explain how the same P5 had, for example, originally supported absolute sovereignty and now support the Responsibility to Protect doctrine. Evolution depends on changes in political preferences, which are not the focus of the legal literature on the UNSC.

More importantly for this book, because of its insistence on describing the legal basis behind a decision rather than the reasons behind the cooperation leading to such a decision, the legal literature cannot explain any of the UNSC decisions on atrocities investigation. For example, while legal analyses debate the legality of Resolution 955 that created the ICTR, such analyses do not explain why the UNSC members voted in favor of that resolution. Additionally, this literature does not have a framework for explaining why the UNSC members refrained from take certain actions (e.g. no investigation in Burundi). As a result, after having analyzed the legal literature on the UNSC, the question of this book still stands. In the hope of finding an answer, the next section turns to the political science literature.

3.3.2 The Political Science Literature

While the legal literature on the UNSC does not answer the question of this book, the political science writings on the UNSC are more promising. Improving upon the weaknesses of the legal writings, the political science literature presents a robust understanding of how state preferences are aggregated to form decisions at the UNSC. Overall, it presents four categories of explanations for why the UNSC members arrive at common decisions.

The first category of explanations falls under the realist school of thought. According to these analyses, the strongest UNSC members can coerce other UNSC members into specific decisions. Chile, for example, faced significant diplomatic pressure from the United States in the debates over Iraq in 2003.[86] Kuziemko and Werker document how such coercive tactics can even take place through monetary transfers akin to bribes. Non-permanent members of the UNSC receive more foreign aid than their peers who do not serve on the UNSC.[87]

Rational choice scholars have also examined cooperation at the UNSC. For these scholars, decisions at the UNSC depend on reaching cooperative equilibriums. The earliest such works on the UNSC emphasized the value of the veto, and the effect that this voting power has had on all substantive and procedural decisions of the

---

[86] Munoz (2009).

[87] Kuziemko and Werker (2006).

UNSC.[88] More recently, Voeten argues that a superpower's threat to take unilateral action without UNSC approval makes other P5 states reconsider their veto over actions they previously disapproved.[89] In a different rational choice analysis, Thompson asserts that UNSC members arrive at common decisions in an effort to transmit information. Thompson argues that because a UNSC decision provides credible information regarding a state's intentions and the consequences of its policies, it allows a coercing state to clearly signal its intentions to the international community, the target state and its own public.[90]

A constructivist approach also exists on this issue. Hurd, for example, identifies that UNSC members are concerned with the legitimacy of the UNSC because its legitimacy is a source of symbolic power. UNSC members who value this symbolism thus have a strong incentive to reach agreements over issues such as peacekeeping missions and the UNSC's general agenda. Additionally, weaker states can couch their arguments in terms of the UNSC's symbolic power, and in turn influence the UNSC members to backtrack on their original positions in order to protect the UNSC's long-term legitimacy. In a similar approach, Johnstone suggests that legal discourse at the UNSC, through its discursive properties, has an independent influence over the decisions of the UNSC members.[91]

Finally, through the writings of Prantl,[92] institutionalism is the last school of thought that provides an answer to the question of cooperation at the UNSC. Prantl argues that informal groups of states within the UNSC have proliferated as a response to the post-Cold War systemic change in international affairs. These informal groups provide an escape from the stifling structure of the P5 and a platform for those who are actually affected by a conflict. In doing so, the informal groups narrow the participatory gap at the UNSC, as the E10 states that are more knowledgeable have a say in the creation of the UNSC's response. As a result, these informal groups enable the members of the UNSC to reach effective responses to international crises. They also allow for diplomatic problem solving, a task that is often difficult for the P5.

Admittedly, some political science analyses of cooperation at the UNSC cross several of the above schools of thought. Voeten, for example, presents an analysis of cooperation at the UNSC that depends both on legitimacy and rational choice. In the absence of an enforcement mechanism for the decisions of the UNSC, Voeten argues that cooperation at the UNSC for the provision of public goods, such as peace and security, requires the existence of a social norm.[93] Similar to elite pacts, the non-majoritarian nature of the UNSC's decision-making procedures allows its decisions to signal out those specific acts that transgress commonly accepted social norms. In case of a specific war, for example, the UNSC members are expected to

[88] See e.g. Padelford (1948); Rudzinski (1951).

[89] Voeten (2001).

[90] Thompson (2006).

[91] Johnstone (2003a).

[92] Prantl (2005).

[93] Voeten (2005).

cooperate when they want to signal that the war has transgressed or will transgress a limit that should be defended. Additionally, Malone explains why and how the UNSC reacted to the political crises in Haiti from 1990 to 1997. In his analysis, all the elements identified by the above schools of political science come into play. Malone thus comes to see "the Security Council as one continuous evolving part of a pattern of global politics in which principles, laws, institutions, diplomacy, power politics, and changing perceptions of interest all have important roles, with chance and paradox ever waiting in the wings."[94] Similarly, Luck evaluates the work of the UNSC on the basis of its founding vision, its tools and challenges, subtly accepting that all schools of political thought influence the UNSC's works. Through historical analysis, Luck concludes that the UNSC "as an institution has proven repeatedly adaptable to a range of conditions, demands, and opportunities."[95]

The analyses presented by these four schools of political science provide critical insight into how the UNSC arrives at its decisions, and build on the writings of the legal community in a number of important ways. First, these analyses provide the correct orientation for understanding how the UNSC works, where the preferences of the various states form the basis of actions, while the law (i.e. the UN Charter and the Rules) provides the channel for arriving at the preferred result. Hurd, for example, argues that Pakistan has consistently desired to keep the situation in Kashmir on the UNSC's agenda due to the symbolic value of that agenda. Understanding this political desire should come before examining the analysis by Sievers and Daws into the various legal tools a state can use to set the agenda at the UNSC.[96]

Additionally, by emphasizing the variation in bargaining dynamics at the UNSC, the political science literature recognizes the circumstances under which decision-making gridlock can be overcome. Prantl, for example, demonstrates how, after years of impasse, the emergence of an informal group of states interested in the independence of Namibia led to a negotiated settlement proposal ultimately ending that conflict. In providing such explanations, the political science literature also offers insight into important case studies. Voeten's outside option, for example, provides a good frame of reference for understanding the 1998 UNSC debates surrounding the Kosovo war, one that cannot be perceived just by looking at the UN Charter's rules on the use of force.

Finally, the four explanations suggested by the political science literature seem to explain why some atrocities investigations never happened. With its focus on the role of power, the realist school explains why an investigation has never looked into atrocities committed in Pakistan or Colombia. As both of these states are powerful international actors that within the UNSC enjoy the regular support of the United States, an attempt to create an investigation would have to overcome significant power-related barriers within (and outside of) the UNSC. Similarly, echoing the *complicity* category presented in Part I above, the rationale choice school explains why the UNSC has never considered creating an investigation into atrocities com-

[94] Malone (1998).

[95] Luck (2006).

[96] Sievers and Daws (2014).

mitted in Chechnya, Tibet or Iraq. Since these atrocities would likely implicate one of the P5, the possible use of a veto prevents any action from ever taking place. Additionally, constructivist analyses offer guidance into the lack of an atrocities investigation into Burundi. As detailed in Chap. 6, the UNSC's decision not to create an investigation was a result of its preoccupation with its own legitimacy, rather than dealing with the local atrocities. Finally, the institutionalist literature sheds some light into the lack of investigations into the atrocities of El Salvador. Prantl documents how the Group of Friends of the Secretary-General on El Salvador (i.e. Colombia, Mexico, Spain, Venezuela and later the United States) provided crucial support to the mediation efforts to end the local civil war.[97] Because the primary objective of the Group of Friends was obtaining peace, they focused their diplomatic efforts on this goal at the exclusion of all others, such as financial development and atrocities investigations.

Despite these advantages, the political science literature has three significant shortcomings. First, it is not clear if the explanations provided in these writings can be generalized to all situations that occur at the UNSC. To the contrary, it often appears as if the analyses apply only to the few case studies presented by their authors. Malone's explanation on the UNSC's responses to the political crisis in Haiti is too case specific to be applicable beyond the case study on Haiti.[98] Voeten's outside option clearly occurred during the UNSC deliberations on the use of force in Kosovo (1998) and Iraq (2003).[99] It is not clear, however, that it was used in any other instance. Thompson's informational model also suffers from similar drawbacks, as it cannot be easily applied beyond the Gulf War (1990–1991) and the invasion of Iraq (2003).[100] Hurd's analysis on legitimacy at the UNSC—a concept that should always be present at the UNSC—is equally difficult to apply.[101] Was legitimacy, for example, a factor in the UNSC's decisions on sanctions on Iran? Furthermore, Johnstone's observations on the value of a legal discourse merit attention when the UNSC members actually discuss a certain situation, as they did over Kosovo, but appear inapplicable to the majority of issues at the UNSC that are barely debated (e.g. Burundi).[102] Paradoxically, these explanations appear to be applicable to issues that arise in other institutions. The outside option may, for example, be useful in a monetary union (e.g. potential exit of Greece from the Eurozone). Yet, they seem unable to explain the majority of the UNSC's work (e.g. renewal of UNFICYP, diplomacy in Burundi, negotiations over Syria). The UNSC, therefore, seems to remain an institution that has "generated so much commentary yet so little systematic analysis."[103]

---

[97] Prantl (2005).

[98] Malone (1998).

[99] Voeten (2001). There are reasons to suggest that Voeten's rationale was also at play in the 2011–2013 debates over Syria.

[100] Thompson (2006).

[101] Hurd (2002).

[102] Johnstone (2003a).

[103] Luck (2006).

Additionally, the political science literature seems indifferent towards most of the practical steps of the UNSC's operations, which form the basis of the legal literature. As a result, political scientists do not venture outside the veto rule in considering the effect that the UN Charter and the Rules have on the UNSC's decisions. Hurd, as a lone exception, evaluates only the agenda setting elements of the Rules, but nothing more.[104] As a result, the political science literature assumes that the regulations that control the work of the UNSC have no effect, neither substantive nor procedural, on the decisions of the UNSC. However, this assumption is never examined, even though it has long been recognized that the decision-making regulations affect the outcome of other institutions.[105]

Finally, the political science literature does not offer a satisfactory explanation for the reasons behind the UNSC's decision to create international criminal investigations. To begin with, there is only scant evidence to support the theories of the realist and the rational choice schools when applied to the UNSC's actions on atrocities investigations. As the following Chapters will show in more detail, it is not clear that a P5 state has ever used its power to convince weaker non-permanent members to vote in favor or against an atrocities investigation. In the case of Darfur, the United States allowed the investigation even though it had opposed the ICC. The explanations of the rational choice school are similarly inapplicable. As a state cannot create an international investigation alone, there is neither an outside option nor an informational advantage in acting through the UNSC on this topic.

The constructivist and instrumentalist explanations may be applicable in the UNSC's decisions to create atrocities investigations. The explanations that focus on legitimacy may be applied for the creation of international investigations. In line with Hurd's writings, for example, it is credible to assert that atrocities investigations are created for their symbolic value. The institutionalist writings of Prantl can also explain why informal group of states arise to support the creation of some investigations. In the investigation into Darfur, for example, the "ICC-9" were of critical importance (see Chap. 7). But, these explanations do not explain the disparity in the actions of the international actors in the area of international justice. How, for example, did symbolism lead to action with respect to Rwanda, yet failed to do so for Burundi? Why did the ICC-9 not exert pressure for an investigation into Sri Lanka? As a result, the question posed in this book remains unanswered.

3.4 Conclusion

This Chapter has examined the existing literature on atrocities investigations, as well as the political science and legal literature on the UNSC, with a goal of identifying why the UNSC members create investigations for specific atrocities.

---

[104] Hurd (2007).

[105] See e.g. McCubbins et al. (1987); O'Halloran (1994).

As described above, the four categories of explanations against atrocities investigations (*complicity, war, alliance, ideology*) indicate why a state would not support an atrocities investigation, but are factually not relevant for the majority of states that have experienced atrocities. By contrast, the four categories of explanations in favor of atrocities investigations (*victorious, idealist*, *identity* and *liberal)* explain the preferences individual states may have towards the creation of atrocities investigations. Yet, these categories cannot be applied to the UNSC in a satisfactory manner, as they are state-centric and do not account for the coordination and cooperation dilemmas faced by the UNSC members.

Beyond the reasons a state would oppose and support an atrocities investigation, this Chapter examined past analyses of the UNSC's work to evaluate whether these provide an answer to the present question. The legal literature offers valuable insight to understand the methods through which the UNSC arrives at its decisions. It fails, however, to appreciate the role of political preferences in this process. The political science literature corrects this by focusing on how the preferences of 15 UNSC members align to achieve cooperation. In doing so, however, it provides answers that (i) are not generalizable beyond a few case studies, (ii) do not appreciate the procedural intricacies of the UNSC's work, and (iii) fail to explain why the UNSC creates some but not other international atrocities investigations.

As a result, the question posed by this book (i.e. why the UNSC decided to investigate certain atrocities but not others?) remains unanswered. The next Chapter suggests a new answer to this question, which corrects for the shortcomings of the existing analyses and accounts for the facts presented in Chap. 2.

References

Interviews

Interview No: 10; Interview Details: Diplomat from France, New York (October 7, 2013).
Interview No: 13; Interview Details: Diplomat from Russia, New York (November 26, 2013).
Interview No: 14; Interview Details: Diplomat from United States, Washington, D.C. (December 4, 2013).
Interview No: 20; Interview Details: Diplomat from Guatemala, New York (January 21, 2014).

Books and Articles

Akhavan, Payam. 1996. The International Criminal Tribunal for Rwanda: The Politics and Pragmatics of Punishment. *American Journal of International Law* 90 (3): 501–510.
Alvarez, Jose E. 1996. Judging the Security Council. *American Journal of International Law* 90 (1): 1–39.
Arendt, Hannah. 1963. *Eichmann in Jerusalem*. Penguin.
Barltrop, Richard. 2011. *Darfur and the International Community: The Challenges of Conflict Resolution in Sudan*. Palgrave MacMillan.

Bass, Gary Jonathan. 2000. *Stay the Hand of Vengeance: The Politics of War Crimes Tribunals*. Princeton: Princeton University Press.

Bass, Gary J. 2004. Jus post bellum. *Philosophy & Public Affairs* 32 (4): 384–412.

Bassiouni, M. Cherif. 1996. Searching for Peace and Achieving Justice: The Need for Accountability. *Law and Contemporary Problems* 59: 9–28.

Black, David R., and Paul D. Williams, eds. 2010. *The International Politics of Mass Atrocities: The Case of Darfur*. London: Routledge.

Bosco, David. 2009. *Five to Rule Them All: The UN Security Council and the Making of the Modern World*. Oxford: Oxford University Press.

———. 2014. *Rough Justice: The International Criminal Court's Battle to Fix the World, One Prosecution at a Time*. Oxford: Oxford University Press.

Bracher, Nathan. 1999. La Mémoire vive et conclusive: The Papon Trial and France's Passion for History. *The French Review* 73 (2): 314–324.

Brosché, Johan, and Daniel Rothbart. 2012. *Violent Conflict and Peacebuilding, the Contuing Crisis in Darfur*. London: Routledge.

Burke-White, William W. 2005. Complementarity in Practice: The International Criminal Court as Part of a System of Multi-level Global Governance in the Democratic Republic of Congo. *Leiden Journal of International Law* 18: 557–590.

Châtaignier, Jean-Marc. 2005. *L'ONU dans la crise en Sierra Leone*. Paris: Éditions KARTHALA.

Chirac, Jacques. 1995. *Speech on the Commemoration on the Deportation of Vel d'Hiv* (July 16, 1995). Available at http://www.levendel.com/En/html/chirac-s_speech.html.

Doyle, Michael W. 2015. *The Question of Intervention, John Stuart Mill & the Responsibility to Protect*. New Haven: Yale University Press.

Elster, Jon. 1998. Coming to Terms with the Past: A Framework for the Study of Justice in the Transition to Democracy. *Archives Europeennes de Sociologie* 39 (1): 7–48.

Evans, Gareth. 2009. The Responsibility to Protect: Ending Mass Atrocity Crimes Once and for All. *Irish Studies in International Affairs* 20 (1): 7–13.

Franck, Thomas M. 2003. What Happens Now? The United Nations After Iraq. *American Journal of International Law* 97: 607–620.

Funk, Kevin, and Steven Fake. 2009. *Scramble for Africa: Darfur-Intervention and the U.S.A.* Montreal: Black Rose Books Ltd.

Huntington, Samuel P. 1991. *The Third Wave: Democratization in the Late Twentieth Century*. Norman: University of Oklahoma Press.

Hurd, Ian. 2002. Legitimacy, Power, and the Symbolic Life of the UN Security Council. *Global Governance* 8: 35–54.

———. 2007. *After Anarchy: Legitimacy and Power in the United Nations Security Council*. Princeton: Princeton University Press.

Jessup, Philip C. 1970. To Form a More Perfect United Nations. *Columbia Journal of Transnational Law* 9: 177–193.

Jo, Hyeran, and Beth A. Simmons. 2016. Can the International Criminal Court Deter Atrocity? *International Organization* 70: 443.

Johnstone, Ian. 2003a. Security Council Deliberations: The Power of the Better Argument. *European Journal of International Law* 14 (3): 437–480.

———. 2003b. The Role of the UN Secretary-General: The Power of Persuasion Based on Law. *Global Governance* 9: 441–458.

Kabbah, Ahmed Tejan. 2010. *Coming Back from the Brink in Sierra Leone*. Accra: EPP Book Services.

Keating, Colin. 2004. Rwanda–An Insider's Account. In *The UN Security Council: From the Cold War to the 21st Century*, ed. David M. Malone. Boulder: International Peace Academy/Lynne Rienner.

Kovanda, Karel. 2010. The Czech Republic on the UN Security Council: The Rwandan Genocide. *Genocide Studies and Prevention* 5 (2): 192–218.

Ku, Julian, and Jide Nzelibe. 2006. Do International Criminal Tribunals Deter or Exacerbate Humanitarian Atrocities? *Washington University Law Review* 84: 777.

Kuziemko, Ilyana, and Eric Werker. 2006. How Much Is a Seat on the Security Council Worth? Foreign Aid and Bribery at the United Nations. *Journal of Political Economy* 114 (5): 905–930.

Luck, Edward C. 2006. *UN Security Council, Practice and Promise*. Abingdon: Routledge.

Macedo, Stephen, ed. 2006. *Universal Jurisdiction: National Courts and the Prosecution of Serious Crimes Under International Law*. Philadelphia: University of Pennsylvania Press.

Malone, David, ed. 1998. *Decision-Making in the UN Security Council, The Case of Haiti, 1990–1997*. Oxford: Clarendon Press.

McCubbins, Mathew D., Roger G. Noll, and Barry R. Weingast. 1987. Administrative Procedures as Instruments of Political Control. *Journal of Law, Economics, and Organization* 3: 243–277.

Meron, Theodore. 1998. *War Crimes Law Comes of Age: Essays*. Oxford: Oxford University Press.

Moreno-Ocampo, Luis. 2013. The Gaddafi Case (Draft Paper). *NYU School of Law's Hauser Colloquium on International Law* (September 2013).

Mullins, Christopher. 2010. Conflict Victimization and Post-Conflict Justice, 1945–2008. In *The Pursuit of International Criminal Justice: A World Study on Conflicts, Victimization, and Post-Conflict Justice*, ed. M. Cherif Bassiouni, Vol. 1. Intersentia.

Munoz, Ambassador Heraldo. 2009. *A Solitary War: A Diplomat's Chronicle of the Iraq War and Its Lessons*. Golden: Fulcrum.

O'Halloran, Sharyn. 1994. *Politics, Process, and American Trade Policy*. Ann Arbor: University of Michigan Press.

Orentlicher, Diane. 1991. Settling Accounts: The Duty to Prosecute Human Rights Violations of a Prior Regime. *The Yale Law Journal.* 100: 2537.

Padelford, Norman J. 1948. The Use of the Veto. *International Organization* 2 (2): 227–246.

Prantl, Jochen. 2005. Informal Groups of States and the UN Security Council. *International Organization* 59 (03): 559–592.

Prunier, Gérard. 2005. *Darfur: The Ambiguous Genocide*. Ithaca: Cornell University Press.

Randall, Kenneth C. 1987. Universal Jurisdiction Under International Law. *Texas Law Review* 66: 785.

Ratner, Steven, Jason Abrams, and James Bischoff. 2009. *Accountability for Human Rights Atrocities in International Law: Beyond the Nuremberg Legacy*. 3d ed. New York: Oxford University Press.

Rostow, Nicholas. 2010. UN Realities. In *Looking to the Future, Essays on International Law in Honor of W. Michael Reisman*, ed. Mahnoush H. Arsanjani, Jacob Cogan, Robert Sloane, and Siegfried Wiessner. Leiden: Martinus Nijhoff.

Rudolph, Christopher. 2001. Constructing an Atrocities Regime: The Politics of War Crimes Tribunals. *International Organization* 55 (03): 655–691.

Rudzinski, Alexander W. 1951. The So-Called Double Veto. *The American Journal of International Law* 45 (3): 443–461.

Ruiz, Gaetano Arangio. 1979. *The United Nations Declaration on Friendly Relations and the System of the Sources of International Law*. Alphen aan den Rijn: BRILL.

Sadat, Leila Nadya. 2002. The Trial of Slobodan Milosevic. *Insights of American Society of International Law* 7: 10.

Sanders, Barrie. 2015. Justice and Identity: A Retrospect on the Eichmann Trial in Light of Isreali Hostility to the ICC. *Justice in Conflict Blog* (February 2, 2015). Available at http://justiceinconflict.org/2015/02/02/justice-and-identity-a-retrospect-eichmann-trial-in-light-of-israeli-hostility-to-the-icc.

Schabas, William A. 2004. United States Hostility to the International Criminal Court: It's All About the Security Council. *European Journal of International Law* 15 (4): 701–720.

Schachter, Oscar. 1964. The Quasi-Judicial Role of the Security Council and the General Assembly. *American Journal of International Law* 58: 960–965.

———. 1968. Intervention and the United Nations. *Stanford Journal of International Studies* 3: 5–12.

Scharf, Michael P. 1997. *Balkan Justice: The Story Behind the First International War Crimes Trial Since Nuremberg*. Durham: Carolina Academic Press.
Scheffer, David J. 1999. The United States and the International Criminal Court. *American Journal of International Law* 93: 12–22.
———. 2013. *All the Missing Souls: A Personal History of the War Crimes Tribunals*. Princeton: Princeton University Press.
Serrano, Mónica, and Thomas G. Weiss. 2014. *The International Politics of Human Rights: Rallying to the R2P cause?* London: Routledge.
Sievers, Loraine, and Sam Daws. 2014. *The Procedure of the UN Security Council*. Oxford: Oxford University Press.
Sikkink, Kathryn. 2011. *The Justice Cascade: How Human Rights Prosecutions are Changing World Politics*, The Norton Series in World Politics. New York: WW Norton & Company.
Stedjan, Scott, and Colin Thomas-Jensen. 2010. The United States. In *The International Politics of Mass Atrocities: The Case of Darfur*, ed. David R. Black and Paul D. Williams. London: Routledge.
Stimson, Henry Lewis, and McGeorge Bundy. 1948. *On Active Service in Peace and War*. Vol. 2. New York: Harper.
Szasz, Paul C. 2002. The Security Council Starts Legislating. *American Journal of International Law* 96: 901–905.
Thompson, Alexander. 2006. Coercion Through IOs: The Security Council and the Logic of Information Transmission. *International Organization* 60 (01): 1–34.
Totten, Samuel, and Eric Markusen, eds. 2006. *Genocide in Darfur: Investigating the Atrocities in the Sudan*. New York: Routledge.
Trindade, A.A. Cançado. 1976. The Domestic Jurisdiction of States in the Practice of the United Nations and Regional Organisations. *International and Comparative Law Quarterly* 25: 715–765.
Valentino, Benjamin, Paul Huth, and Dylan Balch-Lindsay. 2004. 'Draining the Sea': Mass Killing and Guerrilla Warfare. *International Organization* 58 (02): 375–407.
Voeten, Erik. 2001. Outside Options and the Logic of Security Council Action. *American Political Science Review* 95 (4): 845–858.
———. 2005. The Political Origins of the UN Security Council's Ability to Legitimize the Use of Force. *International Organization* 59 (03): 527–557.
Werle, Gerhard. 2005. *Principles of International Criminal Law*. The Hague: TMC Asser Press.
Wood, Nancy. 1999. Memory on Trial in Contemporary France: The Case of Maurice Papon. *History and Memory* 11 (1): 41–76.
Zahar, Alexander, and Göran Sluiter. 2008. *International Criminal Law*. Oxford: Oxford University Press.

News Sources

New York Times

Myers, Lee Stevens, *Making Sure Ware Crimes Aren't Forgotten*, The New York Times (September 22, 1997).
Neier, Aryeh, *An Arab War-Crimes Court for Syria*, The New York Times (April 4, 2012).
Nechepurenko, Ivan and Nick Cumming-Bruce, *Russia Cuts Ties With International Criminal Court, Calling it 'One-Sided'*, The New York Times (November 16, 2016).
Sengupta, Somini, *French Push UN to seek war crimes case in Syria*, The New York Times (April 4, 2014).
Sengupta, Somini, *UN will weigh asking court to investigate war crimes in Syria*, The New York Times (May 21, 2014).

The Guardian

Gillet, Kit, *Romania confronts communist past in trial of prison camp chief*, The Guardian (September 24, 2014).

Various News Sources

[anonymous], *15 April 2014 – Security Council Meeting on the "Caesar" Report Concerning Mass Torture Perpetrated by the Syrian Government*, French Mission to the United Nations, Press Release (April 15, 2014) (at http://www.franceonu.org/france-at-the-united-nations/press-room/speaking-to-the-media/remarks-to-the-press/article/15-april-2014-security-council).

[anonymous], *Ivory Coast's Laurent Gbagbo arrives in the Hague*, BBC November 30, 2011 (at http://www.bbc.co.uk/news/world-15946481).

[anonymous], *Vichy était la negation de la France*, Le Monde (October 23, 1997).

Butty, James, *Burundi Officially Informed UN of Intent to Leave ICC*, VOA News (October 27, 2016) (at http://www.theeastafrican.co.ke/news/ICC-is-not-targeting-Africa-it-is-responding-to-African-calls/2558-2661408-item-2-67dh7oz/index.html).

Oladimeji, Ramon, *ICC not biased against Africa countries – Bensouda*, Punch (April 12, 2016) (at http://punchng.com/icc-not-biased-against-african-countries-bensouda/).

Taub, Ben, *The Assad Files, Capturing the top-secret documents that tie the Syrian regime to mass torture and killings*, The New Yorker (April 18, 2016) (at http://www.newyorker.com/magazine/2016/04/18/bashar-al-assads-war-crimes-exposed).

Court Documents

International Criminal Court

Gaynor, Fergal, Letter on behalf of victims of *Kenyatta* case (November 3, 2013), accessible at http://www.iccnow.org/documents/Letter to UNSC from the Victims Lawyer in the Kenyatta case.pdf.

Statement of the Prosecutor of the International Criminal Court, Fatou Bensouda, on opening a Preliminary Examination into the situation in Burundi (April 25, 2016), available at https://www.icc-cpi.int/Pages/item.aspx?name=otp-stat-25-04-2016.

International Criminal Tribunal for the Former Yugoslavia

Prosecutor's Report on Nato Bombing Campaign, Press Release, ICTY, The Hague (June 13, 2000).

Prosecutor v. Slobodan Milosevic, Defence Opening Statement, ICTY, The Hague (August 31, 2004).

International Military Tribunal at Nuremberg

Opening Statement, Chief U.S. Prosecutor, Justice Robert Jackson (November 20, 1945).

Government Documents

Documenting Atrocities in Darfur, State Publication 11182, Released by the Bureau of Democracy, Human Rights, and Labor and the Bureau of Intelligence and Research (September 2004), available at http://2001-2009.state.gov/g/drl/rls/36028.htm.

UN Documents

Reports

A/HRC/RES/33/24, Situation of human rights in Burundi (October 5, 2016).
A/HRC/32/CRP.2, "They came to destroy": ISIS Crimes Against the Yazidis (June 15, 2016).
A/RES/71/248, International, Impartial and Independent Mechanism to Assist in the Investigation and Prosecution of Persons Responsible for the Most Serious Crimes under International Law Committed in the Syrian Arab Republic since March 2011 (January 11, 2017).
Office of the High Commissioner for Human Rights, *Too long a wait for peace and justice – Commission on Inquiry* (July 1, 2016) (available at http://www.ohchr.org/EN/NewsEvents/Pages/Syriapeacejusticecannotwait.aspx).

Records of United Nations Security Council Meetings

S/PV.3453, The situation concerning Rwanda (November 8, 1994).

Letters

S/2014/361, Letter dated 19 May 2014 from the Permanent Representative of Switzerland to the United Nations addressed to the Secretary-General, (May 19, 2014).

Resolutions

S/2014/348, Draft Resolution referring the situation in the Syrian Arab Republic to the International Criminal Court (May 22, 2014).
S/RES/2139, Middle East situation - Syria (February 22, 2014).

Chapter 4
The Argument: Three Procedural Steps

The representative of the USSR agreed that the part of the resolution relating to the maintenance on the Council's agenda of the Spanish question was procedural, but other parts of the resolution were matters of substance. If the resolution was voted upon as a whole, then he would vote against its adoption.

He added that if there was any objection to his interpretation of the case, he would ask the Council to decide whether the resolution was of a procedural or substantive character.

The Spanish Question, Report of the Security Council to the General Assembly covering the period from 17 January to 15 July 1946.
(A/93, Official Records of the Second Part of the First Session of the General Assembly, Supplement No. 1 (October 3, 1946))

Abstract To understand why the UNSC has created only a few atrocities investigations, this Chapter focuses on the role of the UNSC procedure in decision-making. A decision by the UNSC is a committee process, which can only be concluded if the UNSC members overcome significant uncertainty and apprehension over each other's preferences, and coordinate or cooperate towards a common outcome. The UNSC members are able to overcome these difficulties through the UNSC procedural rules, which allow the UNSC members to coordinate and cooperate, and thereby create an atrocities investigation. This Chapter explains how the UNSC's procedure contributes to the creation of atrocities investigations, specifies the boundaries of this argument and presents the research design for the following chapters.

Building on the two previous chapters, the first of which presented the facts while the second focused on the literature review, this Chapter presents the argument of this book. To understand why the UNSC has created only a few atrocities investigations, this Chapter focuses on the role of the UNSC procedure in decision-making.

C. Kaoutzanis, *The UN Security Council and International Criminal Tribunals: Procedure Matters*, Studies in Global Justice 20,
https://doi.org/10.1007/978-3-030-23777-6_4

A decision by the UNSC is a committee process, which can only be concluded if the UNSC members overcome significant uncertainty and apprehension over each other's preferences, and coordinate or cooperate towards a common outcome. The UNSC members are able to overcome these difficulties through the UNSC procedural rules, which allow the UNSC members to coordinate and cooperate, and thereby create an atrocities investigation. Understanding these procedural rules and their main elements is central to answering the question posed in this book.

To develop the argument, this Chapter starts, in Sect. 4.1, by briefly summarizing the existing limitations in answering the present question. Section 4.2 then documents how the UNSC's procedure contributes to the creation of atrocities investigations. The significance of the procedural argument is developed in Sect. 4.3, while Sect. 4.4 specifies the boundaries of this argument. Section 4.5 presents the research design used in the subsequent chapters to develop and test this procedural argument.

4.1 Existing Limitations

While atrocities have occurred in 92 states since the end of the Cold War, the UNSC has created an investigation into the atrocities committed in only 11 of these states. As the previous Chapter documents, the literature on atrocities investigations offers four categories of explanations for why states oppose an atrocities investigation. Yet, these explanations have limited applicability to the existing facts, as they only explain the UNSC's actions in 19 of the 92 states. The literature on atrocities investigations presents four separate categories for why a state would support the creation of atrocities investigations. Yet, these four categories are state-centric and do not explain how individual state preferences are aggregated when it comes to decision making at the UNSC. Similarly, the legal literature on the UNSC explains how the rules governing the UNSC can be used to create international atrocities investigations, but does not examine how the members of the UNSC arrive at a decision on these investigations. Political science writings explain how the UNSC members arrive at a decision, but present answers that are not generalizable to the creation of atrocities investigations, do not appreciate the procedural intricacies of the UNSC's work, and do not answer the question of this book.

In addition to the shortcomings of the existing literature, there is an additional complication in the contextual background of this analysis. Diplomats at the UNSC constantly indicate that a single reason or a consistent set of reasons for the occurrence of atrocities investigations does not exist. The UNSC, after all, is an evolving institution, the decisions of which are affected by numerous evolving political calculations. While a causal explanation based on state preferences cannot explain the actions of the UNSC, the argument of this book does not assume that individual state preferences do not matter. They do. Yet, an explanation that focuses on the preferences of the individual UNSC members would not explain the mechanism by which preferences of 15 UNSC members are aggregated into a single UNSC decision, and the ways in which this mechanism can lead UNSC members to modify their preferences over atrocities investigations. It would also fail to explain the double-standards of the UNSC's actions on atrocities investigations, where similar atrocities over which all 15 UNSC members have similar preferences have received disparate treatment.

4.2 Importance of Procedure

To overcome these limitations, this book looks at the one constant feature of the UNSC, its decision-making procedure. International cooperation behind the UNSC's decisions to create international atrocities investigations can be examined through the prism of the UNSC decision-making procedure. As outlined in Chap. 2, there are three steps in the decision-making process at the UNSC, namely (i) the preliminary steps (i.e. awareness of a situation and setting the agenda), (ii) the deliberations and (iii) the issuance of the decision. This three step decision-making process does not determine the outcome of the UNSC actions. But, the political decisions taken at the three steps of the decision-making process allow the UNSC members to channel their priorities and arrive at acceptable common decisions. In doing so, the three procedural steps allow the UNSC members to overcome their coordination and cooperation dilemmas. *As a result, to understand why UNSC members arrive at an agreement on creating certain atrocities investigations, the characteristics of each of these three steps deserve special attention.*

First, not all atrocities are discussed at the UNSC. As a result of its limited institutional capacity, the UNSC cannot prioritize or even allocate time equally to all events in the international system. Historically, the UNSC has tended to prioritize those events that have a patron; a diplomat that supports their cause within the UNSC. A diplomat from one of the UNSC members thus has to insist on bringing up a specific topic for consideration by convincing other UNSC members that it is worth their time and effort to deliberate on a specific topic. In the case of the Rwandan genocide, this support came from Ambassador Keating, of New Zealand, and Ambassador Kovanda, of the Czech Republic. For the atrocities in Burundi, this support came from the African diplomats at the UNSC. Based on a review of the UNSC's work since the end of the Cold War, Map 4.1 indicates that atrocities committed in only 52 states, out of the 92 that experienced atrocities in this period, benefitted from the attention of a UNSC diplomat. To understand the scarcity of UNSC international atrocities investigations, it is important to examine why certain UNSC diplomats decide to focus on and prioritize specific atrocities. Chapter 5 considers this question.

Once the attention of the UNSC members has been seized on certain atrocities, it becomes important to understand how, during their deliberations, the UNSC members evaluate their options. On a substantive level, the UNSC does not deliberate about its response to atrocities in a vacuum. *Quid pro quos*, alliances, diplomatic ties, the stance of the Secretary-General and a host of other factors become important in forming the UNSC's response. The UNSC members, however, also seek the recommendation of a third-party (e.g. the Secretary-General, the sanctions

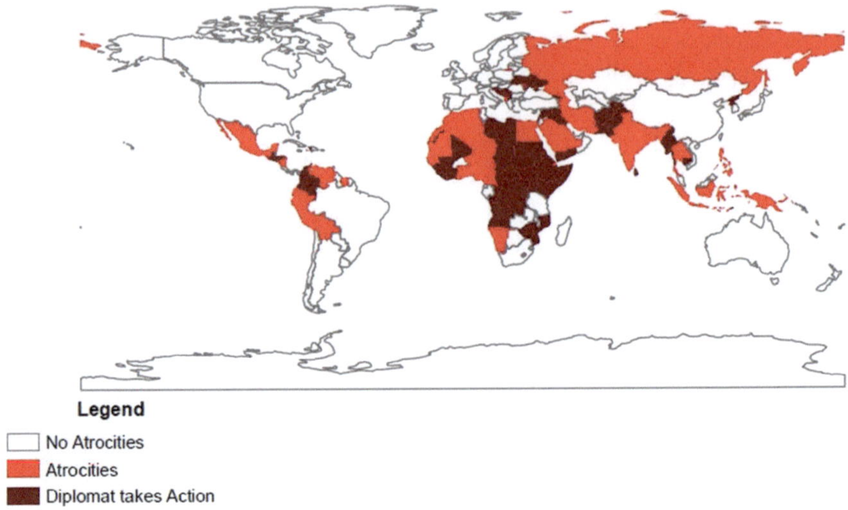

Map 4.1 Atrocities that received the attention of a UNSC diplomat

committee, a fact-finding mission) before taking any action. For the authorization of atrocities investigations, the UNSC has consistently requested the opinion of a fact-finding mission, and has abided by that opinion.[1] The support, for example, from the International Commission of Inquiry on Darfur put significant pressure on the UNSC for the referral of the atrocities in Darfur to the ICC. By contrast, the recommendation of the International Commission of Inquiry Concerning Burundi against creating an investigation into the atrocities committed in Burundi brought those efforts to a sudden halt.

Out of the 52 states with a patron diplomat, Map 4.2 highlights that the UNSC used a third-party for only 20 states. The recommendations of the third-party are always based on findings of facts and law. Similar to the decisions of a prosecutor to investigate a crime (see Introduction), the decisions of the third-party are not political. The UNSC decision, however, to use a third-party and follow its recommendations is inherently political. To understand the scarcity of UNSC international atrocities investigations, it is important to examine why the UNSC outsources part of its decision-making process to a third-party and follows the decision of this third-party. Chapter 6 turns to this question.

Finally, once the UNSC members have focused on certain atrocities through the insistence of a patron diplomat and have received a supporting recommendation from an independent third-party, they deliberate as to the proper course of action. At that moment, the leading states put forth draft resolutions with their proposals and try to convince other UNSC members to support these. Once again, it is expected

[1] One exception to this statement is Libya, where the investigation came after Resolution 1970. For more on this, see Chap. 6.

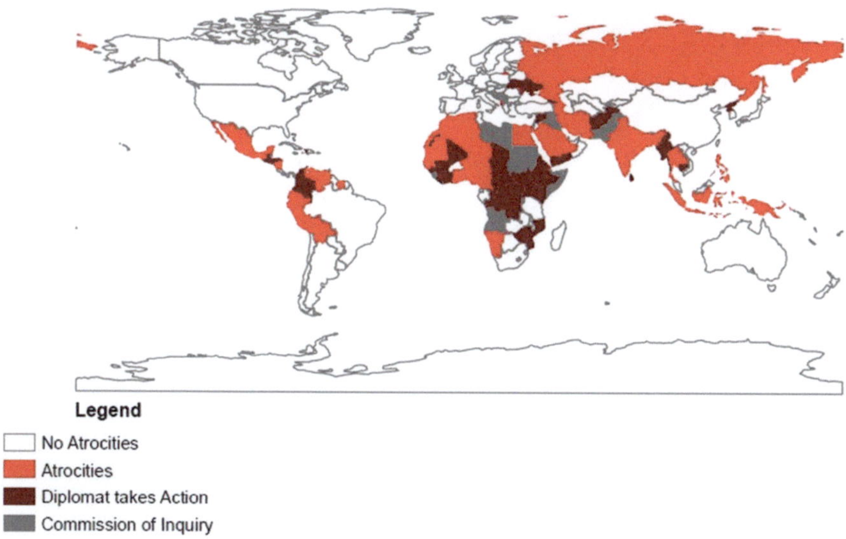

Map 4.2 Atrocities examined by a Commission of Inquiry

that those UNSC members with an interest in a specific outcome will use myriads of political tools to convince the other UNSC members on a certain course of action. As highlighted above, however, significant arguments among UNSC members are also expected to take place on the textual provisions of the draft resolution. With regards to the investigation in Darfur, for example, France and the United States jousted for several days over the text of the resolution. They only come to a common agreement by relying on prior UNSC precedent. Map 4.3 indicates that the UNSC agreed on a resolution to create an investigation into 11 out of the 20 states with atrocities that had both benefitted from a patron diplomat and for which the UNSC relied on a third-party that agreed with an investigation. As a result, to understand the scarcity of investigations, it is important to examine why the UNSC members rely on precedent in the formulation of their resolutions. Chapter 7 examines this question.

This book explains how institutional rules of the UNSC guide the UNSC's actions on atrocities investigations. Its main argument is that the UNSC created five atrocities investigations for only 11 of the 92 states that experienced atrocities from 1990 to 2014, because only these 11 (i) had a patron diplomat, (ii) received a supportive recommendation from a third-party, and (iii) could be based on UNSC precedent. While not sufficient, each of these steps is necessary for the creation of an atrocities investigation. The following three Chapters identify the conditions behind each of these three steps in the UNSC's institutional process.

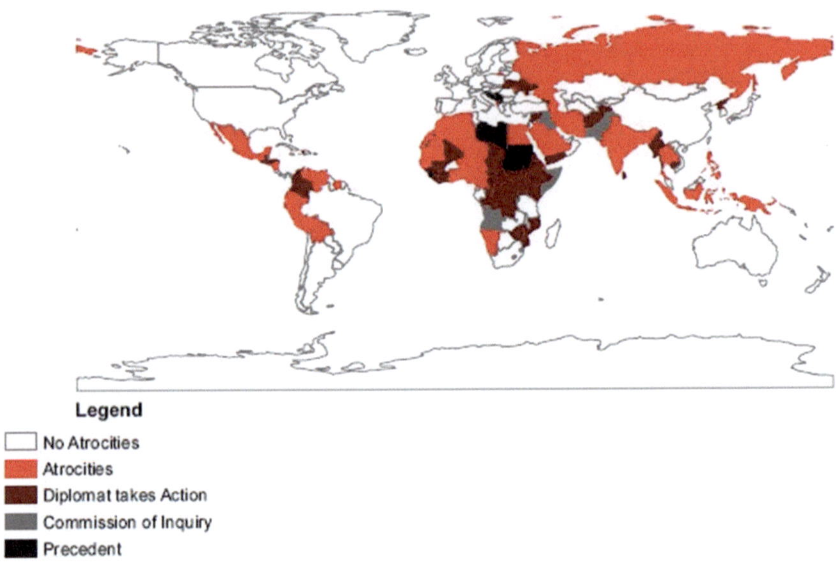

Map 4.3 Use of precedent for atrocities

4.3 The Significance of the Argument

While the three steps leading to the creation of a UNSC atrocities investigation are separate and distinct within the UNSC's decision-making process, they highlight how the UNSC members rely on specialized professional expertise in reaching a decision. Through such expertise, the UNSC is able to mitigate the difficulties it faces in dealing with atrocities.

The UNSC is in a bind when faced with atrocities. If the UNSC creates an investigation into events that were not atrocities (i.e. if it commits a Type I error, or reaches a false positive), it would lose some of its credibility in international affairs. It would also waste precious financial and political resources. Yet, if the UNSC fails to create an investigation for events that were atrocities (i.e. if it commits a Type II error, or reaches a false negative), it would again lose some of its credibility in international affairs. It will also squander an opportunity to use justice as a peacebuilding tool. As a result, the UNSC faces negative externalities both from (i) creating an investigation when atrocities were not perpetrated, and (ii) not creating an investigation where atrocities were perpetrated.

To avoid the negative externalities of a wrong action, the UNSC has a great incentive at resorting to atrocities investigations only for those cases that involve confirmed atrocities. But, making this determination is a difficult task for the UNSC members. To begin with, there is no exact definition of what constitutes an atrocity. As a result, the UNSC members have no precise model to apply or relevant factors to weigh in determining if certain facts rise to the level of atrocities. Additionally, the difficulty of such a determination is compounded by the absence of credible information on the commission of atrocities. As a result, the UNSC often does not know whether certain events were atrocities and whether reports on those facts are reliable. Finally, the UNSC members have capacity constraints, which restrain them from prolonged focus and examination of any particular instance of atrocities. In such a fluid context, it is hard for the UNSC members to evaluate and predict the negative externalities of their actions.

Past studies highlight how decision-makers faced with such uncertainty over complex or technical issues often delegate some powers to a common agent (e.g. the EU Commission, the WTO Dispute Settlement Body, the International Court of Justice).[2] The UN Charter and the Rules, however, restrain the UNSC from delegating decisions over atrocities to a common agent. The absence of common state preferences among the UNSC members makes such delegation even less likely to happen in practice. To the contrary, across all issues, the UNSC consistently acts as executor, legislator and adjudicator.[3]

In the absence of clear facts and a common agent, past studies argue that uncertainty over complex or technical issues provides fertile ground for the rise of powerful epistemic communities.[4] These are organized groups of professionals, who share beliefs and ideas, and who are able to help their states and institutions through their expertise and judgment by framing issues, defining interests, overcoming technical uncertainties and even suggesting innovative policy options.[5] While there is no evidence that such epistemic communities exist at the UNSC level, the following three Chapters illustrate that, through their expertise and judgment, diplomats, third-party commissions and the resort to precedent take on a similar function within the UNSC's decision-making process. In the Conclusion, this book returns to this point and evaluates the role of specialized professional expertise within the actions of the UNSC.

4.4 The Boundaries of the Argument

By focusing on the effect of the UNSC's procedural rules on its outcomes, this book asserts that procedure can control the relationship between cause and effect at the UNSC. Yet, this book does not advance a procedural argument by comparing it against counterfactual explanations based on the existing literature. Such a comparison would be futile, as the existing explanations do not capture the UNSC's activities on atrocities investigations. Additionally, this argument does not assume that state preferences are subsumed by the powers of the UNSC's institutional procedure. State preferences remain the background conditions to the process, as states

[2] Mallard (2014); Mavroidis and Wolfe (2015).

[3] Johnstone (2008); Alvarez (1996); Malone (1998).

[4] Haas (1992).

[5] Haas (1992); Adler and Haas (1992).

need to sponsor, support or acquiesce with a decision of the UNSC. Yet, interests are expressed, formed and altered through the institutional process. If the process was different (e.g. one of a different international institution), the same states faced with the same atrocities would likely reach different outcomes. As the previous three Maps indicate, the procedural aspects shape the expression of state preferences, and thus the work of the UNSC. *Because these procedural aspects are constant, contrary to state preferences that routinely vary, their influence on the UNSC's decisions deserves separate attention.* This focus is the distinguishing feature of the argument presented in this book.

A brief comparison can provide useful context for the importance of focusing on the UNSC's procedure. The New York County District Attorney, Cyrus Vance, Jr., and the Prosecutor of the ICC, Fatou Bensouda, have (at least) one thing in common. They both have a preference to prosecute crime.[6] If a crime takes place in New York County, however, District Attorney Cyrus Vance, Jr. has a relatively easy task before taking the suspect to trial: all he has to do is to convince a grand jury. In New York County, a grand jury is comprised of 23 individuals, who only hear the evidence presented by assistant district attorneys and decide if the investigation should proceed (i.e. if a case against a suspect should go to trial).[7] District attorneys in the United States, such as Cyrus Vance, Jr., are supposed to have an easy task. The grand jury process is believed to be so undemanding for prosecutors, that it is often said that grand juries will even indict a ham sandwich.[8] By contrast, Fatou Bensouda has an uphill battle in taking someone to court. After she investigates the crime, Fatou Bensouda has to convince the Pre-Trial Chamber of the ICC of the worthiness of her case. The Pre-Trial Chamber, which is comprised of three judges, will evaluate Bensouda's facts and legal arguments, listen to alternative facts and counter-arguments presented by the suspect and the suspect's lawyers and take into accounts greater considerations, such as the interests of justice and the interest of the ICC.[9] Presenting a case to the Pre-Trial Chamber takes a considerable amount of effort and is never a guaranteed success for the ICC's prosecutor.[10] It is far from indicting a ham sandwich. Despite their common preferences to fight crime, the different procedures predetermine the scope and number of cases Vance, Jr. and Bensouda

[6] See. e.g. Statement by Manhattan District Attorney Cyrus R. Vance, Jr. on Law Enforcement Action Against Distributors of Synthetic Cannabinoids (September 16, 2015), available at http://manhattanda.org/press-release/statement-manhattan-district-attorney-cyrus-r-vance-jr-law enforcement-action-against; see also Statement of the Prosecutor of the International Criminal Court, Fatou Bensouda, following the transfer of the first suspect in the Mali investigation: "Intentional attacks against historic monuments and buildings dedicated to religion are grave crimes" (September 26, 2015), available at http://www.icc-cpi.int/en-menus/icc/press%20and%20media/press%20releases/Pages/otp-stat-26-09-2015.aspx.

[7] The New York District Attorney's Office, Criminal Justice System: How it Works, available at http://manhattanda.org/criminal-justice-system-how-it-works?s=39.

[8] Reynolds (2013).

[9] See e.g., ICC, Rules of Procedure and Evidence, Chap. 6.

[10] Courtney and Kaoutzanis (2014).

will bring. The three-step decision-making procedure of the UNSC, which relies on a patron diplomat, a commission of inquiry and precedent, has the same effect.

Through its focus on institutional procedure, this book also avoids the shortcomings of the previous analyses. In contrast to the legal literature on the UNSC, this analysis appreciates the importance of each state's political preferences and aims to indicate how these are expressed and developed through the decision-making process. This book equally bypasses the three shortcomings of the political science literature on the UNSC. By focusing on the constant aspects of the UNSC's decision-making process, the argument of this book can be generalized to other UNSC actions, such as sanctions or diplomacy, which are outcomes of the same decision-making process. As a process-based argument, it appreciates the constraints imposed by the rules of the UNSC. And, as the UNSC is a living political body, in which calculations and incentives change constantly, this process based argument presents reasonable answers to the existing differences among the UNSC's decisions to create atrocities investigations.

In addition to these, while a causal explanation based solely on state preferences cannot explain the actions of the UNSC, the argument of this book is not premised on the idea that individual state preferences do not matter. An argument, however, that focuses on the preferences of the individual UNSC members would not explain the mechanism by which preferences of 15 UNSC members are aggregated into a single UNSC decision, and the ways in which this mechanism can lead UNSC members to modify their preferences over atrocities investigations. It would also fail to explain the differences among the UNSC's actions on atrocities investigations, where similar atrocities, over which all 15 UNSC members have similar preferences, have received disparate treatment.

But, state preferences, which are ubiquitous, are critical to the UNSC's decision-making procedure. At one extreme, state preferences can prohibit the decision-making process from taking place. The strong interests, for example, that Russia and the United States have over Syria prohibit any conversation on an investigation in the local atrocities from taking place at the UNSC. At the other extreme, the complete absence of state preferences may de-politicize the decision-making process, making it faster and less contentious. When few member states of the UNSC had *ex ante* preferences on the atrocities committed in Sierra Leone, the United States and the United Kingdom were able to create an investigation with almost no pushback, or input, from other UNSC states.

In between these two extremes, the UNSC member states routinely have some *ex ante* preferences over atrocities. These state preferences are adequately captured by the categories of explanations in favor and against atrocities investigations presented in Chap. 3. The liberal category, for example, explains the Clinton administration's interest in the crimes committed in the former Yugoslavia. The idealist category portrays the preferences many UNSC states had towards creating an investigation for the Rwandan genocide. These *ex ante* state preferences undeniably affect all aspects of the UNSC's procedure. In the first procedural step, these preferences influence a diplomat's knowledge of, and interest in, the atrocities. In the second step, these preferences not only influence the state's attitude towards the creation and work of a commission of inquiry, but also the likelihood that the state will review the commission's report and support its conclusions. Finally, in the third step, these *ex ante* preferences influence the likelihood that a state will search for precedent, and support its use, for the creation of an investigation. As a result, while this book asserts that state interests cannot explain the double-standards of the UNSC's work on atrocities investigations, it recognizes that the presence of factors outlined by the existing literature affects the likelihood that a member state will be supportive of an investigation in each of the three decision-making steps.

In developing this argument, this book mirrors the emphasis political scientists place on the legislative process in understanding the outcome of political bargaining within domestic and international institutions. The preferences of individual legislators are always important to the outcome of the deliberations. Yet, it has also been recognized that the voting procedures can lead to paradoxical results.[11] More recent explanations of such counterintuitive results focus less on the mathematic properties of alternative preferences and more on the power of the decision-making process. It is generally accepted that "[t]he rules employed by legislatures significantly restrict the potential outcomes of the legislative process," as they "prohibit…[options]… from arising for comparison, thus leaving other points invulnerable."[12] Some of the studies that focus on such rules highlight the power of committees on the outcome of deliberations. Committee power, for example, is contingent on its power to *ex ante* or *ex post* terminate (i.e. veto) the decision-making process.[13] Committee power is also contingent on the committee's focus on reelection, power or policy.[14] Other studies of decision-making rules highlight the influence of agenda on the outcome of deliberations. The agenda can completely determine the outcome of a legislative vote by leading to results that were not *ex ante* the most popular.[15] It does so by "limit[ing] the available information that decision makers have and determin[ing] the available strategies."[16] Such is the power of the agenda, that the agenda-setter has the ability to pre-determine the outcome of the deliberations to his or her own preferences.[17]

These studies of legislative bodies shed light on how the decision-making process can control the outcome of the deliberations. They emphasize that the decision-making sequence, power to set the agenda and the power of a committee can have effects that are independent of the decision-makers' preferences. This book advances a similar argument, as the role of diplomats, the use of third-party commissions and the resort to precedent are the three procedural features that guide the decision-making process at the UNSC. In doing so, these features create, aggregate and elim-

[11] E.g. the Condorcet method (Marquis de Condorcet 1785) or the Borda count (de Borda 1781).

[12] Shepsle and Weingast (1981).

[13] Shepsle and Weingast (1987).

[14] Sinclair (1986).

[15] Hammond (1986).

[16] Plott and Levine (1978).

[17] McKelvey (1981).

inate competing preferences of the 15 UNSC member states, thereby contributing to the differences among the UNSC's actions on atrocities.

4.5 Research Design

Before proceeding further, it is important to understand the methodology used in the following Chapters to examine each of the three procedural steps of the UNSC. As highlighted in the Introduction, this book relies on a robust historical record of the work of the UNSC, derived from primary and secondary sources and supplemented with interviews with participants in the UNSC's deliberations on atrocities. As such, the book as a whole uses case studies to develop its procedural argument. Yet, each of the subsequent Chapters uses case studies in a different manner.

4.5.1 Chapter 5: Three Case Studies on Diplomats Relating to Sierra Leone

Chapter 5 investigates the first step of the decision-making process, namely how diplomats set the agenda with respect to specific atrocities. To do so, that chapter relies on case studies of diplomatic action relating to the civil war in Sierra Leone.

In order to identify the relevant case studies, a tripartite research strategy was implemented. First, those diplomats who since the end of the Cold War have been involved on decisions of atrocities investigations at the UNSC were identified. Then, through the use of archival research, historical narratives, diplomatic memoirs and newspaper articles, the research was narrowed to those cases in which diplomats had an active role over the topic of atrocities investigations at the UNSC. Finally, the research had to overcome the limitation that the work of a diplomat is rarely publicly aired. Diplomacy is known to be a secretive profession, in which plans and actions are not mentioned as they might expose a state's preferences to its allies and foes. To overcome this veil of secrecy, the archival research on this topic was supplemented by a series of interviews with the diplomats most active in atrocities investigations at the UNSC, their aides, and members of the civil society observing these diplomats.

In conducting the research, it became apparent that a valuable source of diplomatic activity on atrocities investigations at the UNSC comes from the diplomats of the UN. In a few significant ways, the personnel of the various UN bodies, such as the Department of Peacekeeping Operations and the UN Development Program ('UNDP'), and the numerous Special Envoys or Special Representatives do not work according to customary diplomatic arrangements. For example, the administrator of UNDP reports to the UNDP's Executive Board and can thus defy the instructions of the Secretary-General. Additionally, the heads of departments within the UN are traditionally appointed by state-members of the UN. While these individuals are responsible to the Secretary-General, they often use their contacts with their member state to circumvent the UN's hierarchical process. Despite these differences, it is widely accepted that UN diplomats operate vis-à-vis the Secretary-General much in the same way that diplomats do vis-à-vis their foreign ministries.[18] They have the same incentives and concerns, and play the same role in making UN policies and implementing UN actions as diplomats do for their countries. Their actions were thus included in the research materials.[19]

By focusing solely on actions undertaken by diplomats relating to the conflict in Sierra Leone, Chap. 5 controls for a host of external variables, such as the influence of a country's predetermined foreign policy and the greater role of international relations in the study of diplomatic actions. The civil war in Sierra Leone raged from 1991 to 2002, with the most violent period occurring after 1997. Throughout its history, the Sierra Leonean conflict was never the most prominent issue at the UNSC.[20] In the early years of this civil war, the UNSC had to deal with more significant crises in the former Yugoslavia and in the Great Lakes region of Africa (e.g. Rwanda, Burundi, Uganda, Democratic Republic of the Congo). After 1997, when a series of peace agreements had failed and the atrocities in Sierra Leone escalated (e.g. the RUF's launch of "Operation No Living Thing"), the UNSC had to deal with the events in Kosovo, East Timor's efforts to gain independence, wars between Eritrea and Ethiopia, and conflicts in the Democratic Republic of the Congo, in the Central African Republic and in Liberia.

The conflict in Sierra Leone was also not contested among the P5 or the various E10 that served on the UNSC during the conflict, allowing for diplomats to have a greater role within the decision-making process at the UNSC. Within the UNSC, the United Kingdom, as the former colonial power of Sierra Leone, had the lead (i.e. first role) on all issues relating to the conflict of Sierra Leone.[21] While initially restrained in its involvement, the United Kingdom became keenly interested in stopping the conflict after 1999. The United States also displayed an interest in stopping the conflict, and even appointed a special envoy to the region. It never, however, shifted its primary focus to West Africa. France, while interested in this conflict—mainly because it affected Cote d'Ivoire—maintained a tacit agreement with the United Kingdom not to meddle with its initiatives. For the other two P5 members, Russia and China, the conflict was of no special interest. The E10 were similarly disinterested. One exception came from Nigeria, who sat on the UNSC in 1994 and 1995 and participated, as a very active peacekeeper, in this conflict. The UNSC, however, remained largely passive on this civil war during those 2 years.

---

[18] See Annan (2012, p. 135); Urquhart (1987, p. 208); Bosco (2009, p. 180); Chesterman et al. (2008, p. 132); Interviews: 6, 15, 16, 18.

[19] For a detailed analysis of how even the UN Secretary General acts as a diplomat on behalf of the UN system, see Frohlich and Williams (2018).

[20] See Châtaignier (2005 p. 15).

[21] Interviews: 2, 10, 19.

4.5.2 Chapter 6: Single Case Study on Commission of Inquiry to Burundi

Chapter 6 examines the second step of the UNSC's decision-making process, namely why the UNSC decides to create commissions of inquiry as part of its deliberations. It relies on a detailed case study on the atrocities committed in Burundi in the mid-1990s because the UNSC members were not able to predetermine its outcome (i.e. no selection effects).

To begin with, the UNSC can control the work of a commission of inquiry in three ways. First, the UNSC members could control the budget of the commission of inquiry. Second, the UNSC members could control the facts (i.e. evidence) to which the commission of inquiry would have access. Third, the UNSC members could create a commission of inquiry only for those situations that allow for one outcome (e.g. those places that have undoubtedly experienced significant crimes). All three mechanisms would allow the UNSC members to predetermine the recommendations of the commission of inquiry.

None of these problems plague the commissions of inquiry into atrocities created by the UNSC. First, the UNSC members outsource the formation and budgetary process of all commissions of inquiry to the Secretary-General, who uses the general UN budget for such investigations.[22] Second, all commissions are given broad leeway to investigate all facts and have the power to collect information from any source they find credible.[23] As such, the UNSC members are not guaranteed to successfully spoon-feed evidence to the commission.[24] Third, the UNSC members may create commissions of inquiry only into situations that have experienced significant atrocities, but have not narrowed the mandate of their recommendations to specific questions or issues. The commissions are thus created with the power to opine broadly. In practice, their recommendations have sometimes been unpredictable. The commission of inquiry into Darfur, for example, while staying within its mandate, disagreed with the findings of the United States that the atrocities constituted genocide. Yet, the commission still compiled a list of suspects for crimes against

[22] E.g. Resolution 1012 (1995) ("8. Requests the Secretary-General to establish, as a supplement to financing as an expense of the Organization, a trust fund to receive voluntary contributions to finance the commission of inquiry;").

[23] E.g. Resolution 1012 (1995) ("3. Calls upon States, relevant United Nations bodies and, as appropriate, international humanitarian organizations to collate substantiated information in their possession relating to acts covered in paragraph 1 (a) above, to make such information available as soon as possible and to provide appropriate assistance to the commission of inquiry; … 5. Calls upon the Burundi authorities and institutions, including all Burundi political parties, to fully cooperate with the international commission of inquiry in the accomplishment of its mandate, including responding positively to requests from the commission for security, assistance and access in pursuing investigations, including…").

[24] In Burundi, for example, the commission collected evidence from a broad variety of sources, see S/1996/682 (e.g. pp. 39–43).

humanity and war crime,[25] which was not required by its mandate.[26] The historical record, overall, supports the fact the UNSC members relinquish control over the work and outcome of the commissions of inquiry.

In addition to these, the individuals comprising the commission of inquiry may transform their mandate into a tool for the benefit of certain members of the UNSC. Similar to bureaucracies or institutions, commission of inquiry created by the UNSC are ripe venues for institutional capture,[27] as their individual members are given significant discretion in investigating, compiling a report and suggesting conclusions. In creating, however, commissions of inquiry, the UNSC members minimize the potential for institutional capture by outsourcing the process of selecting individual members to the Secretary-General.[28] The Secretary-General, in turns, chooses legal experts to fill these spots. In doing so, the commissions of inquiry into atrocities end up with independent legal experts beyond the direct reach and influence of any UNSC member state.

This selection process, however, creates concerns about a different sort of institutional capture. By resorting to legal experts, the commissions of inquiry are staffed by individuals generally sympathetic to human rights, international law and the associated norms of combating impunity and ending atrocities. As a result, institutional capture of these commissions, rather than favoring specific UNSC member states, may translate in a general tendency to recommend atrocities investigations. The fact that most commissions of inquiry support the creation of atrocities investigations plays into this potential. It is not, however, clear how this affects the political calculus behind the creation of the investigations. Perhaps, the UNSC members—who know that the commissions will *ex ante* recommend atrocities investigations—are interested in the substance of the investigation's findings. It might also be, however, UNSC members are mostly interested in protecting the legitimacy of the UNSC before deciding to create an atrocities investigation, and resort to the commission for its legitimizing effect than the substance of its decisions.

To deal with this uncertainty, Chap. 6 presents a case study on the commission of inquiry into the atrocities committed in Burundi. From 1993 onwards, Burundi has

---

[25] International Commission of Inquiry on Darfur (2005, p. 133).

[26] The commission's mandate comes from UNSC Resolution 1564 (2004) ("12. Requests that the Secretary-General rapidly establish an international commission of inquiry in order immediately to investigate reports of violations of international humanitarian law and human rights law in Darfur by all parties, to determine also whether or not acts of genocide have occurred, and to identify the perpetrators of such violations with a view to ensuring that those responsible are held accountable, calls on all parties to cooperate fully with such a commission, and further requests the Secretary-General, in conjunction with the Office of the High Commissioner for Human Rights, to take appropriate steps to increase the number of human rights monitors deployed to Darfur;").

[27] Bendor and Moe (1986); Barkow (2010).

[28] E.g. Resolution 1012 (1995) ("2. Recommends that the international commission of inquiry be composed of five impartial and internationally respected, experienced jurists who shall be selected by the Secretary-General and shall be furnished with adequate expert staff, and that the Government of Burundi be duly informed;").

been the scene of significant atrocities, which due to their connection to the Rwandan genocide troubled the UN system. As a result, Burundi received a lot of attention by the UNSC in the mid-1990s. As documented in Chap. 6, Burundi was the destination of two of the UNSC's missions, two missions of the Secretary-General, and, finally, a commission of inquiry. Yet, the commission of inquiry into the atrocities committed in Burundi ended with a clearly *negative* recommendation against creating an atrocities investigation. This conclusion does not only negate the possibility of the commission's institutional capture by pro-accountability lawyers, but also countered the pro-investigation sentiment expressed at the UNSC before the results of the investigation.

Apart from overcoming the possibility for selection effects, the commission of inquiry into Burundi provides, more than any other instance, a clear indication that commissions of inquiry have a real impact on the work of the UNSC. In this case, the UNSC and the Secretary-General accepted the negative recommendations of the commission despite their prior preference to create an investigation. Examining why this commission was given such deference poses a real question for scholars of the UNSC, which is answered in Chap. 6.

4.5.3 Chapter 7: Multiple Case Studies on Role of Precedent

Chapter 7 examines the third step in the UNSC's decision-making process, namely the use of precedent in the issuance of UNSC decisions. It does so through the use of multiple short case studies.

The focus on the UNSC precludes a quantitative analysis on the use of precedent, such as those used in past studies relating to legal opinions.[29] Relying on citations to past cases, those studies created datasets measuring the adherence to a specific opinion in subsequent cases and identifying the judges who supported or refuted their prior decision(s). At the UNSC, the possibility that a disagreeing state can halt the decision-making process before arriving at an official disagreement (particularly if the disagreement comes from a P5) prevents the possibility of a quantitative analysis. It is, for example, impossible to count how many times France has disagreed with a prior UNSC decision by counting the subsequent decisions of the UNSC, as France's disagreement may silently lead to no action (i.e. nothing to observe) by the UNSC on this issue. As dissents are not the only way disagreements may be expressed at the UNSC, a quantitative study would miss substantial information.

Faced with this drawback, Chap. 7 examines case studies on the use of precedent when authorizing an international atrocities investigation. By focusing on the specific issue of international atrocities investigations, a substantial historical record of the UNSC deliberations can be compiled and analyzed, which allows the observation of the otherwise subtle or even silent disagreements among the UNSC members, precisely the items that would have been overlooked in a quantitative analysis.

[29] See e.g. Lupu and Fowler (2013); Pelc (2014); Spriggs and Hansford (2002).

Furthermore, in the past 20 years, the UNSC has debated the text of a resolution on atrocities investigation only a handful of times (the former Yugoslavia, Rwanda, Sierra Leone, Sudan, Libya, Syria). While such a small collection of cases precludes the examination of alternative or interacting explanations, it creates a closed universe of cases, in which it is possible to trace the role of precedent in the otherwise secretive deliberations of the UNSC. Finally, precedent has always been central in the creation of these investigations. In deciding the details of each investigation, the members of the UNSC, academics and commentators have made frequent reference to the precedent set by prior investigations. For example, the 1-year time span for the investigation into Rwanda was regularly compared to the open-ended nature of the precedent investigation into the former Yugoslavia.[30]

Case studies are additionally well suited to overcoming the possible spurious effects of precedent. Previous analyses are divided over the role of precedent. Some argue that precedent has important weight in decision-making both in domestic courts[31] and international courts, such as the WTO.[32] At the UNSC, Johnstone notes that concerns about creating precedent influenced the positions that states held in the debates on the Kosovo intervention.[33] Other studies argue, however, that the use of precedent does not necessarily indicate its causal explanatory power. Precedent may instead be used as an *ex post* legitimating factor in decisions.[34] By focusing on the details of specific case studies, Chap. 7 highlights how, *but-for* precedent, decision-makers would have reached different results, a counter-factual scenario that is difficult to test with quantitative methods.[35]

4.6 Conclusion

This Chapter presented a new alternative explanation on why the UNSC authorizes certain international atrocity investigations, which asserts that the UNSC's procedure is central to overcoming cooperation and coordination problems faced by the UNSC members when dealing with atrocities. As a result, one can only understand the decisions of the UNSC on atrocities investigations, and hence answer the question posed in this book, by focusing on the ways through which the UNSC's procedure guides the UNSC members to a common outcome.

---

[30] Reydams (2005) ("Most striking, however, is the different temporal jurisdiction of the Tribunals. The ICTY, established in February 1993, has jurisdiction over serious violations of international humanitarian law committed in the territory of the former Yugoslavia since 1991. The jurisdiction of the ICTR, on the other hand, is limited to the period 1 January 1994–31 December 1994—an artificial and politically convenient time-frame.").

[31] See e.g. Knight and Epstein (1996).

[32] See e.g. Pelc (2014).

[33] Johnstone (2003).

[34] Segal and Spaeth (1996a, b).

[35] Pelc (2014).

As outlined above, an examination of the UNSC's procedures demonstrates that three necessary steps must be completed for the UNSC members to agree to create an atrocities investigation. First, one or more diplomats from a UNSC member state must persistently raise the fact that the atrocities are occurring at the UNSC. Second, an independent third-party must recommend to the UNSC that an atrocities investigation should take place in a specific case. Finally, the UNSC members must arrive at a consensus over the text of the authorizing resolution. The politics behind each of these steps will be analyzed in the following three Chapters.

References

Interviews

Interview No. 2; Interview Details: Member of UN Office of Legal Affairs, on Skype (June 24, 2013).

Interview No. 6; Interview Details: Member of UN Office of Legal Affairs, New York (August 6, 2013).

Interview No. 10; Interview Details: Diplomat from France, New York (October 7, 2013).

Interview No. 15; Interview Details: Member of UN Office of Legal Affairs, New York (December 6, 2013).

Interview No. 16; Interview Details: Member of UN Office of Legal Affairs, New York (December 6, 2013).

Interview No. 18; Interview Details: Diplomat from United Kingdom, London (January 7, 2014).

Interview No. 19; Interview Details: Diplomat from Greece, on Skype (January 19, 2014).

Books and Articles

Adler, Emanuel, and Peter M. Haas. 1992. Conclusion: Epistemic Communities, World Order, and the Creation of a Reflective Research Program. *International Organization* 46 (01): 367–390.

Alvarez, Jose E. 1996. Judging the Security Council. *American Journal of International Law* 90 (1): 1–39.

Annan, Kofi. 2012. *A Life in War and Peace*. Penguin.

Barkow, Rachel E. 2010. Insulating Agencies: Avoiding Capture Through Institutional Design. *Texas Law Review* 89: 15.

Bendor, Jonathan, and Terry M. Moe. 1986. Agenda Control, Committee Capture, and the Dynamics of Institutional Politics. *American Political Science Review* 80 (4): 1187–1207.

Chesterman, Simon, Thomas M. Franck, and David M. Malone. 2008. *Law and the Practice of the United Nations*. Oxford University Press.

Bosco, David. 2009. *Five to Rule Them All: The UN Security Council and the Making of the Modern World*. New York: Oxford University Press.

Châtaignier, Jean-Marc. 2005. *L'ONU dans la crise en Sierra Leone* (Éditions KARTHALA).

Courtney, Jocelyn, and Christodoulos Kaoutzanis. 2014. Proactive Gatekeepers: The Jurisprudence of the ICC's Pre-trial Chambers. *Chicago Journal of International Law* 15: 518.

de Borda, Jean-Charles. 1781. Mémoire sur les Élections au Scrutin. *Mémoires de l'Académie Royale des Sciences*.

Frohlich, Manuel, and Abiodun Williams. 2018. *The UN Secretary-General and the Security Council: A Dynamic Relationship*. Oxford: Oxford University Press.

Haas, Peter M. 1992. Introduction: Epistemic Communities and International Policy Coordination. *International Organization* 46 (1): 1–35.
Hammond, Thomas H. 1986. Agenda Control, Organizational Structure, and Bureaucratic Politics. *American Journal of Political Science* 30: 379–420.
Johnstone, Ian. 2003. Security Council Deliberations: The Power of the Better Argument. *European Journal of International Law* 14 (3): 437–480.
———. 2008. Legislation and Adjudication in the UN Security Council: Bringing Down the Deliberative Deficit. *American Journal of International Law* 102: 275–308.
Knight, Jack, and Lee Epstein. 1996. The Norm of Stare Decisis. *American Journal of Political Science* 40: 1018–1035.
Lupu, Yonatan, and James H. Fowler. 2013. Strategic Citations to Precedent on the U.S. Supreme Court. *The Journal of Legal Studies* 42 (1): 151–186.
Mallard, Graham. 2014. Static Common Agency and Political Influence: An Evaluative Survey. *Journal of Economic Surveys* 28 (1): 17–35.
Malone, David. 1998. *Decision-Making in the UN Security Council, the Case of Haiti, 1990–1997*. Oxford: Clarendon Press.
Marquis de Condorcet, Marie Jean Antoine Nicolas de Caritat. 1785. Essai sur l'application de l'analyse à la probabilité des décisions rendues à la pluralité des voix.
Mavroidis, Petros C., and Robert Wolfe. 2015. From Sunshine to a Common Agent. The Evolving Understanding of Transparency in the WTO. *The Evolving Understanding of Transparency in the WTO (February 2015). Robert Schuman Centre for Advanced Studies Research Paper No. RSCAS.*
McKelvey, R.D. 1981. A Theory of Optimal Agenda Design. *Management Science* 27 (3): 303.
Pelc, Krzysztof J. 2014. The Politics of Precedent in International Law: A Social Network Application. *American Political Science Review* 108 (3): 547.
Plott, Charles R., and Michael E. Levine. 1978. A Model of Agenda Influence on Committee Decisions. *The American Economic Review* 68 (1): 146–160.
Reydams, Luc. 2005. The ICTR Ten Years on Back to the Nuremberg Paradigm? *Journal of International Criminal Justice* 3 (4): 977–988.
Reynolds, Glenn Harlan. 2013. Ham Sandwich Nation: Due Process When Everything Is a Crime. *Columbia Law Review Sidebar* 113: 102–109.
Segal, Jeffrey A., and Harold J. Spaeth. 1996a. The Influence of Stare Decisis on the Votes of United States Supreme Court Justices. *American Journal of Political Science* 40 (3): 971–1003.
———. 1996b. Norms, Dragons, and Stare Decisis: A Response. *American Journal of Political Science* 40 (4): 1064.
Shepsle, Kenneth A., and Barry R. Weingast. 1981. Structure-Induced Equilibrium and Legislative Choice. *Public Choice* 37 (3): 503–519.
———. 1987. The institutional foundations of committee power. *American Political Science Review* 81 (01): 85–104.
Sinclair, Barbara. 1986. The Role of Committees in Agenda Setting in the U. S. Congress. *Legislative Studies Quarterly* 11 (1): 35–45.
Spriggs, James F., and Thomas G. Hansford. 2002. The U.S. Supreme Court's Incorporation and Interpretation of Precedent. *Law and Society Review* 36: 139–160.
Urquhart, Brian. 1987. *A Life in Peace and War*. New York: Harper & Row.

Court Documents

International Criminal Court

International Commission of Inquiry on Darfur, Report (January 25, 2005), accessible at http://www.icc-cpi.int/NR/rdonlyres/F87E244D-B27C-4A0A-BE1B-D27CECB5649E/278008/Report to UN on Darfur.pdf.

Rules of Procedure and Evidence, accessible at https://www.icc-cpi.int/iccdocs/PIDS/legal-texts/RulesProcedureEvidenceEng.pdf.

Statement of the Prosecutor of the International Criminal Court, Fatou Bensouda, following the transfer of the first suspect in the Mali investigation: "Intentional attacks against historic monuments and buildings dedicated to religion are grave crimes" (September 26, 2015), available at http://www.icc-cpi.int/en_menus/icc/press%20and%20media/press%20releases/Pages/otp-stat-26-09-2015.aspx.

Government Documents

The New York District Attorney's Office, Criminal Justice System: How it Works, available at http://manhattanda.org/criminal-justice-system-how-it-works?s=39.

The New York District Attorney's Office, Statement by Manhattan District Attorney Cyrus R. Vance, Jr. on Law Enforcement Action Against Distributors of Synthetic Cannabinoids (September 16, 2015), available at http://manhattanda.org/press-release/statement-manhattan-district-attorney-cyrus-r-vance-jr-law enforcement-action-against-.

UN Documents

Reports

A/93, Official Records of the Second Part of the First Session of the General Assembly, Supplement No. 1 (October 3, 1946).

Letters

S/1996/682, Letter dated 25 July 1996 from the Secretary-General addressed to the President of the Security Council (August 22, 1996).

Resolutions

S/RES/1012, Burundi (1995).

S/RES/1564, Sudan (September 18, 2004).

Chapter 5
The First Step: Preliminary Steps: The Role of A Patron Diplomat

> *I had these instructions which made no sense at all…I felt that I would get a better hearing if I called the National Security Council [rather than the State Department], which I did, and they said, "Well, no, we're worrying about this, and these are your instructions." I actually screamed into the phone. I said, "They are unacceptable. I want them changed." So they told me to chill out and calm down. But ultimately, they did send me instructions that allowed us to do a reinforcement of UNAMIR.*
>
> *Madeleine Albright, U.S. Permanent Representative to the UN Security Council on the reauthorization of UN Assistance Mission in Rwanda, April 1994.*
>
> (Albright 2003)

Abstract In the first step of the UNSC decision-making process, the creation of an atrocities investigation requires that a diplomat of a UNSC member state brings the atrocities to the attention of the UNSC. It is commonly accepted that diplomats do so (i) at the instruction of their states, (ii) at the discretion afforded to them by their states, and (iii) rarely, against the instruction of their states. This chapter advances the understanding of the role diplomats play in the UNSC's decision-making process by examining how atrocities often come to the attention of the UNSC as the outcome of a disagreement between the diplomats at the UNSC and their superiors. It also highlights, through three case studies relating to the civil war in Sierra Leone, how the work of diplomats is far from mechanical and full of political interactions.

The UNSC does not investigate most atrocities that take place in the world. Due to their limited institutional capacity, the UNSC members cannot allocate time to all events in the international system. Additionally, as explained in Chap. 2, the UNSC has no legal obligation to focus on those events brought to its attention by outsiders. In practice, because of the institutional procedure at the UNSC, the UNSC prioritizes those events that have a patron; a diplomat that advocates for their cause within the

C. Kaoutzanis, *The UN Security Council and International Criminal Tribunals: Procedure Matters*, Studies in Global Justice 20,
https://doi.org/10.1007/978-3-030-23777-6_5

UNSC. A diplomat from one of the UNSC members thus has to insist on bringing up a specific topic for consideration by convincing other UNSC members that it is worth their time and effort to deliberate on that specific topic. Out of the 92 states that have experienced atrocities since 1990, a diplomat at the UNSC has brought to the attention of the UNSC atrocities committed in 52 of these states (see Map 4.1 above and Table 5.1a below). Accordingly, in order to understand why the UNSC chooses to create an investigation for certain atrocities, one must first understand *why certain UNSC diplomats decide to advocate for the investigation of those specific atrocities.*

This Chapter turns to this task. It proceeds in three parts. Section 5.1 presents three existing explanations of diplomatic engagement, namely that diplomats act (i) at the instruction of their government, (ii) within the discretion afforded to them by their government and (iii) against their government's instructions. It also indicates how these explanations capture the work of the UNSC in the field of atrocities investigation. As the epigraph illustrates, however, sometimes diplomats act beyond these three methods, as they voice their disagreement and convince their own states to change their preferences. Section 5.2 explores this type of diplomatic action and

Table 5.1a Atrocities with a Patron Diplomat

1. Afghanistan	27. Kosovo
2. Angola	28. Kuwait
3. Bosnia	29. Lebanon
4. Burma	30. Liberia
5. Burundi	31. Libya
6. Cambodia	32. Mali
7. Central African Republic	33. Montenegro
8. Chad	34. Mozambique
9. Colombia	35. North Korea
10. Congo	36. Pakistan
11. Cote d'Ivoire	37. Palestine
12. Croatia	38. Rwanda
13. Democratic Republic of the Congo	39. Serbia
14. East Timor	40. Sierra Leone
15. El Salvador	41. Slovenia
16. Eritrea	42. Somalia
17. Ethiopia	43. South Sudan
18. FYROM	44. Sri Lanka
19. Georgia	45. Sudan
20. Guatemala	46. Syria
21. Guinea	47. Tajikistan
22. Haiti	48. Uganda
23. Honduras	49. Ukraine
24. Iraq	50. Western Sahara
25. Israel	51. Yemen
26. Kenya	52. Zimbabwe

Table 5.1b Atrocities without Patron Diplomat

1. Albania	21. Lesotho
2. Algeria	22. Mauritania
3. Armenia	23. Mexico
4. Azerbaijan	24. Moldova
5. Bangladesh	25. Morocco
6. Bahrain	26. Namibia
7. Benin	27. Nepal
8. Bhutan	28. Nicaragua
9. Bolivia	29. Niger
10. Cameroon	30. Nigeria
11. Comoros	31. Papua New Guinea
12. Djibouti	32. Peru
13. Ecuador	33. Philippines
14. Egypt	34. Russia
15. Ghana	35. Saudi Arabia
16. Guinea-Bissau	36. Senegal
17. India	37. Suriname
18. Indonesia	38. Thailand
19. Iran	39. Togo
20. Laos	40. Venezuela

suggests a framework for understanding the success of such disagreements. Nevertheless, the four sources of diplomatic activity presented in Sects. 5.1 and 5.2 appear mechanical, devoid of any actual political interactions. Section 5.3 corrects for this impression by presenting three case studies of diplomatic activities at the UNSC from the Sierra Leonean civil war. The goal of these case studies is to highlight the intricacies of how diplomats advocate for the investigation of those specific atrocities within the larger, and moving, constellation of international affairs.

5.1 Three Existing Explanations

The UNSC's actions in the field of international criminal justice are replete with stories relating to individuals. Madeleine Albright is remembered as the moving force behind the creation of the ICTY and Colin Keating for the creation of the ICTR. David Scheffer had a critical role in the operation of the Extraordinary Chambers in the Courts of Cambodia ('ECCC'), while Jean-Marc de la Sablière played a similar role for the referral of the Darfur case to the ICC. There are three reasons for which scholars of international affairs should not be surprised by the extent of diplomatic actions in the field of international criminal justice.

First, diplomats are empowered to act on behalf of their states. Often times, these diplomats will take an important decision for international criminal justice acting on behalf of their state, and at the instruction of their states.[1] As described in Chap. 3, there are numerous reasons for which UNSC member states would prioritize specific atrocities. Domestic politics in the United States led the George W. Bush administration to focus on the genocide in Darfur.[2] Colonial ties with Sierra Leone made the Blair administration in the United Kingdom more responsive to the atrocities of that conflict.[3] Commercial ties with a specific state may also play an important role. For example, the Chinese government was intent on letting the Darfur genocide go unnoticed due to its oil interests in Sudan.[4] Power, domestic-politics, cultural ties are all valid reasons for which a state will instruct its diplomat at the UNSC to focus on specific atrocities.

Because of these various reasons, UNSC members instruct their diplomats to take specific positions (including voting in a specific manner) when the UNSC is considering specific atrocities. In 2005, for example, Anne Patterson, the Deputy U.S. Permanent Representative to the UNSC, abstained from Resolution 1593 on the referral of the Darfur case to the ICC on instructions from Washington. Similarly, towards the end of the negotiations on the same resolution, Mr. Li Baodong, the Chinese diplomat at the UNSC, was instructed from his capital to abstain, rather than veto, the resolution.[5] Finally, each of the Russian and Chinese vetoes to draft resolution S/2014/348 on an atrocities investigation for Syria also originated in Moscow and Beijing.

Second, beyond acting at the instruction of their capitals, diplomats take important actions on issues of international criminal justice by acting within the margin of discretion afforded by their states.[6] Most states do not have the capacity to remain appraised and interested in all developments of international affairs. In such instances, the diplomats at the UNSC often have the flexibility to act as they please, so long as they do not offend their state's interests and partners. As principal-agent theory predicts, in such instances, diplomats are given considerable discretion.

In practice, this creates an interesting comparison between the diplomats of the P5 and those of the E10, as the P5 have larger and more sophisticated foreign policy apparatuses than their counterparts at the E10.[7] At first, it may appear that diplomats of the E10 are often less constrained in their decision-making that those of the P5 because of the limited institutional capacity of the small states at the UNSC. Yet, evidence from interviews shows that even the E10 spend important resources on the policies that affect their own state, a P5 or a patron-state of their country.[8] Diplomats

[1] See Nye and Keohane (1971).

[2] Hamilton (2011); Stedjan and Thomas-Jensen (2010); Hamilton and Hazlett (2007).

[3] Châtaignier (2005); Kampfner (2004).

[4] Hamilton (2011); Mody (2010).

[5] Interviews: 1, 9, 13.

[6] See e.g. Johnson and Urpelainen (2014); Pickering and Naim (2001).

[7] Interviews: 1, 3, 4.

[8] Interviews: 7, 17, 19, 20.

from Greece, for example, were given considerable latitude to act on issues relating to Africa. But, they were instructed by the Greek foreign ministry to avoid any action on issues that might irritate any of the P5 without consulting with Athens.[9] As such, while diplomats from the P5 are generally expected to be on a tight leash, the discretion afforded to diplomats from the E10 may vary considerably from issue to issue.

There are several examples in which diplomats acted within their discretion on issues of atrocities investigation. Most famously, Ambassador Keating of New Zealand and Ambassador Kovanda of the Czech Republic were instrumental in the creation of the ICTR. As New Zealand and the Czech Republic had no interests in Rwanda, their governments did not pay attention to events in that country and gave their diplomats at the UNSC discretion to act as they saw fit. Keating and Kovanda could thus make their own decisions on how best to respond to the genocide.[10] This space to maneuver enabled them to suggest an international atrocities investigation to the other UNSC members and to keep working towards its creation. A similar example of discretionary action took place in 2000 and involved the French Deputy Permanent Representative to the UNSC, Yves Doutriaux. France and the United Kingdom had long accorded their diplomats leeway to accommodate each other's preferences in Africa. As part of his discretionary actions, Doutriaux thus voted in favor of the creation of the SCSL, which was supported by the United Kingdom.

Third, in very rare cases, diplomats will violate their states' instructions. While such transgressions are not likely to happen often, since a diplomat's career can be terminated for insubordination, they are anticipated under the concept of shirking in principal-agent's theory.[11]

Interestingly, shirking has taken place at the UNSC in a few highly publicized occasions. For example, in the 2003 debates regarding the invasion of Iraq, Mexico's Ambassador Adolfo Aguilar Zinser opposed a U.S.-sponsored resolution against the instructions of Mexican President Vicente Fox.[12] In the area of atrocities, the most famous case of shirking took place in 2011 and involved the Libyan diplomat at the United Nations, Ibrahim Dabbashi. Dabasshi in open defiance of the instructions of the Libyan government of Colonel Qaddafi defected from the regime and called for an ICC investigation into the Libyan atrocities. The impact of his actions was magnified by the publicity of his defiance, which took place through a declaration to the media.

Overall, diplomats are instrumental in bringing atrocities to the attention of the UNSC and insisting that such atrocities receive an investigation. As past analyses indicate, diplomats take such actions (i) at the instruction of their government, (ii) within the discretion afforded to them by their government, and (iii) rarely, against their government's instructions. None of these three categories of diplomatic activi-

[9] Interview: 19.

[10] Kovanda (2010) (p. 196).

[11] See e.g. McCubbins (1985) (defining shirking as the instances in which "an agent pursues his objectives to the detriments of the principal"); Bendor et al. (2001).

[12] DePalma, New York Times, June 7, 2005.

ties are surprising. A diplomat's actual engagement, however, with such issues is much more complicated and far less mechanical that than these three descriptive categories suggest. The case studies presented in Sect. 5.3 correct for this impression. Before turning to those, the next Section presents one more way that diplomats may act in favor of international atrocities investigations.

5.2 Diplomatic Disagreements

Beyond the three sources of diplomatic activities mentioned above, the historical records, the epigraph of this Chapter and the interviews of this book indicate that diplomats sometimes disagree with their own superiors and advocate for change to the scope of their instructions. In turn, after having successfully changed their state policy vis-à-vis certain atrocities through their disagreement, diplomats bring these atrocities to the attention of the UNSC.

This fourth source of diplomatic activity is controversial, as it challenges common assumptions of foreign policy. A disagreement can be defined as "an argument caused by people having different opinions about something."[13] The expression of disagreement with one's instructions inverts a foundation of principal-agent theory, according to which the principal decides and the agent—as the name indicates—acts. Diplomats, apparently, do not always "argue for policies in which they do not personally believe."[14] By raising a disagreement and managing to obtain new instructions, the agent is no longer a recipient and becomes an instigator. It, moreover, appears that foreign policy is not formulated by a distinct set of actors and continuously adhered to by others. Instead, the practice of foreign policy may be better depicted as an interactive process, one with many participants, that is in constant flux.

Despite being non-conventional, disagreements within hierarchies are conducive to positive results,[15] as they encourage innovation, goal-driven results and facilitate better cooperation across decision-makers. To the contrary, groupthink and obedience to instructions is a recipe for policy disaster.[16] It hinders change, promotes uniformity and restrains creative thinking. In practice, the benefits of disagreements far outweigh the transaction costs from the lack of coordination.

There are at least three factors that increase the likelihood that a diplomat would prevail in a disagreement with his or her capital. First, the diplomat's personality is an important factor. A diplomat's knowledge of his or her capital's preferences is an additional important factor. Finally, a diplomat is more likely to prevail over disagreements on specific actions rather than foreign policy at large.

[13] Merriam Webster Dictionary (2015).

[14] Clark (1973, p. 82).

[15] Eisenhardt et al. (1997); Schweiger et al. (1986).

[16] Janis (1972, 1982).

First, the personality of the diplomat may be important in convincing his or her capital to change its instructions.[17] Past studies of decision-making teams have highlighted how a diplomat's likelihood of prevailing in disagreements with his or her capital depends on the character, upbringing, professional background and temperament of each diplomat.[18] Age, experience and education are all conducive to such disagreements.[19] Additionally, such traits are more successful in heterogeneous teams (i.e. teams whose members have varying ages, gender and functional backgrounds).[20]

Similar explanations may account for the success of diplomatic disagreements at the UNSC. After all, each diplomat carries with him or her experiences and personality traits during his or her service at the UNSC. Additionally, the diplomat in New York is part of a team, with colleagues of different ages, genders and preferences. These micro-level elements of a diplomat's life affect the quality of his or her arguments and the gravitas of his or her stance vis-à-vis his superiors. As a result, individual-centered elements can influence the success of a diplomatic disagreement at the UNSC.

The second factor for which a diplomat may prevail in a disagreement is because he or she will disagree only when his or her view is likely to succeed. At the UNSC, there are several ways in which such internal knowledge may be important. For one, a diplomat may know when to disagree through his or her relationship to his or her state. As diplomats are agents of the state, various elements of principal-agent theory explain how a diplomat's relationship to his or her state is likely to guide the diplomat in voicing his or her disagreements. A series of studies use formal models to argue that a principal will grant an agent greater discretion when they share similar preferences.[21] According to this *ally principle*, we should expect that diplomats with preference similarity to their superiors will voice their disagreements more than those diplomats without preference similarity. Beyond the ally principle, several formal models suggest that discretion is more likely to be given to an agent when the principal has low search costs and there is transparency, which together allow the principal to monitor and *ex post facto* punish the agent's defections or reward his or her obedience.[22] The ability to oversee and punish the agent gives the principal comfort that the agent's actions will not stray from, or in any way undermine, the principal's general aims. A diplomat is more likely to voice disagreements when the principal has such comfort. Finally, the conduct of foreign policy is a specialized field. A few past studies have highlighted that, in such fields, discretion

[17] For such approaches to the study of international relations, see Offer (1995); Byman and Pollack (2001).

[18] See Diplomat (1937); Bertrand and Schoar (2003); Janis (1972, 1982); Eisenhardt et al. (1997).

[19] Bertrand and Schoar (2003).

[20] Eisenhardt et al. (1997).

[21] On ally principle, see Huber and McCarty (2004); Johns (2007); Bendor et al. (2001).

[22] On monitoring of agent, see Huber and McCarty (2004); Johnson (2013a).

increases with the need for *expertise*.[23] As a result, disagreements are likely to increase in tandem with a diplomat's expertise.

Anecdotal evidence from the UNSC supports the three above explanations. The former U.S. Permanent Representative to the UNSC, Susan Rice is said to have leveraged her relationship with President Obama towards the negotiation of Resolution 1970, authorizing the ICC's intervention in Libya.[24] At the same time, the Obama administration monitored her performance at the UNSC and, on that basis, attempted to *ex post facto* reward her by elevating her to Secretary of State despite public perception that she was not the best suited for the job.[25] Finally, in comparison to some of her predecessors in the George W. Bush administration, such as John Bolton and Zalmay Khalizad, the Obama administration gave Rice more leeway on issues relating to conflict in Africa, a topic that she had worked on for over 20 years.[26] Similar observations can be made with respect to Russian foreign minister, and former permanent representative to the United Nations, Sergey Lavrov.

In the third factor, a diplomat's disagreement may depend on the stage of the decision-making process.[27] A diplomat may provide input in at least two steps of the decision-making process: (i) the formulation of policy and (ii) the execution of a specific action under this foreign policy. Foreign policy can be defined as "a goal-oriented or problem-oriented program by authoritative policymakers (or their representatives) directed toward entities outside the policymakers' political jurisdiction."[28] To the contrary, a specific action can be defined as one of the steps taken towards executing this program.

Because of his or her expertise, a diplomat will not only understand the problems with a specific foreign policy and the implementing actions, but is also more likely to convince his or her superiors of the need to avoid such problems. An erroneous foreign policy or course of action is likely to have negative consequences for a diplomat's state, which he or she is supposed to protect as part of his or her employment obligations.[29] Furthermore, an erroneous foreign policy or course of action will likely have negative personal repercussions for the diplomat's supervisors in the state's foreign ministry. In extreme cases, if the decision proves entirely misguided or results in negative consequences, the diplomat's supervisors may be

[23] On need for expertise, see Johnson and Urpelainen (2014); Johnson (2013b); Bendor and Meirowitz (2004); McCubbins (1985).

[24] Cooper and Myers, New York Times (March 18, 2011).

[25] This example also highlights the perils of not objecting to a mistake of your superior. Rice withdrew her name from consideration for the State Department because of Republican opposition to her role in delivering a mistaken report on the death of Ambassador Stevens in Libya.

[26] Interviews: 9, 13.

[27] Prior studies adopting a similar approach include those that focus on bureaucratic politics, see e.g. Allison and Halperin (1972); Legro (1996); Jervis (1976, p. 24).

[28] Hermann (1990).

[29] Though disputed, an ambassadorial action that is suggested to have caused trouble to the United States relates to Ambassador's April C. Glaspie meeting with Iraqi President Saddam Hussein, on July 25, 1990, before the invasion of Kuwait. For more, see New York Times (July 31, 1991).

removed from office.[30] For more ordinary cases, the government will no longer consider such supervisors to be capable foreign policy players and will likely doubt their subsequent decisions.[31]

States have an incentive to listen to the opposition voiced by their diplomats over taking a specific course of action to implement its foreign policy. In their everyday activities, diplomats are instructed by their states to act on specific issues, and are routinely given some discretion in order to accomplish their states' pre-defined goals. Diplomats, however, also bring their own experience to the execution of their mission. A mainstay of this experience is a diplomat's awareness of the immediate consequences of a particular action. For two reasons, this awareness may not be shared by the state. First, by being part of an institution or by living in a host country, a diplomat gains an insider's understanding into the issues and problems of the local environment, one that is not shared by his or her state.[32] Second, through involvement in the day-to-day practice of foreign policy, a diplomat may appreciate the practical differences of each foreign policy action much better than his or her more distant colleagues in the capital.[33] As a result of this expertise, a state is likely to change its policy, if a diplomat voices a disagreement that relates to specific foreign policy action.

States also have great incentives to listen to the opposition voiced by their diplomats when it comes to formulating foreign policy. First, diplomats enjoy participating in the formulation of foreign policy.[34] Moreover, diplomats have valuable expertise on the debated issues. The diplomats, for example, who are staffed at the U.S. Department of State Office of Global Criminal Justice are hired precisely to help formulate U.S. policy on issues of international criminal justice. Finally, as part of the larger bureaucratic machinery, diplomats promote the interests and the agendas of their office.[35] To guarantee that all relevant views are heard, particularly when many other agencies have their own views, each state is likely to actively engage with its relevant diplomats in the policy formation process.[36]

But, for two reasons, changes in state practice are more likely to be fueled by disagreements over concrete particularized steps rather than larger foreign policy. To begin with, in formulating their foreign policy, states place an "over-emphasis on

---

[30] It is believed, for example, that Antonis Samaras was dismissed as Greek foreign minister, in April of 1992, over his actions relating to the recognition of the fifth breakaway republic of the former Yugoslavia under the name of Macedonia. For more, see Eleftherotypia (September 4, 2005).

[31] Such doubts were voiced within the Kennedy cabinet over the use of Adlai Stevenson at the UNSC during the Cuban Missile Crisis, as Stevenson had a reputation of avoiding confrontation.

[32] Talbott (2003, p. 115); Clark (1973, p. 72).

[33] Keating (2004, p. 503); Kovanda (2010); Interview: 7 (explaining how the diplomats at the UNSC could speak to the Claude Dusaidi, an RPF (i.e. Tutsi) representative in New York and knew more about the conflict in Rwanda than their capitals, which got information only from the official Hutu government or press).

[34] Pickering and Naim (2001); Munoz (2009, p. 180).

[35] See Introduction, note 15.

[36] Clark (1973, p. 49).

caution."[37] As a result, because of its risk adverse nature, a state may be less likely to revise its position on issues for a disagreeing diplomat, even when this diplomat has an informational advantage over his or her superiors. Additionally, a state's incentive to change its foreign policy may be undermined by the uncertain nature and fast-paced developments in the context of international conflicts. Conflicts are most often carried out in fluid contexts, where events run ahead and guide subsequent diplomatic actions. A state dealing with a dissenting diplomat may try first to gauge the future of a conflict, and how this future relates to the foreign policy opposed by the diplomat, before changing that policy. As presented in the following case studies on the conflict in Sierra Leone, the United States and the United Kingdom were given a new opportunity to act due to the RUF's recalcitrant actions. They were able to fulfill the preferences of certain of their diplomats (i.e. Scheffer, and Short and Greenstock, respectively), without having to upset their foreign affairs with a midcourse change in policy. A state, however, dealing with a disagreement over a specific step of foreign policy has no such luxury. As illustrated again in the following case studies, the United Nations could not prevent or delay the signing of the Lomé Peace Accords. A diplomatic 'fight or flight syndrome' seems more likely to appear in such crammed decision-making grounds.

Overall, while diplomatic disagreements in which a diplomat disagrees with his or her own superiors and advocates for change to the scope of their instructions may be a source of diplomatic activity, as discussed above, the conditions for such fruitful disagreements are limited. As such, states are likely to heed to disagreements in a few limited circumstances.

5.3 The Case Studies

Part I of this Chapter highlighted three traditional sources of diplomatic activity, namely that diplomats take action (i) at the instruction of their government, (ii) within the discretion afforded to them by their government, and (iii) rarely, against their government's instructions. Part II presented a framework for understanding the more controversial, and previously unrecognized, fact that diplomats also act after having convinced their states to change their policies. Yet, the above two Parts give the impression that diplomatic activity is mechanical, devoid of any color. To the contrary, the following case studies highlight the intense and passionate nature of the work diplomats undertake at the UNSC within the four sources of diplomatic activity.

This Part proceeds in three sections, each of which presents one case study from the Sierra Leonean civil war in chronological order. The first case study details how Hans Correll disagreed with Kofi Annan and managed to change Annan's decision over the use of amnesty in Sierra Leone. The second case study highlights how David Scheffer came about to receiving specific instructions from the U.S. State

[37] Clark (1973, p. 23).

Department over the creation of the SCSL. Finally, the third presents how Sir Jeremy Greenstock acted within the discretion afforded by the U.K. government when evaluating the role that Foday Sankoh was playing in Sierra Leone.

5.3.1 *Case Study of Disagreement: The UN and Amnesty (at the Lomé Peace Accords)*

The first case study of diplomatic action relating to international atrocities investigations occurred the few days before the signing of the Lomé Peace Accords and involved the Special Representative of the Secretary-General, Francis Okelo, the United Nations Office of Legal Affairs ('OLA') and the Secretary-General, Kofi Annan. The staff members of the OLA disagreed with Okelo's and Annan's intention to sign on to the amnesty provisions of the Lomé Peace Accords. This section first provides the context of the events and then explains why Kofi Annan changed policy and agreed with the position of the OLA.

The Secretary-General, Kofi Annan, had long been aware of the atrocities being committed in Sierra Leone. Initially, the Secretary-General "expressed [his] deep regret at the violence, loss of life and property and immense suffering undergone by the people of Sierra Leone since the coup d'état…"[38] He later informed the UNSC that the atrocities committed by the rebel AFRC/RUF alliance[39] reached severe proportions.[40] The shock and awe value of the Secretary-General's description of atrocities is noteworthy:

> As ECOMOG troops approached [Koindu and Buedu], armed former junta elements attacked the local civilian population, killing, raping and mutilating hundreds of them, causing tens of thousands of Sierra Leoneans to flee into Liberia and Guinea in the last few weeks and tens of thousands to flee into the interior of Sierra Leone. Hundreds of patients have been admitted to hospitals suffering from amputation of limbs and ears and severe lacerations. Humanitarian organizations fear that the actual number of victims may be much larger…..
>
> Of those victims who have received treatment, most are male, ranging in age from 8 to 60 years. The youngest amputee admitted to hospital is, however, a six-year-old girl, one of

[38] Secretary-General's Report, S/1998/249.

[39] The civil war in Sierra Leone started in 1991, when, under the leadership of Foday Sankoh and with significant help from Charles Taylor in Liberia, the Revolutionary United Front ('RUF') rebels attacked eastern Sierra Leone. As the civil war violence continued, in May 1997, rogue elements of the Sierra Leonean army removed President Kabbah from power. The putschist movement was named the Armed Forces Revolutionary Council ('AFRC'), and was led by Major Johnny Paul Koroma. The latter invited the RUF to join the AFRC and form a people's army. As a reaction to the RUF-AFRC cooperation, that same month, both forces of the Economic Community of West African States Monitoring Group ('ECOMOG') landed in Sierra Leone, and local militias—which had been protecting their neighborhoods from the RUF and now the AFRC—integrated into the Civil Defense Forces ('CDF'). The civil war thus became a five-way struggle, with the RUF-AFRC forces fighting against the ECOMOG troops, the remnants of the Sierra Leone army and the CDF.

[40] Secretary-General's Report, S/1998/486.

> whose arms was completely severed. Victims also report that babies have been taken from their mothers' arms and burned alive. There are numerous reports of rape, including one of the multiple rape of a 12-year-old girl. Doctors at one hospital state that lacerations inflicted on one 60-year-old woman are the result of a failed attempt to behead her.....
>
> From all parts of the country there are reports of extrajudicial killings, rape, arbitrary detention, including for purposes of sexual abuse, torture of children (especially child-combatants), forced labour and the looting and destruction of residential and commercial premises and property.

As a result of the continued fighting, on July 13, 1998, the UNSC established the United Nations Observer Mission in Sierra Leone ("UNOMSIL") with up to 70 military observers and a small medical staff. UNOMSIL was led by the Special Representative for Sierra Leone, a position that had been created to subsume that of the Secretary-General's Special Envoy.[41] Francis Okelo, a national of Uganda, long-time UN administrator and, up to then, Special Envoy to Sierra Leone, was named the Special Representative.

For the subsequent period of the conflict, the Special Representative for Sierra Leone had a central role in negotiating and handling the political aspects of the civil war. With the backdrop of the international community condemning the atrocities that had been committed and with the UNSC having authorized a peacekeeping force, the Special Representative and the Secretary-General attempted to build momentum for a peace deal. This process culminated in late May 1999,[42] when all warring parties, together with the governments of "Benin, Burkina Faso, Cote d'Ivoire, Ghana, Guinea, Liberia, Libyan Arab Jamahiriya, Mali, Nigeria, Togo, the United Kingdom and the United States of America" as well as the UN, the Organization of African Unity, the ECOWAS, and the Commonwealth of Nations, met in Lomé—the capital of Togo—to negotiate a peace agreement.[43] After more than a month of negotiations, the agreement was signed on July 7, 1999. The events of this first case study took place in the days before the signing of this agreement.

As the warring sides were approaching the conclusion of the peace agreement, it became apparent that the government of President Kabbah was ready to include amnesty provisions to placate demands from the rebels and to entice them to participate in the agreement. Kabbah was no stranger to this procedure, which he had first agreed to in the 1996 Abidjan Peace Accords.[44] Earlier in 1999, in a private meeting with U.S. Ambassador-at-Large for War Crimes David Scheffer, Kabbah had privately conceded that amnesty for all rebels—including the top commanders—could be negotiated as part of a peace agreement.[45] During the Lomé talks, Kabbah formally accepted this rebel demand.[46] So did all of the other parties to the Lomé talks.

[41] Resolution 1181 (1998).

[42] Secretary-General's Report, S/1996/645.

[43] Lomé Peace Accords.

[44] Abidjan Peace Accords (Article 14); Kabbah (2010) (chapter 6).

[45] Scheffer (2013, p. 306).

[46] Kabbah (2010) (chapter 7).

As part of his duties, Francis Okelo frequently reported on the progress of the peace-talks to the UN headquarters. Following this procedure, after a draft of the accords had been finalized, Okelo sent this draft to the UN Headquarters and waited for his instructions regarding whether he should sign the accord on behalf of the United Nations, as a guarantor. The UN Secretariat was initially positive towards the text of the peace accord and was inclined to sign on.[47] Okelo, however, had also sent the draft of the peace accords to the OLA.[48] Once the text of the agreement arrived at the OLA, a series of staff members voiced their disagreement with the amnesty provisions of the accord internally, within the OLA.[49] These UN lawyers, on the basis of their expertise and experience with past conflicts, argued forcefully against the amnesty provision, which they perceived it to be in violation of international criminal law. It would also counter the developing trend towards accountability for those most responsible for committing atrocities.

Hans Corell, Under-Secretary-General for Legal Affairs, shared the feelings of his staff members[50] and decided to take up the issue with the Secretary-General.[51] Corell and Okelo cooperated very closely with their superior, Kofi Annan. In line with the three factors outlined in the framework set forth in the previous Section, they used their close relationship as leverage for their argument. Beyond their close professional ties, they also knew that Annan was particularly sympathetic to the idea of providing accountability for atrocities.

In his conversation with Annan, Corell acknowledged the positive elements of the accord and then voiced his disagreement with the amnesty provision in a detailed and forceful manner.[52] His arguments focused on the two consequences of the amnesty provision. First, such a provision would tarnish the image of the United Nations. Corell asserted that the general trend of international law had shifted towards a paradigm of accountability and that the United Nations—as a guardian of international law—should not agree to a provision that violated established legal practice. How could the United Nations sign onto an agreement that would give the murderous Sankoh a blank sheet when it was putting pressure on numerous governments to surrender war criminals to the ICTY and the ICTR? Second, the amnesty provision would harm peace efforts in Sierra Leone and beyond. Judging by the precedent of the Abidjan accords, Corell considered that an amnesty provision gave the rebels a perverse incentive not to cease from committing atrocities, since a future amnesty provision would always appear possible. Beyond Sierra Leone, the use of an amnesty clause in Lomé could set a negative precedent for other conflicts.

Throughout their disagreement, both the OLA lawyers and Corell did not attack the remaining provisions of the agreement. They agreed with the UN's policies towards the Sierra Leonean conflict, which involved a combination of forceful mea-

[47] Interviews: 6, 15.

[48] Interviews: 6, 15, 16.

[49] Interviews: 6, 15, 16.

[50] The OLA falls under the supervision of the Under-Secretary-General for Legal Affairs.

[51] Interview: 15.

[52] Interview: 15.

sures (sanctions, peacekeeping) and increased diplomatic efforts.[53] All of these policies seemed to have been incorporated into the Lomé Peace Accords. Understanding the difficulties of the negotiations between the various warring parties and cognizant of the grim realities of the continued conflict in Sierra Leone, Corell and his staff were as eager as all other parties to conclude a peace agreement. But, despite their agreement with the larger policy, stemming from their expertise on international criminal justice, they were also in the best position to appreciate the shortcomings of the proposed amnesty. Their only concern centered on their preference not to preclude a future possibility of justice in order to have peace in the short term. Their opposition to an unqualified approval of the agreement was the message that Corell conveyed to Kofi Annan. Corell also suggested a different step, namely signing the agreement and simultaneously adding a reservation.[54]

Annan found Corell's points compelling. He changed his initially unqualified optimism towards the text of the accords. As he writes in his memoirs, he "took the very unusual step of instructing his Special Representative to Sierra Leone, Francis Okelo, to write into the agreement *by hand* that for the UN, there could be no amnesty for genocide, war crimes or crimes against humanity"[55] (emphasis in original). Okelo did just that.

5.3.2 *Case Study of Instructions: United States and Atrocities in Sierra Leone (Immediately After the Lomé Peace Accords)*

The second case study of diplomatic actions took place after the signing of the Lomé Peace Accords and involved the U.S. Ambassador-at-Large for War Crimes, David Scheffer, and the foreign policy apparatus of the U.S. government. As was done for the previous case study, this section first provides the context for the events. Then it explains the discussions and actions among several high-ranking members of the Clinton administration over the amnesty language in the Lomé Peace Accords, and how these ended in specific instructions for Scheffer.

The United States paid close attention to the events in Sierra Leone and to the Lomé Peace Accords. After the Clinton administration's abject failure to act during the Rwandan genocide and the administration's repeated internal and external criticisms over that failure, Africa had become a new priority.[56] Yet, events in both the international and domestic sphere had rendered the Sierra Leonean conflict of secondary significance. Only when circumstances changed, following the RUF's capture of 150 peacekeepers in April 2000, did the Clinton administration focus on

[53] Interviews: 6, 15, 16.

[54] Interviews: 5, 15, 16.

[55] Annan (2012, p. 155).

[56] See e.g. Albright (2003, p. 173).

the conflict. Under increased domestic and international pressure, the United States decided to support forceful measures to stop the conflict, including the creation of an international criminal tribunal. The events examined here took place before that change in policy, during a period that the United States was striving for "peace on the cheap."[57]

With the United States focused on events in the former Yugoslavia, Saddam Hussein's intransigence in Iraq, and a multitude of other conflicts, the events in Sierra Leone did not draw the full attention of the U.S. government until 1999. After the RUF/AFRC attack on Freetown in late December 1998, codenamed "Operation No Living Thing," ECOMOG placed renewed efforts to stop the Sierra Leonean civil war. These efforts led to the Lomé Peace Accords in July 1999, in which the United States participated as an outside observer and guarantor. The amnesty provisions of the Lomé Peace Accords were included in the presence of the U.S. team, which was led by the Reverend Jesse Jackson.

The position of the United States on the Lomé Peace Accords was a result of Jackson's initiative. After he secured the Africa-American vote for the Bill Clinton's 1996 re-election campaign, Jackson became an informal advisor to the President. For his help in the re-election campaign, President Clinton appointed Jackson as his Special Envoy to Africa.[58] In a time in which U.S. attention to Africa's problems was overshadowed by a host of international crises, Jackson had significant leeway in making policy decisions. Jackson was active on the ground in West Africa. In July 1998, for example, Jackson brokered a meeting between President Kabbah of Sierra Leone, President Taylor of Liberia, who was a staunch supporter of the RUF, Secretary-General Annan, and Nigerian President Abubakar.[59]

While the Sierra Leonean conflict continued, Jackson's connection with President Clinton had grown even closer, with the former becoming the latter's spiritual advisor over the Monika Lewinsky scandal that had broken out in early 1998. As a result, during the negotiations of the Lomé Peace Accords, Jackson was able to arrange for President Clinton to telephone both President Kabbah and RUF leader Sankoh to put pressure on both towards accepting the agreement.[60] When the agreement was negotiated and concluded, Jackson, to the surprise of several individuals within the State Department, failed to object to the amnesty language.[61] By failing to do so he sided with President Kabbah of Sierra Leone, who considered the amnesty to be the *quid pro quo* for the RUF's cessation of hostilities.[62]

David Scheffer, the U.S. Ambassador-at-Large for War Crimes, was among those dismayed by the use of the amnesty provisions in the Lomé Peace Accords. He was the person most responsible for the implementation of zero tolerance to atrocities within U.S. foreign policy. On a parallel track with Jackson's forays into peace-

[57] Reno, New York Times (May 11, 2000).

[58] White House Press Secretary (October 8, 1997).

[59] Secretary-General's Report, S/1998/750.

[60] Karon, Time Magazine (May 12, 2000).

[61] Scheffer (2013, p. 311).

[62] Kabbah (2010, p. 133–135).

building for Sierra Leone, Scheffer had, in 1998, travelled to Sierra Leone to confront both the Kabbah government and the rebels over the need to end the atrocities and seek accountability. Upon returning from his trip, where he realized the gravity of what was occurring, he held several meetings with other State Department officials and with the Atrocities Prevention Interagency Working Group to argue for a swift judicial process for those most responsible for the atrocities. In the end, despite his ambassadorial rank and interest in Sierra Leone, Scheffer "had not been privy to the final days of negotiations" on the Lomé Peace Accords. He "was taken aback to read the breadth of [the Accords'] terms on pardon and amnesty."[63] Scheffer realized that "the priority for the Africa specialists in the State Department was a peace deal, apparently at whatever cost to justice."[64] Mirroring this observation, the official U.S. statement on the Lomé Peace Accords congratulated both sides for working together and expressed support for the agreement "which will bring to an end the tragic war of Sierra Leone."[65]

Scheffer's surprise was not limited to Jackson's decision to support the agreement despite the amnesty clause. Throughout his career, Scheffer opposed any dichotomy between peace and justice, and saw the two as intertwined and inseparable. In the case of Sierra Leone, others in the State Department considered that the amnesty provision offered an opportunity for Sankoh to transform the RUF into a political party. Scheffer found the hope that such amnesty would lead to national reconciliation to be "almost unbearable gobbledygook."[66] Additionally, as a practical matter, Scheffer believed that international criminal law would override any agreement on amnesty for war crimes and crimes against humanity committed in Sierra Leone.[67] In his eyes, the preference for "peace on the cheap" was practically and legally wrong.

Despite Scheffer's personal preferences, the Lomé Peace Accords were signed and no one in the U.S. government publicly spoke up in favor of justice. In October 1999, 3 months after the signing of the Lomé Peace Accords, U.S. Secretary of State Albright formally visited Freetown. Her visit was emblematic of the administration's approach. It included a visit to a recovery camp for war amputees, $55 million in aid, and $65 million in debt forgiveness. Yet, Secretary Albright also had a private meeting with RUF leader Sankoh and AFRC leader Koroma. When asked about the issue of an amnesty in the Lomé Peace Accords, Albright conceded that "[u]ltimately, the only way that reconciliation really can come is if people have a sense that justice has been done and those who have perpetrated the terrible crimes are punished individually." But, she prioritized consolidating peace before proceeding with justice.[68]

---

[63] Scheffer (2013, p. 311).

[64] Scheffer (2013, p. 312).

[65] Statement by the United Kingdom and United States of America (July 6, 1999).

[66] Scheffer (2013, p. 312).

[67] Sierra Leonean News (February 11, 1999).

[68] Onishi, New York Times (October, 19, 1999).

The events on the ground proved that the Clinton administration's approach was misguided, as the RUF violated the terms of the peace accords and continued carrying out atrocities. Even after the capture by the RUF of 150 peacekeepers in late April 2000, the administration followed Jackson's advice. In a statement on May 12, 2000, President Clinton clarified that "I have asked Reverend Jesse Jackson, my special envoy for democracy in Africa, to return to the region to work with leaders there for a peaceful resolution of this crisis."[69] But, before landing in Freetown, Jackson managed to make himself irrelevant to the process. He first supported that Sankoh has to be brought back to a political position. Then, he notoriously compared the murderous Sankoh to Nelson Mandela. Sierra Leoneans were furious. Abu Mbawa Kongonba, a Sierra Leonean legislator, captured the general mood in saying that "I cannot help believing that the Rev. Jackson is a collaborator of Foday Sankoh….he has a hidden agenda."[70] The Kabbah government clarified that it could not guarantee Jackson's safety in Freetown, effectively making him a *persona non grata*.

While the peacekeepers were released through Jackson's contacts with Liberian President Charles Taylor, the poor performance of the Clinton administration over the Sierra Leonean crisis incited a litany of complaints. Initially, the international community and the UN criticized the administration for discriminating against African problems. Why was the United States involved in Kosovo and East Timor, but not in a brutal civil war in Sierra Leone? Powerful Republicans also voiced strong opposition to maintaining the Lomé framework. Republican Senator Judd Gregg, of New Hampshire, head of the Senate's appropriations subcommittee and advisor to the 2000 presidential campaign of George W. Bush, opposed the Lomé Peace Accords by blocking $368 million in State Department funds from going to United Nations peacekeeping missions.[71] Finally, the public pressure culminated in July 2000 with the publication of Ryan Lizza's account of the Clinton administration's actions in Sierra Leone. Characterized as "the most grotesque," and "a policy of coercive dishonesty," Lizza asserted that Clinton's policy towards Sierra Leone sent a positive message towards the RUF atrocity perpetrators.[72] The administration's foreign policy on Sierra Leone was thus entirely exposed and it was obvious to most that it was in need of a significant change.

Meanwhile, Scheffer renewed his efforts to convince the various State Department offices of the need for accountability in the efforts to stop atrocities from recurring. To that end, he travelled—in February 2000—to Sierra Leone to meet with the local government, the UN peacekeeping mission and the victim groups. During the spring of 2000, Scheffer presented the options for accountability in meetings with senior State Department officials and pressured Secretary of State Albright to include accountability in the Sierra Leonean peace process.[73] In May 2000, he also met with

[69] Lewis, New York Times (May 12, 2000).

[70] Onishi, New York Times (May 19, 2000).

[71] New York Times (June 6, 2000).

[72] Lizza, The New Republic (July 24, 2000).

[73] Scheffer (2013, p. 320).

Under-Secretary-General for Legal Affairs Hans Corell to explore the options for a UN court in Sierra Leone.[74] As a result, by late Spring 2000, less than a year after the Lomé Peace Accords, confidential sources informed the New York Times that high level political appointees within the Clinton Administration, such as Harold Koh, assistant secretary of state for human rights, Julia Taft, assistant secretary of state for refugees, and David Scheffer opposed power-sharing with the RUF in Sierra Leone.[75] Scheffer continued building his case for accountability up until June 3, 2000, when Richard Holbrooke, U.S. Ambassador to the United Nations, informed him that the United States would propose to the UNSC the creation of an international criminal tribunal for the atrocities committed in Sierra Leone. Scheffer was explicitly instructed to act towards the creation of such a tribunal. In his own words, "[t]hat was the green light [he] had been waiting for."[76]

5.3.3 Case Study of Discretion: United Kingdom and Foday Sankoh (After the Lomé Peace Accords)

The third case study of diplomatic activity took place after the signing of the Lomé Peace Accords and involved Jeremy Greenstock and Clare Short and the foreign policy apparatus of the U.K. government. Greenstock and Short used the discretion afforded to them as part of their official duties to evaluate and question the role assigned to RUF leader Foday Sankoh in the post-Lomé political system of Sierra Leone. Once again, this section provides the context for the events and then explains the debates among several high-ranking members of the Blair administration on the role Sankoh should have in Sierra Leone following the Lomé Peace Accords.

As described in Tony Blair's memoirs, the United Kingdom did very little with regards to Sierra Leone's civil war before 2000.[77] In its early years in power, the Blair cabinet was focused on the international crises in the former Yugoslavia—particularly Kosovo—and the attempted inspections of Saddam Hussein's WMD programs in Iraq. In 1999, once a large number of atrocities started receiving international attention, the United Kingdom slightly shifted its interest towards Sierra Leone. The Blair family had some personal ties to Sierra Leone, as Blair's father had been a lecturer at the Sierra Leone University in Freetown.[78] The United Kingdom also had colonial ties with that country, a reality that influenced the perception of U.K. policy-makers towards the civil war.[79] These ties were so important that the BBC coverage remained the primary news media not only for the U.K. gov-

[74] Scheffer (2013, p. 320); Interview: 15.

[75] Crossette, New York Times (May 20, 2000).

[76] Scheffer (2013, p. 322).

[77] Blair (2010, p. 246).

[78] Short (2004, p. 4).

[79] Blair (2010, p. 246).

ernment, but also for all fighting parties in the civil war. More importantly, another former U.K. colony—Nigeria—had taken the lead in fighting the AFRC/RUF rebels. Mindful of the atrocities and of Nigeria's financial difficulties in fighting this war, the Blair government decided to contribute £1 million to the logistical needs of ECOMOG forces in January 1999.[80] By January 20, 1999, in its effort to bolster the anti-rebel front, the United Kingdom had also sent a frigate to Freetown.[81] At the same time, however, Blair was also preparing for an air campaign against Serbia for the protection of Kosovar Albanians.

The contrast between the United Kingdom's interest towards the war in Kosovo and general apathy towards Sierra Leone's civil war could not have been starker. The double-standard was not lost on *The Guardian*, which reported that "[t]he UN's consolidated humanitarian appeal for Kosovo is $690 m[illion], of which 58% has been met, while $2.1b[illio]n has just been pledged for regional reconstruction. A UN appeal for $25 m[illion] for Sierra Leone met profound international indifference and a mere 32% of the appeal has been covered."[82] Various commentators—such as the UN Human Rights Commissioner Mary Robinson—tried to galvanize the United Kingdom's attention to Sierra Leone by noting that there were more atrocities in Sierra Leone than in Kosovo.

In contrast to its intervention in Kosovo, the United Kingdom favored a power-sharing agreement with the goal of national reconciliation for Sierra Leone. In July 1999, at the same time that U.K. ground troops entered the war in Kosovo, the Lomé Peace Accords on Sierra Leone were signed. In an effort to support the peace process held in Lomé, the U.K. government paid for the costs of the month-long negotiations.[83] Then, upon the completion of the negotiations, the United Kingdom encouraged the warring parties to abide by their agreement.[84]

The United Kingdom was willing to work with the text of the Lomé Peace Accords despite the significant concessions made by Kabbah's government to the rebels. The United Kingdom's comments on the Lomé Peace Accords indicated support for the agreement while recognizing its flaws. The inclusion, for example, of an amnesty provision was "one of the many hard choices that the Government and the people of Sierra Leone had to make in the interests of securing a workable agreement."[85] Similarly, the U.K. Foreign Secretary—in answering questions to Parliament—acknowledged that Sankoh's appointment to the Ministry for Mining, which oversaw the lucrative diamond trade—a major source of rebel funding, was integral to the deal and, thus, an important step towards peace.[86]

---

[80] Norton-Taylor and Whitehouse, The Guardian (January 14, 1999).

[81] Goldman, The Guardian (January 20, 1999).

[82] Britain, The Guardian (August 4, 1999).

[83] Châtaignier (2005, p. 89).

[84] Statement by the United Kingdom and United States of America (July 6, 1999).

[85] Deputy Permanent Representative of the United Kingdom to the UNSC, Steward Eldon, Statement at UNSC (August 20, 1999).

[86] Questions to Parliament (May 23, 2000).

In its efforts to support the reconciliation effort, the U.K. government became increasingly invested in the post-Lomé peace process by cooperating with the government of President Kabbah in the efforts to end the civil war. The United Kingdom shipped armaments and ammunition to the government of Sierra Leone.[87] It sponsored a UNSC resolution on the creation of a 6,000 soldier strong peacekeeping force, which was eventually adopted in late October 1999. Again, at the request of the United Kingdom, the UNSC increased this mission to 11,000 troops in February of 2000. A U.K. police officer was also assigned to retrain the Sierra Leonean police.[88] The Inspector General of Sierra Leone, Keith Biddle, came from the United Kingdom. The U.K. Department of Foreign International Development ('DfID') further undertook a significant task in the process of disarmament, demobilization, and reintegration of the former rebels. Clare Short, the DfID Minister "became very involved personally and travelled to Sierra Leone many times to try to get the demobilization process going."[89] DfID also funded the creation of political structures that would "challenge the endemic corruption" in Sierra Leone.[90] In an effort to deprive a principal source of the rebels' income, the U.K. Foreign Secretary, Robin Cook, proposed a restriction in the sale of uncut diamonds.[91] Finally, the United Kingdom committed to pay £250,000 to the creation of a Truth and Reconciliation Commission. By early 2000, the U.K. commitments to Sierra Leone thus amounted to £40–50 million.[92]

The United Kingdom's insistence on supporting the Lomé Peace Accords continued despite several indications that the RUF was not abiding by the terms of the agreement. In January 2000, Sankoh had a "businesslike" meeting with U.K. Foreign Office Minister for Africa, Peter Hain, and admitted that—while he supported the Lomé Peace Accords—there would be a delay in disarming his supporters in eastern Sierra Leone.[93] In February 2000, Sankoh violated an international travel ban and went to South Africa, where he was arrested and deported. He was rumored to have travelled there to strike an arms deal.[94] A few days later, staff of the United Nations World Food Program were temporarily taken hostages by RUF rebels. RUF rebels blocked other UN troops from access to several towns in Eastern Sierra Leone.[95]

Not all members of the United Kingdom's foreign policy apparatus, however, believed in the potential success of the Lomé Peace Accords. The U.K. Permanent Representative at the UNSC, Sir Jeremy Greenstock, together with Clare Short, the DfID Minister,[96] began having doubts about the applicability of the Lomé Peace

[87] Sierra Leone News (October 6, 1999).

[88] Woollacott, The Guardian (April 14, 2000).

[89] Short (2004, p. 100).

[90] Short (2004, p. 101).

[91] Sierra Leonean News (September 28, 1999).

[92] Sierra Leonean News (January 25, 2000).

[93] Sierra Leonean News (January 26, 2000).

[94] Foreign Pages, The Guardian (February 23, 2000).

[95] Sierra Leonean News (February 24, 2000).

[96] Short broke away from Blair over the Iraq war and became a vocal critique of the Blair administration. See e.g. Short (2004, p. 212–257).

Accords. In early March of 2000, Sir Jeremy Greenstock's visit to Freetown, as part of an official UNSC mission to Sierra Leone, coincided with Clare Short's trip, which was part of a DfID mission. As senior officials, Greenstock and Short both enjoyed significant discretion in their actions. In their trip to Sierra Leone, they also had to avoid creating false impressions or expectations about the UK's preferences.

Acting within the discretion afforded to them as part of their official duties, Greenstock and Stock had a joint private meeting with Foday Sankoh.[97] They both reported that this meeting proved unnerving at the time. Sankoh refused to admit that the RUF was impeding the peace process. Moreover, Sankoh gave the appearance of a man with a deeply flawed character, "confused" and "worried about his own position."[98] For Greenstock and Short, accepting this person as an honest interlocutor in the peace process appeared impossible. Including Sankoh in the rebuilding efforts, such as disarmament or amnesty, no longer made sense since Sankoh thought "that he must retain a military option."[99]

Despite Greenstock's and Short's initiative to meet with Sankoh and the conclusions they relayed to London, the United Kingdom's foreign policy in Sierra Leone stayed the same with regards to Sankoh. The United Kingdom abandoned the Lomé framework only after the RUF took peacekeepers as hostages, in May 2000. Secretary Annan increased the pressure on powerful governments to intervene. No longer bogged down in Kosovo, Blair had a good opportunity to implement his principled view of foreign policy in Africa.[100] At this time, in a cabinet meeting over the events in Sierra Leone, many cabinet members proposed military action.[101] The public also appeared to be supportive of such action.[102] After the Kosovo experience, Blair did not even think about seeking UNSC approval.[103] Seven hundred paratroopers were—unilaterally and—rapidly deployed to secure the airport serving Freetown, in the neighboring town of Lingui. Blair's spokesperson clarified that "it would be wrong [for the United Kingdom] not to be there."[104]

The United Kingdom's military presence turned the tide of events. Soon after, Sankoh was arrested by a mob in Freetown and handed over to the Kabbah regime. This detention marked the last turn towards the end of the civil war in Sierra Leone. Some years later, Secretary-General Annan wrote that:

> Rather than watch Sierra Leone fall into another bout of atrocious civil war of the kind that had devastated the country throughout the 1990s, what followed in May 2000 was a deci-

[97] Interview: 18.

[98] Sierra Leonean News (March 13, 2000); Interviews: 15, 16, 18.

[99] Sierra Leonean News (March 13, 2000).

[100] Blair (2010, p. 246).

[101] Short (2004, p. 101).

[102] Showcross, The Guardian (May 10, 2000); Snow, The Guardian (May 10, 2000).

[103] Blair (2010, p. 431).

[104] Ellison et al., The Guardian (May 12, 2000).

> sive military intervention by a British military task force that routed the rebel factions and returned the balance to Sierra Leone's political system.[105]

In the words of a Sierra Leonean folk expression, the military intervention indicated that the United Kingdom would no longer 'try to scare the monkey with a dead baboon.'[106] It also signaled the end of the Lomé framework. In reality, the conclusions reached by Short and Greenstock were validated, as Sankoh proved that he could not be trusted. Subsequently, in July 2000, Greenstock negotiated with his U.S. counterparties at the UNSC over the creation of an international criminal trial for the Sierra Leonean civil war, which the UNSC approved in August of that year. Sankoh died in prison, awaiting trial.

5.4 Conclusion

Diplomats matter. And, they matter in many different ways. This Chapter explains why a diplomat becomes the patron-supporter of specific atrocities. As the literature on diplomatic actions has recognized, diplomats decide to seize the attention of the UNSC on specific atrocities according to (i) the instructions of their state, (ii) the discretion afforded to them by their state, or (iii) rarely, by disregarding the instructions of their state. This Chapter also explains that diplomats can do so (iv) by disagreeing with their state and convincing the state of the need for new instructions.

The theoretical expectations, however, on diplomatic actions are full of mechanical steps. If for, example, a diplomat receives instructions, a diplomat is expected to act. Additionally, if a diplomat has some discretion, a diplomat may take a stance. Yet, in reality, diplomatic life is complicated and multi-faceted. This color in the diplomacy relating to atrocities investigation is depicted in the three case studies from the Sierra Leonean civil war. Viewed together, these case studies indicate that diplomats are active participants within the foreign policy process, whose actions are influenced by, and can only be understood within, a constant movement of international affairs.

Once a patron diplomat brings specific atrocities to the attention of the UNSC, the UNSC begins its deliberations. As Table 5.1a indicates, a patron diplomat has brought to the attention of the UNSC the atrocities committed in 52 of the 92 states. With the attention of the UNSC seized, the UNSC members commence their deliberations on the appropriate responses, entering thereby the second step of the UNSC's decision-making process. The following Chapter looks into the events of this second step.

---

[105] Annan (2012, p. 117).

[106] Snow, The Guardian (May 16, 2000).

References

Interviews

Interview No. 1; Interview Details: Diplomat from United Kingdom, New York (June 13, 2013).
Interview No. 3; Interview Details: Diplomat from the United Kingdom, New York (July 11, 2013).
Interview No. 4; Interview Details: Diplomat from United States, New York (July 12, 2013).
Interview No. 5; Interview Details: Member of NGO Security Council Report (July 31, 2013).
Interview No. 6; Interview Details: Member of UN Office of Legal Affairs, New York (August 6, 2013).
Interview No. 7; Interview Details: Diplomat from New Zealand, New York (August 23, 2013).
Interview No. 9; Interview Details: Official from the International Criminal Court, New York (September 9, 2013).
Interview No. 13; Interview Details: Diplomat from Russia, New York (November 26, 2013).
Interview No. 15; Interview Details: Member of UN Office of Legal Affairs, New York (December 6, 2013).
Interview No. 16; Interview Details: Member of UN Office of Legal Affairs, New York (December 6, 2013).
Interview No. 17; Interview Details: Diplomat from Colombia, New York (December 17, 2013).
Interview No. 18; Interview Details: Diplomat from United Kingdom, London (January 7, 2014).
Interview No. 19; Interview Details: Diplomat from Greece, on Skype (January 19, 2014).
Interview No. 20; Interview Details: Diplomat from Guatemala, New York (January 21, 2014).

Books and Articles

Albright, Madeleine. 2003. *Madame Secretary: A Memoir*. New York: Hyperion.
Allison, Graham, and Morton Halperin. 1972. Bureaucratic Politics. *World Politics* 24: 40–79.
Annan, Kofi. 2012. *A Life in War and Peace*. London: Penguin.
Bendor, Jonathan, and Adam Meirowitz. 2004. Spatial Models of Delegation. *American Political Science Review* 98 (02): 293–310.
Bendor, Jonathan, Amihai Glazer, and Thomas Hammond. 2001. Theories of Delegation. *Annual Review of Political Science* 4 (1): 235–269.
Bertrand, Marianne, and Antoinette Schoar. 2003. Managing with Style: The Effect of Managers on Firm Policies. *The Quarterly Journal of Economics* 118 (4): 1169–1208.
Blair, Tony. 2010. *A Journey: My Political Life*. New York: Knopf.
Byman, Daniel, and Kenneth Pollack. 2001. Let Us Now Praise Great Men: Bringing the Statesman Back In. *International Security* 25: 107–146.
Châtaignier, Jean-Marc. 2005. *L'ONU dans la crise en Sierra Leone*. Paris: Éditions KARTHALA.
Clark, Eric. 1973. *Diplomat the World of International Diplomacy*. New York: Taplinger Publishing Company.
Diplomat, H. 1937. The Modern Diplomat. *Foreign Affairs* 15: 3.
"disagreement." *Merriam-Webster.com*. Merriam-Webster, 2011 (30 March 2015) at http://www.merriam-webster.com.
Eisenhardt, Kathleen, Kahwajy Jean, and L.J. Bourgeois III. 1997. Conflict and Strategic Choice: How Top Management Teams Disagree. *California Management Review* 39 (2): 42–62.
Hamilton, Rebecca. 2011. *Fighting for Darfur.* Palgrave Macmillan.
Hamilton, Rebecca, and Chad Hazlett. 2007. Not on Our Watch: The Emergence of the American Movement for Darfur. In *The War in Darfur*, ed. Alex de Waal. Cambridge, MA: Global Equity Initiative.

Hermann, Charles F. 1990. Changing Course: When Governments Choose to Redirect Foreign Policy. *International Studies Quarterly* 34 (1): 3–21.
Huber, John D., and Nolan McCarty. 2004. Bureaucratic Capacity, Delegation, and Political Reform. *American Political Science Review* 98 (03): 481–494.
Janis, Irving L. 1972. *Victims of Groupthink: A Psychological Study of Foreign-Policy Decisions and Fiascoes*. Boston: Houghton, Mifflin.
———. 1982. *Groupthink: Psychological Studies of Policy Decisions and Fiascoes*. Boston: Houghton, Mifflin.
Jervis, Robert. 1976. *Perception and Misperception in International Politics*. Princeton: Princeton University Press.
Johns, Leslie. 2007. A Servant of Two Masters: Communication and the Selection of International Bureaucrats. *International Organization* 61 (2): 245–275.
Johnson, Tana. 2013a. Institutional Design and Bureaucrats' Impact on Political Control. *The Journal of Politics* 75 (01): 183–197.
———. 2013b. Looking Beyond States: Openings for International Bureaucrats to Enter the Institutional Design Process. *The Review of International Organizations* 8 (4): 499–519.
Johnson, Tana Lynn, and Johannes Urpelainen. 2014. International Bureaucrats and the Formation of Intergovernmental Organizations: Institutional Design Discretion Sweetens the Pot. *International Organization* 68 (1): 177–209.
Kabbah, Ahmed Tejan. 2010. *Coming Back from the Brink in Sierra Leone*. Accra: EPP Book Services.
Kampfner, John. 2004. *Blair's Wars*. New York: Free Press.
Keating, Colin. 2004. Rwanda–An Insider's Account. In *The UN Security Council: From the Cold War to the 21st Century*, ed. David M. Malone. Boulder: International Peace Academy.
Kovanda, Karel. 2010. The Czech Republic on the UN Security Council: The Rwandan Genocide. *Genocide Studies and Prevention* 5 (2): 192–218.
Legro, Jeffrey. 1996. Culture and Preferences in the International Cooperation Two-Step. *American Political Science Review* 90: 118–137.
McCubbins, Mathew D. 1985. The Legislative Design of Regulatory Structure. *American Journal of Political Science* 29: 721–748.
Mody, Bella. 2010. *The Geopolitics of Representation in Foreign NEWS – Explaining Darfur*. Lanham, Rowman & Littlefield Publishers.
Munoz, Ambassador Heraldo. 2009. *A Solitary War: A Diplomat's Chronicle of the Iraq War and Its Lessons*. Golden: Fulcrum.
Nye, Joseph S., and Robert O. Keohane. 1971. Transnational Relations and World Politics: An Introduction. *International Organization* 25: 329–349.
Offer, Avner. 1995. Going to War in 1914: A Matter of Honor. *Politics and Society* 23: 213–241.
Pickering, Thomas, and Moisés Naim. 2001. The FP Interview: Mr. Diplomat. *Foreign Policy* (July 2001).
Scheffer, David. 2013. *All the Missing Souls: A Personal History of the War Crimes Tribunals*. Princeton: Princeton University Press.
Schweiger, David M., William R. Sandberg, and James W. Ragan. 1986. Group Approaches for Improving Strategic Decision Making: A Comparative Analysis of Dialectical Inquiry, Devil's Advocacy, and Consensus. *Academy of Management Journal* 29 (1): 51–71.
Short, Clare. 2004. *An Honourable Deception? New Labour, Iraq, and the Misuse of Power*. London: Free Press.
Stedjan, Scott, and Colin Thomas-Jensen. 2010. The United States. In *The International Politics of Mass Atrocities: The Case of Darfur*, ed. David R. Black and Paul D. Williams. London: Routledge.
Talbott, Strobe. 2003. *The Russia Hand, A Memoir of Presidential Diplomacy*. New York: Random House.

News Sources

New York Times

[Anonymous reporting on Iraq], The New York Times (July 31, 1991).
[Anonymous reporting on Sierra Leone], The New York Times (June 6, 2000).
Cooper, Helene, and Steven Lee Myers, *Obama Takes Hard Line with Libya After Shift by Clinton*, The New York Times (March 18, 2011).
Crossette, Barbara, *UN Expands Troop Limit For Mission In Sierra Leone*, The New York Times (May 20, 2000).
DePalma, Anthony, *Adolfo Aguilar Zinser, Blunt Mexican Envoy, Dies at 55*, The New York Times (June 7, 2005).
Lewis, Neil A., *Clinton Offers Military Aid To Help Calm Sierra Leone*, The New York Times (May 12, 2000).
Onishi, Norimitsu, *Sierra Leone Victims and Rebels Hear Albright's Message of Peace*, The New York Times (October 19, 1999).
Onishi, Norimitsu, *Sierra Leone's Wobbling Government Talks of Peace*, The New York Times (May 19, 2000).
Reno, William, *When Peace Is Worse Than War*, The New York Times (May 11, 2000).

The Guardian

[anonymous on the Foreign Pages], *Rebel Leader Deported*, The Guardian (February 23, 2000).
Britain, Victoria, *Unrealistic Humanitarians; No One Thought the War in Sierra Leone Would End; Not That It Has the West Must Suspend Its Criticisms*, The Guardian (August 4, 1999).
Ellison, Michael, Richard Norton-Taylor and Ewen MacAskill, *UN Sees British Forces as only Hope; Troops Involvement Stepped Up But London Denies Combat Role*, The Guardian (May 12, 2000).
Goldman, Antony (Senior Africa Editor, Economist Intelligence Unit), *Luanda loses to Kosovo*, The Guardian Leader Pages (January 20, 1999).
Norton-Taylor, Richard and Tom Whitehouse, *Search for Sierra Leone deal Intensifies*, The Guardian Foreign Page (January 14, 1999).
Showcross, William, *Send in the Mercenaries if Our Troops Won't Fight*, The Guardian (May 10, 2000).
Snow, Tom, [untitled], The Guardian Education Pages (May 16, 2000).
Snow, Tom, *An Ethnical Foreign Policy*, The Guardian Leader Pages (May 10, 2000).
Woollacott, Martin, *Desperation for Money Is Africa's Political Currency; When Income Starts to Run Out Leaders Behave like Mugabe*, The Guardian (April 14, 2000).

Sierra Leonean News (Reporting on Diplomacy relating to Civil War, Available at http://www.sierra-leone.org/Archives/)

February 11, 1999.
October 6, 1999.
September 28, 1999.
January 25, 2000.
January 26, 2000.
February 24, 2000.

March 13, 2000.
March 13, 2000.

Various News Sources

Karon, Tony, *The Resistible Rise of Foday Sankoh*, Time Magazine (May 12, 2000).
Lizza, Ryan, *Where Angels Fear to Tread*, The New Republic (July 24, 2000).
Η σύσκεψη του '92 και η αποπομπή του Σαμαρά (translated as: "The meeting of '92 and the dismissal of Samaras"), Eleftherotypia (September 4, 2005) (available at http://web.archive.org/web/20091109021328/archive.enet.gr/online/online_text/c=110,dt=09.04.2005,id=29616224.).

Government Documents

Peace Agreement between the Government of Sierra Leone and the Revolutionary United Front of Sierra Leone, November 20, 1996 (Abidjan Peace Accords).
Peace Agreement between the Government of Sierra Leone and the Revolutionary United Front of Sierra Leone, July 7, 1999 (Lomé Peace Accords).
Questions to Parliament, *Members in the Commons Hansard Written Answers for Tuesday 23 May 2000*, Column 413W (May 23, 2000).
United Kingdom and United States of America, *Statement on Signing of the Sierra Leone Peace Agreement* (July 6, 1999).
White House Press Secretary, *Statement* (October 8, 1997) (Appointment of Reverend Jesse Jackson as Special Envoy for the President and the Secretary of State for the Promotion of Democracy in Africa).

UN Documents

Reports

S/1998/486, UN Secretary-General's Report, Sierra Leone (fifth progress report) (June 9, 1998).
S/1998/750, UN Secretary-General's Report, Sierra Leone (first progress report) (August 12, 1998).
S/1998/249, UN Secretary-General's Report, Sierra Leone (fourth progress report) (March 17, 1998).
S/1996/645, UN Secretary-General's Report, Sierra Leone (sixth report) (June 4, 1999).
S/2005/158, Letter dated 11 March 2005 from the Secretary-General address to the President of the Security Council (March 11, 2005).

Records of United Nations Security Council Meetings

S/PV. 4035, Sierra Leone (August 20, 1999) (Mr. Steward Eldon, Representative of the United Kingdom, Statement at Meeting of the UN Security Council).

Resolutions

S/RES/1181, Sierra Leone (July 13, 1998).
S/RES/1606, Burundi (June 20, 2005).

Chapter 6
The Second Step: The Deliberations: The Use of Third-Parties

Acting under Chapter VII of the United Nations Charter, on 18 September 2004 the Security Council adopted resolution 1564 requesting, inter alia, that the Secretary-General 'rapidly establish an international commission of inquiry in order immediately to investigate reports of violations of international humanitarian law and human rights law in Darfur by all parties, to determine also whether or not acts of genocide have occurred, and to identify the perpetrators of such violations with a view to ensuring that those responsible are held accountable'.

Report of the International Commission of Inquiry on Darfur to the United Nations Secretary-General, Geneva, 25 January 2005.
(International Commission of Inquiry on Darfur (2005))

Abstract In the second step of the UNSC decision-making process, the creation of an atrocities investigation by the UNSC requires that the UNSC members collectively believe that the investigation will benefit their states and the UNSC. The UNSC members are capable of weighing the material benefits of the investigation. They are, however, also concerned about the legitimacy of their action. Chapter 6 explains that UNSC members resort to the use of an independent third-party to bridge the gap between these two competing concerns. A case study on the UNSC's decision to create an international commission of inquiry into Burundi in 1995 provides support for this explanation.

Once a patron diplomat has brought specific atrocities to the attention of the other UNSC members, the UNSC members begin their deliberations. At that point, while deliberating whether or not to create an atrocities investigation, the UNSC members

C. Kaoutzanis, *The UN Security Council and International Criminal Tribunals: Procedure Matters*, Studies in Global Justice 20,
https://doi.org/10.1007/978-3-030-23777-6_6

Table 6.1 Diplomat patron and commission of inquiry

Patron diplomat but no commission on inquiry	Patron diplomat and commission on inquiry
1. Afghanistan	1. Angola
2. Burma	2. Bosnia
3. Cambodia	3. Burundi
4. Central African Republic	4. Croatia
5. Chad	5. East Timor
6. Colombia	6. FYROM
7. Congo	7. Iraq
8. Cote d'Ivoire	8. Israel
9. Democratic Republic of the Congo	9. Kosovo
10. El Salvador	10. Kuwait
11. Eritrea	11. Lebanon
12. Ethiopia	12. Libya
13. Georgia	13. Montenegro
14. Guatemala	14. Pakistan
15. Guinea	15. Palestine
16. Haiti	16. Rwanda
17. Honduras	17. Serbia
18. Kenya	18. Sierra Leone
19. Liberia	19. Slovenia
20. Mali	20. Somalia
21. Mozambique	21. South Sudan
22. North Korea	22. Sudan
23. Sri Lanka	
24. Syria	
25. Tajikistan	
26. Uganda	
27. Ukraine	
28. Western Sahara	
29. Yemen	
30. Zimbabwe	

have consistently sought the advice of a commission of inquiry.[1] In numbers, as noted in Table 6.1 and Map 3.2, the UNSC has created a commission on inquiry only in 20 of the 52 states that had experienced atrocities and had a patron diplomat at the UNSC. With the exception of Libya, which is discussed in the Conclusion of this Chapter, the UNSC has created a commission of inquiry for all the atrocities

[1]The UNSC has only authorized one international atrocities investigation, the one into Libya (2011), without the affirmative opinion of a commission of inquiry. In that instance, the Human Rights Council had created a commission of inquiry, which was still conducting its research when the UNSC referred the case to the ICC.

that received an investigation. Finally, the UNSC has never acted against the recommendations of a commission of inquiry.

But, *why would the UNSC members seek help from, and follow the recommendations of, a third-party in an otherwise straightforward decision?*[2] And, why would the use of third-parties become part of the UNSC's *de facto* institutional procedures, even though it is not *per se* required by the Charter or the Rules (see Chap. 2)? Finally, why did only 20 cases of atrocities, out of the 52 that had a patron diplomat, receive a commission of inquiry? This Chapter answers these questions.

In brief, the UNSC members' decisions to use third-parties before deciding on the creation of an atrocities investigation can be explained by examining the interplay of power and legitimacy at the UNSC. The authority of the UNSC is a function of *both* its power and its legitimacy.[3] But, power and legitimacy actually often clash, rather than complement each other. The use of third-party mechanisms allows the members of the UNSC to square these two sources of authority. Surprisingly, despite the numerous past studies on the use of third-parties, only Johnstone has recognized the importance of legitimacy in their use (but focused only on the Secretary-General). This Chapter thus contributes to filling this gap in the literature.[4]

Parenthetically, it is interesting to note that this Chapter applies beyond the UNSC's work on atrocities. Third parties are used in most other areas of the UNSC's operations. The UNSC members, for example, routinely seek information and recommendations relating to a specific conflict situation from the Special Envoys of the Secretary-General and the Department of Peacekeeping Operations, which have regular contacts with that conflict. When deliberating about the use of sanctions or terrorism, the UNSC also uses the advice of the Sanctions Committee and the Counter-Terrorism Committee. Additionally, the questions of this Chapter are important to the broader literature on international organizations. Some international organizations, such as NATO, never use third-parties; others use third-parties in a few instances, such as the WTO dispute settlement body that sometimes relies on scientific experts; others still, such as the UNSC, the Human Rights Council and UNDP, use third-parties constantly. By presenting one new reason behind the use of third-parties at the UNSC, this Chapter sheds light on this larger variation.

To answer the above questions and develop the argument that commissions of inquiry are used to bridge the gap between power and legitimacy at the UNSC, this Chapter starts, in Sect. 6.1, by explaining how, despite the fact that power and legitimacy are both sources of authority, they clash at the UNSC. Section 6.2 then illustrates how a third-party, such as a commission of inquiry, can bridge the gap between considerations of power and legitimacy. Section 6.3 presents other competing explanations on the use of third-parties by UNSC members. The UNSC's decision

---

[2] Borrowing from the economics literature, a third-party can be defined as an entity that is not currently affected by, and will not in the future be affected by its decision on, the present situation. See e.g. Basu (2003).

[3] Claude (1966).

[4] One exception, Johnstone (2003b).

to use a commission of inquiry into the atrocities committed in Burundi is used, in Sect. 6.4, to test and illustrate the argument of this Chapter.

6.1 Interplay of Power and Legitimacy

Third-parties are used in order to bridge the gap between power and legitimacy at the UNSC. Yet, before understanding how that bridge is constructed, it is important to first understand how power and legitimacy operate at the UNSC and appreciate the multiple dimensions in the decision-making process over which they conflict. To that end, this Section starts by explaining how considerations of power and legitimacy both independently compel the UNSC to take specific actions. Then, this Section presents the clash between these two sources of UNSC actions.

6.1.1 The Role of Power

Power-politics are instrumental in most UNSC decisions with regards to a threat to international peace and security. Power-politics, which mirror the 'logic of consequences' category developed by March and Olsen,[5] are based on rationalist cost-benefit calculations. The initial design of the UNSC, in Yalta and Dumbarton Oaks, was predicated on such calculations.[6] It was agreed then that each great power would have an exclusive geographic sphere of influence, and would maintain its tenure over its sphere without interfering in the other spheres. The polarization of the Cold War further supported the same reasoning, and also gave rise to *quid pro quo* solutions to international problems. After weighing the pros and the cons, Soviet missiles were, for example, removed from Cuba and North Atlantic Treaty Organization ('NATO') missiles from Turkey.[7] Even today, such considerations continue to be anecdotally referenced on all UNSC issues.[8] It is constantly rumored that the P5 tacitly agree that France, for example, gets its preferred results with regards to the situation in Ivory Coast; Russia in Georgia; China in Sri Lanka; and the United States in Afghanistan. Additionally, as outlined in Chap. 3, many academics have recognized that rationalist calculations of the UNSC members are central to the actions of the UNSC.[9] Finally, some proposals for UNSC reform are also based on rationalist calculations. For these, it makes little sense that India is not a

[5] March and Olsen (1989).

[6] Bosco (2009).

[7] Allison (1969).

[8] For such rumors, see Doyle (2004) (p. 90).

[9] See e.g. Padelford (1948); Rudzinski (1951); Voeten (2001); Thompson (2006).

P5, while France holds such a seat, since the former surpasses the latter in most measures of material strength.[10]

Power-politics explain why some diplomat-backed atrocities never received a commission of inquiry. In the case of Sri Lanka, for example, allegations of war crimes emerged after the end of the local civil war in 2009. In particular, the magnitude of the allegations against the Sri Lankan government was such that diplomats from several of the E10, including Japan, Costa Rica, Mexico and Austria, are rumored to have persistently kept the matter at the attention of the other UNSC members. Yet, as the Sri Lankan government enjoyed the diplomatic and financial support of China, the UNSC never considered creating a commission of inquiry. It is because of this context that the Secretary-General stepped into the vacuum left by the UNSC and created, in June 2010, the Panel of Experts on Accountability in Sri Lanka. Even though the panel's mandate did not extend to fact-finding or investigations, its report is replete with details of atrocities.[11] Yet, the report did not overcome China's support for Sri Lanka. To the contrary, in reacting to the report, China suggested that the domestic government of Sri Lanka should be allowed to take its own measures for accountability,[12] thereby conclusively ending the possibility of a UNSC commission of inquiry, or other involvement, in these atrocities.

6.1.2 The Role of Legitimacy

Considerations of legitimacy also empower the UNSC to act when it comes to threats to international peace and security. Classified by March and Olsen under the 'logic of appropriateness,'[13] the legitimacy of the UNSC 'pulls' other actors to abide by its decisions.[14] The significance of maintaining legitimacy for the UNSC was not lost on the drafters of the UN Charter. In the aftermath of World War II, it is very likely that the great powers could have imposed the UN Charter on the lesser powers. Yet, as Hurd demonstrates,[15] they chose to hold the San Francisco conference and to allow lengthy debates on all of the Charter's provisions. As outlined in Chap. 3, academics have also recognized that legitimacy is important to the actions of the UNSC and its members.[16] Finally, debates at the UNSC also highlight the important role that the UNSC's legitimacy has in international relations. In 1995, for example, the UNSC debated the Secretary-General's Agenda for Peace, which outlines the ways that the UN can promote and safeguard peace in the post-Cold

[10] Khator (2010).

[11] Report of the Secretary-General's Panel of Experts on Accountability in Sri Lanka (March 31, 2011).

[12] Chinese Foreign Ministry (April 30, 2011).

[13] March and Olsen (1989).

[14] Franck (1988).

[15] Hurd (2007).

[16] See e.g. Claude (1966); Caron (1993); Voeten (2005); Hurd (2002).

War era. During that debate, the representative of Nigeria, Ambassador Ibrahim Gambari, asserted that the UNSC should support the goals of this Agenda "so that the continuing legitimacy of the United Nations can be assured."[17]

The UNSC's preoccupation with its legitimacy may explain why a commission of inquiry was never considered for some atrocities that were supported by a patron diplomat. The UNSC has, for example, been involved in Western Sahara since 1991,[18] when it empowered the Secretary-General to hold a referendum for the independence of Western Sahara and also authorized a peacekeeping mission (MINUSRO). Since then, the UNSC has heard regular briefings from the representatives of the Secretary-General on this issue and has followed the various peace talks among the different sides. Were the UNSC to create a commission of inquiry, it would be admitting that its diplomatic efforts over the past 25 years did not rectify or account for past atrocities. More importantly, a commission of inquiry would also question the role of the MINUSRO peacekeepers and the various special representatives, as it would recognize that, despite their efforts, atrocities (such as the continued separation of Sahrawis due to the existence of the Moroccan sand berms or Polisario's treatment of refugees in the Tindouf Refugee Camps in Algeria) continue to take place.[19]

6.1.3 Clash Between Power and Legitimacy

Power-politics and legitimacy are both important sources of authority for the UNSC. Often, they feed off each other, as power increases legitimacy by its dissuasive effect on potential violators and legitimacy supplements power by its normative pull on potential challengers. But, there are three significant reasons for which these two sources of authority do not always go hand-in-hand. Legitimacy can be broadly defined as "a normative belief by an actor that a rule or institution ought to be obeyed."[20] *A UNSC decision will thus be considered legitimate if (i) the actor evaluating the decision's legitimacy (ii) believes it ought to (iii) respect that UNSC decision.* An action taken under a rationale of power-politics conflicts in significant ways with these three foundational elements of legitimacy.

The role of legitimacy at the UNSC, first, presupposes that the UNSC members will take an interest in what other actors think about their actions. With the end of the Cold War and an increasingly globalized world, such "other actors" have become a more divergent group, and now include other member states of the UN, citizens groups, NGOs and academic commentators. Yet, under rationalist considerations,

[17] S/PV.3492 (January 18, 1995), Agenda for Peace, Supplement to an Agenda for Peace: position paper of the Secretary-General on the occasion of the fiftieth anniversary of the United Nations (S/1995/1).

[18] S/RES/691 (1991).

[19] See e.g. Human Rights Watch (2014).

[20] This definition is borrowed from Hurd (2007).

each UNSC member is expected to define its material gains foremost in terms of itself. The priorities of other actors, which are crucial for the legitimacy of a UNSC action, are not important for any action taken under a power-politics rationale. The interests of other actors will, for example, be left by the wayside, if Kosovo and South Ossetia are recognized as independent states as part of a U.S.-Russian *quid pro quo.*[21]

A rationalist approach towards the UNSC decisions also clashes with the way that the belief of legitimacy is formed. A legitimate action is one that is respected not because of coercion or self-interest.[22] While there is some disagreement among scholars of legitimacy on how such non-materialistic beliefs are formed, most emphasize the roles that procedural and substantive fairness play in this process. UNSC actions taken under considerations of power-politics clash with both.

Procedural fairness requires that a decision "was made and is applied in accordance with the 'right process.'"[23] While often the adherence to the process in place is considered sufficient to satisfy the requirements of procedural justice, many argue that a correct procedure requires some minimum guarantees. Among these, various thinkers highlight the value of a proper debate. Rousseau, for example, insisted on the participation of all citizens in the decision-making process.[24] Habermas equally highlighted the importance of discourse.[25] Rawls identified as legitimate a decision taken under a constitution (i.e. decision-making process) accepted by all citizens.[26] Weiler uses the term "social legitimacy" to convey a similar belief.[27] Under this line of thought, a decision will enjoy procedural fairness if the process by which it is reached upon allows all affected parties to voice their concerns.

Yet, as compared to both western democracies and other international institutions (e.g. EU, WTO), at the UNSC "procedures are opaque and unfair."[28] As highlighted in Chap. 2, the UNSC ordinarily decides behind closed doors, often after the initiation of the P5, who also usually start deliberating after the P3 have reached a preliminary agreement as to a certain topic. Sometimes, at the request of a non-UNSC state, the UNSC allows a concerned state to participate in its debate and even to speak in favor or against a specific issue. Such comments take place, however, in the UNSC's public sessions, which are routinely held after the UNSC has already decided an issue.

Precisely because of this opaque nature of deliberations, the European Court of Justice, in the prominent *Kadi* case, which involved the legal status of a UNSC resolution in the European Union (i.e. whether EU states have to comply with a UNSC

---

[21] For a slightly different approach, see Doyle (2008) (p. 67) (arguing that the UNSC is "widely representative of the international community").

[22] See e.g. Hurd (2007).

[23] Franck (1988).

[24] Rousseau (1762).

[25] Habermas (1979).

[26] Rawls (1993).

[27] Weiler (1999).

[28] Voeten (2005).

resolution), found that UNSC resolutions on sanctions lacked procedural justice and thus violated fundamental freedoms of EU citizens, such as the right to be heard and the right to an effective legal remedy.[29] A few exceptions exist to this opacity, when the UNSC holds public debates on specific issues. These debates are considered very important to the non-UNSC members, who get to voice their concerns. But, even then the deliberation is deficient.[30] And, such debates usually lead to broad decisions, which enjoy support among the UN member states (e.g. commitment to protect women or children in conflicts), but do not immediately change the situation on the ground vis-à-vis any particular threat to international peace and security. As UNSC decisions are generally not made under transparent conditions and after proper debate,[31] they thus suffer from a lack of procedural fairness.

In addition to shortcomings vis-à-vis procedural fairness, decisions taken under rationalist-based calculations also lack substantive fairness. Past studies highlight that substantive fairness requires consistent action across similar cases. Franck, for example, argues that when the other sources of legitimacy "are dispensed capriciously, the desired effect of legitimization may not accrue."[32] For Chayes and Chayes equally, consistent compliance with international norms is a prerequisite for substantive fairness.[33] Hurd summarizes the above by noting that legitimacy includes "a sense that [the decision-maker] treats people fairly."[34] When such a sense is lacking, the legitimacy of the decision-making institution itself is challenged.[35]

Because of power-politics, the UNSC will often resort to different solutions when faced with almost identical problems. In the mid-1990s, for example, peacekeepers and multiple diplomatic missions were sent to the former Yugoslavia, while almost nothing happened for Rwanda. From a rationalist viewpoint, such distinctions make sense—after all, the former Yugoslavia is located in Europe on the east-west fault line—while few states had any interests in Rwanda. The consequences, however, of this distinction for the legitimacy of the UNSC were far-reaching, as they indicated a lack of substantive fairness by the UNSC.[36]

It is, finally, difficult to square considerations of power-politics at the UNSC with the third foundational element of legitimacy, namely its normative characteristics. The latter presupposes a common understanding. Yet, norms in the international system are often contested. It is extremely rare for the UNSC to deal with conflicts

---

[29] Kadi Case, ECJ (2005, paras. 344–354).

[30] Johnstone (2008).

[31] Kirgis (1995) considers that this fact alone distracts from the UNSC's goal to ensure peace and security.

[32] Franck (1988). This corresponds to Franck's idea of coherence.

[33] Chayes and Chayes (1995).

[34] Hurd (2007).

[35] Franck (1988).

[36] The former Secretary-General Boutros-Boutros Ghali summed up this feeling in an interview with PBS, saying that "in Yugoslavia the international community was interested, was involved. In Rwanda nobody was interested. So we have to fight two problems. The tragedy as such and the indifference of the international community." Ghosts (2004).

like the 1990 invasion of Kuwait, which all actors believed to be a condemnable act of aggression. When acting, however, on the basis of power-politics, the UNSC does not take into account the normative preferences of all actors. Ordinarily, the preferences of the weaker actors (i.e. Thucydides' Melians) are the ones to be left unsatisfied. These actors then question the legitimacy of the UNSC's actions. A vivid illustration of this comes from the debates on humanitarian intervention and the responsibility to protect in Libya, where some of the P5 suggested actions (i.e. regime change) contradicted the normative understanding of the other P5 and E10. A more mundane example comes from the creation of the ICTR. The UNSC knew that the creation of the ICTR was opposed by the Tutsi government in Rwanda, which represented the victims of the genocide. In the eyes of the Tutsi government, the ICTR should have investigated additional crimes and should have been secondary to the domestic courts of Rwanda. By alienating the victims of the genocide from the ICTR—which was explicitly designed to punish the genocidaires—the UNSC actions led to more disagreement over the legitimacy of this tribunal and decreased the likelihood that other actors in the international system would consider it a legitimate attempt at securing justice.

As a result, when the UNSC members decide on the basis of power-politics, they are often undermining the UNSC's legitimacy because:

1. By remaining focused only on their own material interests, the UNSC members and, namely, the P5, do not deal with the concerns of the other international actors;
2. The lack of procedural and substantive fairness in the UNSC decision-making process leads few actors to believe they ought to (i.e. due to non-material reasons) follow the UNSC's decision; and
3. A decision by the UNSC does not reflect a common international normative understanding, because it does not resolve and may even exacerbate the normative disagreements over a specific course of action.

Two past studies have attempted to demonstrate how power and legitimacy considerations can become complimentary in the context of the UNSC.[37] In the first study, Claude argues that legitimization at the UN takes place through the UN General Assembly, which includes more actors and, in Claude's view, was[38] less polarized than the UNSC.[39] For Claude, a state will consider a UNSC decision to be legitimate if, after its procedure of open debate and majority vote, the UN General Assembly agrees with the UNSC decision. Yet, Claude's argument does not explain how the members of the UNSC can *ex ante* predict the subsequent actions of the UN General Assembly. For example, before its decision to create the ICTR, how could the UNSC know if the UN General Assembly would support this tribunal without

[37] Others have attempted to reduce the role of power-politics. See e.g. Bowett (1994) (suggesting judicial review of UNSC decisions).

[38] On a side note, it is doubtful that the UN General Assembly was ever less polarized than the UNSC, particularly after decolonization started in 1960.

[39] Claude (1967).

Table 6.2 Power-politics and legitimacy

	Element	Mechanism for legitimacy
1	Actor	All international actors
2	Beliefs	Procedural and substantive fairness
3	Ought to be respected	Agreement over norms

openly seeking a vote on the matter? Additionally, Claude relies too much on the value of the majority vote at the UN General Assembly. This vote can also produce unfair results, whose legitimacy will be contested. The General Assembly has, for example, consistently voted against Israel's actions in Palestine, even in situations in which most commentators and P5 members side with Israel. Since such votes appear to be politically biased, they lack substantive fairness and do not engender respect for their outcome. The legitimacy, therefore, of the UNSC's actions cannot be satisfactorily judged by the UN General Assembly.[40]

In the second study, Hurd advances a different line of thinking.[41] Assuming that legitimacy is a subjective quality and that all goal-driven actors are conditioned by their social context, Hurd argues that it is almost impossible to decouple any decision from considerations of legitimacy. The present question of how the UNSC maintains its legitimacy in light of power-politics is impossible to evaluate without considering that the UNSC (the agent) and the notions of legitimacy and power-politics (each, a structure) are intertwined. Hurd explains how actors do not evaluate the legitimacy of a UNSC decision (i.e. not a 'yes' or 'no' answer), but fight over it just as they fight over material gains. In a detailed and persuasive analysis, Hurd traces how rationalist-states contest the symbolic power of the UNSC and try to appropriate its language and arguments. A drawback, however, of Hurd's analysis is its lack of clarity on the possibility of time-lagged reactions to the UNSC's legitimacy. In many instances, the legitimacy of a UNSC action is challenged months or years after it was taken, a possibility that is accounted for in Hurd's case studies.[42] Hurd, however, does not explain how, at the moment they take a decision, the members of the UNSC prepare themselves for the possibility that their actions will be contested at some point in the future.[43] The explanation suggested in this Chapter addresses this limitation.

Before proceeding any further, a short summary of the previous discussion is in order (see also Table 6.2). The UNSC derives its authority from its material power and its legitimacy. Yet, the exercise of material power contradicts three main prerequisites for legitimacy, leading to a clash between the two sources of authority. The next Section proposes a manner through which power-politics and legitimacy can be squared, namely the use of a third-party.

[40] It is, nevertheless, important to note that Claude's idea has some proponents. For a more recent similar take, see Reisman (1993).

[41] Hurd (2007).

[42] See e.g. Libya's actions in Hurd's case study, Hurd (2005, 2007).

[43] For an illustration of how considerations of legitimacy are time sensitive, see Hooghe (2005).

6.2 Third-Party to Avoid Clash

The members of the UNSC can bridge the gap between power-politics and legitimacy by seeking a recommendation from a third-party on the decision they are deliberating to adopt. Such third-parties may include the Secretary-General, Special Envoys or Special Representatives of the Secretary-General, fact-finding missions, commissions of inquiry, and special rapporteurs.[44] The use of third-parties can help to overcome the clash between power and legitimacy that was highlighted in the previous section.

First, a third-party can be more capable than the members of the UNSC at considering the preferences of all international actors.[45] A third-party that does not have a constituency of its own and whose members are selected for their skills, rather than their material interests, can probe into both the preferences of the P5 and the other UN member states, and also examine the positions of the targeted state and the other international actors (e.g. NGOs, religious leaders, and journalists). By being independent, a third-party can also suggest a course of action that better reflects the priorities of all international actors, rather than only those of the UNSC members.

A third-party is, furthermore, capable of arriving at its conclusions through a process that is both procedurally and substantively fair. A third-party can act as a jury, hearing evidence from all sides, giving the target a chance to rebut any allegations against it, distancing itself from the actual UNSC decision and justifying its decisions in writing. The contribution of third-parties to the procedural fairness of the UNSC has already been recognized by the UNSC itself. In response to the criticism that the UNSC received for its lack of procedural fairness from the European Court of Justice in the *Kadi* case, the UNSC created the office of an independent Ombudsman to oversee the creation of the UNSC sanctions lists.[46] A third-party can also use past UNSC decisions or international law as a guidepost for its suggestions, thereby bridging the gap between the pressing rationalist-based preferences of the UNSC members and the need—under considerations of legitimacy—for substantive fairness across decisions. The recommendations, therefore, of such a third-party are more likely to be perceived as legitimate, rather than as part of the power-based calculations of the UNSC members.

The suggestions of a third-party are also better suited to dealing with normative disagreements over the issues faced by the UNSC. As discussed above, situations that threaten peace and security are rarely neat. A depoliticized body, which is independent from the members of the UNSC, can be well positioned to respond to normative disagreements over a course of action. It may, for example, use deliberative processes to persuade the international audience that a specific norm is not appli-

[44] For an early overview of these third-party roles, see Young (1967).

[45] Prantl (2005) argues that the informal groups of UNSC states also allow the UNSC to access a broader audience. This claim is plausible, but its applicability assumes that the informal group of states will (i) exist vis-à-vis a specific matter in front of the UNSC, (ii) listen to the advice of other non-UNSC states and (iii) be able to influence the P5 decision-making process.

[46] Kokott and Sobotta (2012).

cable to specific facts. It may also become a crusader in favor of developing a more clear normative position vis-à-vis a certain topic.[47]

Finally, a third-party can provide the UNSC members with a great line of defense against subsequent complaints. If the legitimacy of any UNSC action is questioned in the future, the UNSC members can point to the recommendations of a third-party as a way to signal that they performed their due diligence and acted in accordance with the interests of all international actors on the basis of an accepted normative position. Similar to parishioners who ask their priest about a difficult personal decision and later justify their actions by reference to the priest's recommendations, the UNSC can refer its critics to these independent suggestions and maintain an appearance of integrity vis-à-vis the international community.

As the above four paragraphs highlight, the ability of a third-party to legitimize the UNSC in any situation depends on the skill set of the third-party in that specific situation. As a result, the UNSC cannot delegate all of its tasks to the same third-party (e.g. the Secretary-General). If it is interested in its institutional legitimacy, the UNSC has to pick the third-party that best reflects the interests of the international community on that specific issue. Additionally, this third-party has to use a fair and transparent procedure in reaching its decisions with regards to the situation at hand. Its recommendations should be consistent with UNSC actions in similar cases. The third-party should further engage with the normative disagreements relating to the specific situation at issue. Finally, once the third-party has made its recommendations, the UNSC has to abide by them.

There is significant anecdotal evidence that UNSC members use third-parties in this way. The IAEA has, for example, been used by the UNSC members in dealing with Iran over its nuclear program. The UNSC, particularly on issues of nuclear weapons, has the capacity and willingness to take action against proliferating states. If the UNSC members were, however, to demand that Iran take some specific action with regards to its nuclear program, everyone would wonder if that action were legitimate, and one that ought to be obeyed. Such questions become particularly important in this context, where the P5 are all nuclear powers trying to convince Iran not to become one. By including the IAEA in their talks, the UNSC has added a third-party that represents a vast majority of the international community and justifies its decisions through its annual reports. Additionally, as the vanguard of the non-proliferation treaty, the IAEA is the foremost crusader on non-proliferation, uniquely suited to dealing with the obvious normative antithesis of the 'haves' telling others to remain as 'have-nots.' Finally, if in the future others accuse the UNSC's plan with regards to Iran, the UNSC members can always deflect criticism by pointing to the suggestions of the IAEA.

But, such evidence is anecdotal. Similar to the existence of *quid pro quos* at the UNSC, it is easier to base such allegations on conjecture rather than real examples. Section 6.4 presents one such real example, by examining why the UNSC decided to create a commission of inquiry into the 1993 massacres in Burundi rather than proceed with the creation of an international criminal tribunal as it had originally

[47] Johnstone (2003a, b).

planned. Before reaching this case study, however, the next Section presents a few different reasons for which the UNSC may use a third-party.

6.3 The Alternative Explanations

Apart from the above, four other explanations exist for which the UNSC members may decide to use a third-party. This Section presents these alternative explanations and their major characteristics in order to facilitate their examination by the case-study on the creation of an international commission of inquiry into Burundi in the subsequent Section.

International organizations sometimes lack the ability to provide expertise; remain impartial; and maintain their international focus. To overcome these three shortcomings, international organizations routinely resort to third-parties for help. It is also believed that international organizations use third-parties as a way to delay an eventual decision.

International organizations are bureaucratic institutions, which ordinarily lack the capacity to understand and decide on technical matters. They are thus in need of the *expertise* that third-parties can provide. The WHO, for example, delegates some of its tasks to private laboratories and states, as it lacks the in-house capacity to perform complicated tests that require advanced equipment, procedures and materials. In such instances, decision-making bodies will look for third-parties with proficient knowledge of the required task.

In several instances, particularly in situations of conflict, international organizations—due to the heavy influence of certain states—are incapable of appearing *impartial*. In such instances, impartial third-parties have the potential to accomplish the task at hand in a more efficient manner than the organizations. The most known example of such a third-party has been the Secretary-General, who routinely intervenes in conflicts on behalf of the UNSC and the United Nations at large.[48] Similar roles have been played by other international actors (e.g. Pope John Paul II, Julius Nyerere, the Community of Sant' Edigio), who leverage their indifference towards a specific dispute to mediate between the disputing parties. In such cases, the international organization is likely to pick individuals or entities of international significance with no connection to the underlying problem.

Third-parties are also routinely used by international organizations in an effort to keep themselves above the fray of every day politics and remain truly *international* in focus. While the EU Commission is the most notable example of such a third-party—one that is actually tasked with supranational powers—other instances of this type of power delegation occur at the WTO and the ICC. The former includes a secretariat[49] and a dispute settlement body,[50] which is tasked with revising the

[48] Urquhart (1995); Skjelsbaek (1991).

[49] Nordström (2005).

[50] Mavroidis (2013).

incomplete trade treaties and, in turn, maintaining the functionality of the international trade regime. The prosecutor of the latter is positioned to maintain the focus of the court on the work of global justice, rather than veer off towards parochial state preferences.

The UNSC has a long history of using the UN Secretariat, independent commissions of inquiry, fact-finding missions and other third-parties in a consultative function. Sometimes these third-parties fulfill the expertise, impartiality and international roles highlighted above. But, in some instances, the UNSC uses third-parties for tasks that it can accomplish on its own. The UNSC has, for example, consistently commenced investigations into atrocities without having first created an independent commission of inquiry into the facts of the situation. Contrary to the above three categories, the use of third-parties in such instances does not add to the UNSC's decision-making capacity. It only prolongs the decision-making process. For this reason, it is widely believed that the UNSC uses third-parties to *delay* a final decision and avoid committing to a specific position.[51] The UNSC members punt an issue by pushing it to a third-party and hope that they will not have to deal with it. This function of third-parties can be particularly helpful if the debated issue is politically contentious among UNSC members. Anecdotal evidence seems to support the existence of such dilatory use of third-parties. In the 2003 debates on Iraq, for example, the states that opposed a U.S. invasion called for more IAEA inspections.

Prior to turning to the case study, it is important to highlight that the main explanation and the four alternative explanations expect different facts from the historical records of the UNSC's involvement with the atrocities in Burundi. To support the main explanation, the historical records should indicate a significant difference between the power-politics of the UNSC members and the UNSC's need of legitimacy. They would also have to show that the commission of inquiry could have been helpful to bridging this gap. To the contrary, to support the first alternative explanation, the historical records should indicate that the UNSC members were in need of legal expertise in dealing with the atrocities in Burundi and considered the commission of inquiry as a source for such expertise. For the second alternative explanation, the records should demonstrate that the UNSC members were biased in their examination of the atrocities in Burundi and created the commission of inquiry to bring about some impartiality. In the case of the third alternative explanation, the UNSC members should have been plagued with parochial concerns and created the commission of inquiry to act as a common agent on behalf of the international community. Finally, to support the final alternative explanation, the historical records should indicate that the UNSC members had a desire to delay their involvement with the atrocities in Burundi.

---

[51] See e.g. Forsythe (1994) ("The very creation of the Commission [of Experts on the former Yugoslavia] showed a lack of seriousness about war crimes trials. If one wanted to act vigorously and expeditiously, one would have proceeded directly to the appointment of an international prosecutor, with adequate staff.")

With these five different expectations in mind, the next Section turns to the case study on the decision by the UNSC members to create a commission of inquiry into the atrocities committed in Burundi.

6.4 International Commission of Inquiry into Burundi

In 1994, two neighboring African countries, with the same Hutu-Tutsi ethnic composition, were each experiencing grave atrocities. In November 1994, to prosecute the atrocities committed in Rwanda, the UNSC created the ICTR. Earlier, in August 1994, the UNSC also indicated a preference to create a tribunal for Burundi. Then, in September 1994, the warring parties in Burundi all acknowledged that the 1993 atrocities constituted acts of genocide. Yet, instead of an atrocities investigation, the UNSC first created the "International Commission of Inquiry established under resolution 1012 (1995) concerning Burundi." And, when the commission of inquiry advocated against creating an atrocities investigation for the atrocities committed in Burundi, the UNSC members shelved their plans for such an investigation.

So, why did the UNSC create a commission of inquiry for Burundi? And, why did the UNSC follow the negative recommendations of the commission of inquiry? The answer to these questions lies in the UNSC's desire to square its calculations of power-politics with its need for legitimacy. This section first presents the events relating to the commission of inquiry and then explains the reasons for which the UNSC formed it and followed its recommendations. In doing so, it confirms that the alternative four explanations were not at play in the present facts.

6.4.1 Leading Up to the Commission of Inquiry

The atrocities in Burundi began in October 1993, when the majority-elected Hutu Prime Minister Melchior Ndadaye was overthrown in a coup d'état, arrested and executed. By way of background, Burundi achieved independence from Belgium in 1962 and had since undergone several cycles of Hutu-Tutsi interethnic violence, with the worse one being the genocide of Tutsis in 1972. At the same time, none of the world's big powers had a particular interest in this country. To the contrary, only France and the United States had embassies there in 1993.[52] Additionally, the UNSC, and the rest of the UN system, had very little past involvement with Burundi. Burundi, it appeared, largely had been off the international affairs radar until the execution of Prime Minister Ndadaye.

[52] Krueger and Krueger (2007).

In Burundi, following the execution of Prime Minister Ndadaye, Tutsi soldiers took control of the government and attacked Hutu leaders. Soon thereafter, Hutu paramilitary groups attacked Tutsi civilians. A vicious cycle of violence expanded, with the situation soon spiraling out of control. In New York, the UNSC immediately condemned the coup and "the acts of violence and the loss of life."[53] The Secretary-General sent a Special Envoy to the region, who tried to stop the violence and restore democratic rule. On November 16, the UNSC asked the Secretary-General to "consider dispatching…a small United Nations team…for fact-finding."[54] This preparatory mission, composed of Siméon Aké (former foreign minister of Cote d'Ivoire), Martin Huslid (former Permanent Representative of Norway to UN) and Michèle Poliacof (political affairs officer at UN Secretariat), arrived in Bujumbura on March 22, 1994. Two days later, the preparatory mission met with President Cyprien Ntaryamira, and continued its extensive investigation. After Ntaryamira and Rwanda's President Hyabarimana were shot down over Kigali, Rwanda, on April 6, 1994,[55] the commission attended Ntaryamira's funeral in Bujumbura and continued investigating. Its report makes for some somber reading. After estimating that approximately 50,000–100,000 people had been massacred, 700,000 had taken refuge abroad and 200,000 had been internally displaced, the preparatory commission wrote that:

> It will merely stress here that the massacres were carried out with knives, machetes, spears, stakes, bamboo poles, arrows, rocks, fire arms and grenades against men and women, infants and children, young people and adults, old people and the elderly, everywhere in the hills, public places and commercial centres, in fields, on footpaths, in schools and even in churches, as was the case in Rusengo, in the province of Ruyigi.
>
> According to the accounts by witnesses and the written statements, entire families were killed and horrible atrocities were committed in which people, including women, children, infants and elderly persons, were killed and thrown into latrines; others were bound hand and foot and thrown into rivers. Still others, sometimes bound up, were locked in houses and shops which were set on fire in order to burn them alive. This was the case of the secondary-school pupils in the town of Kibimba in the province of Gitega, whose charred bodies were left unburied for several weeks, as well as the peasant farmers from Kibiza in the town of Mwumba, the province of Ngozi, who were burned to ashes in a shop into which soldiers had thrown grenades. This was also the case of the persons who had sought refuge in the bishop's residence in Ruyigi, some of whom also died in bedrooms that had been set on fire, and, lastly, of the young people in the inn in Banga who, in order to escape the killing, had sought safety in a tree which was then doused with gasoline and set ablaze, and the poor people who had died in a room set on fire in the same inn, managed by a congregation of the Bene sisters.
>
> Persons of all categories and walks of life and all ages - peasant farmers executives and militant members of political parties, government agents, medical and paramedical personnel, and lay and religious persons - were killed in atrocious ways in the bloodthirsty mad-

[53] S/26631 (October 25, 1993).

[54] S/1995/157 (p. 4).

[55] This event sparked the Rwandan genocide.

> ness which caused the people of Burundi enormous suffering and which cannot in any way be justified.[56]

Having presented the history, the facts and the causes, the preparatory mission provided some recommendations. Among the recommendations, it suggested that "now that the preparatory Mission has completed its political inquiry … a mission should be sent which would concentrate on the legal aspects, so as to establish more precisely the responsibility for the events of October 1993 and identify the guilty parties so that they can be brought to justice."[57]

The preparatory mission submitted its report to the Secretary-General on May 20, 1994. It was circulated to the UNSC members on February 24, 1995. In the intervening 9 months, the UNSC had undertaken the highly unusual step of visiting Burundi itself, not once but twice.[58]

The first UNSC mission to Burundi took place on August 13–14, 1994. It was composed of four UNSC members (the Czech Republic, Nigeria, the Russian Federation and the United States of America). The mission found "a general breakdown of law and order."[59] "In this context, it stressed that impunity from justice is one of the most serious problems Burundi is facing."[60] Among its nine recommendations, it included:

> Bringing to justice perpetrators of the October 1993 attempted coup d'état and the subsequent massacres, and investigation of violations of international humanitarian law in Burundi as appropriate (possibly by an International Tribunal to be established);

This statement provides important insight into the goals of the UNSC members. On July 1, 1994, the UNSC had established a commission of experts to investigate serious violations of international humanitarian law in Rwanda.[61] Two of the four members of the UNSC mission to Burundi, the Czech ambassador, Karel Kovanda, and the Nigerian Ambassador, Ibrahim Gambari, had taken part in the deliberations leading to the creation of the commission of experts for Rwanda, with Kovanda speaking repeatedly on the record in favor of that commission. In Burundi, by contrast, the UNSC mission did not start by suggesting the need for an independent commission, but recommended upfront the creation of a tribunal.

Following the first UNSC mission to Burundi, and as the massacres were continuing, two significant political events occurred. First, on September 10, 1994, the warring parties in Burundi agreed to the Convention on Governance.[62] Article 11 of the Convention states that the warring factions in Burundi agreed to call the coup d'état and the assassination of President Ndadaye "genocide, without prejudice to

---

[56] S/1995/157 (p. 20–21).

[57] S/1995/157 (p. 29).

[58] To put this number in perspective, it should be noted that the UNSC has only conducted approximately 50 missions since its inception in 1945.

[59] S/1994/1039 (p. 6).

[60] S/1994/1039 (p. 6).

[61] S/RES/935 (1994).

[62] Convention on Governance, S/1995/190 (March 8, 1995).

the findings of the independent national and international investigations."[63] Article 36 of the Convention further "requested that an international judicial fact-finding mission be formed within 30 days" to investigate the events that had been referred to as a "genocide."[64] Second, on November 8, 1994, the UNSC created the ICTR, for the Rwandan genocide.

Following these events, the second UNSC mission to Burundi took place on February 10–11, 1995. This time, the mission was composed of seven UNSC members (China, the Czech Republic, Germany, Honduras, Indonesia, Nigeria, the Russian Federation and the United States of America). The members of the mission again wrote that the situation was "precarious and ... potentially explosive."[65] They also recognized that "the persistence of a culture of impunity constitutes a fundamental problem."[66] Yet, in its recommendations, instead of requesting the establishment of a tribunal, the UNSC mission this time suggested that:

> An international commission of inquiry into the October 1993 coup attempt and the massacres that followed, which was proposed by the Government in accordance with the Convention, should be established as soon as possible.

After an additional meeting on the situation in Burundi,[67] the UNSC explained, on March 29, 1995, that "if acts of genocide are committed in Burundi, it will consider taking appropriate measures to bring to justice under international law any who may have committed such acts."[68] To that end, it requested "the Secretary-General to report to the Council on an urgent basis on what steps should be taken to establish such an impartial commission of inquiry."[69] In order to determine what steps were necessary, Boutros-Boutros Ghali resorted to the services of Dr. Pedro Nikken, who had been the UN Human Rights Committee's Independent Expert on El Salvador from 1992 to 1995.

Nikken, after conducting another detailed fact-finding mission on Burundi, recommended that "neither a commission of the truth on the Salvadoran model nor an international commission of judicial inquiry whose mandate is limited to purely judicial matters would be an adequate response."[70] Instead, "[a]n international judicial commission of inquiry…could be viable and useful if its mandate gave it powers that would guarantee that its conclusions and recommendations would be put into effect and achieve the objective of prosecuting and punishing those responsible"[71] for the atrocities. In arguing that there was a need for effective prosecutions, Nikken highlighted that the national judiciary in Burundi would be unable to punish the

---

[63] Convention on Governance, S/1995/190 (March 8, 1995) (Article 11).

[64] Convention on Governance, S/1995/190 (March 8, 1995) (Article 36).

[65] S/1995/163 (p. 4).

[66] S/1995/163 (p. 4).

[67] S/PV.3506 (March 9, 1994).

[68] S/PRST/1995/13.

[69] S/PRST/1995/13.

[70] S/1995/631 (p. 1).

[71] S/1995/631 (p. 1).

perpetrators or would do so following discriminatory criteria.[72] He also warned that the government of Burundi would be unlikely to cooperate with such prosecutions.[73] The Secretary-General transmitted Nikken's report to the UNSC on July 28, 1995.

After more deliberations on Burundi,[74] the UNSC established, on August 28, 1995, "as a matter of urgency, an international commission of inquiry."[75] Reflecting the concerns of the Nikken report, the commission's mandate was to "establish the facts" and "recommend measures of a legal, political or administrative nature, as appropriate, after consultation with the Government of Burundi, and measures with regards to the bringing to justice of persons responsible for those acts…".[76]

6.4.2 Commission on Inquiry as a Safeguard for the UNSC

The creation of another commission for Burundi may appear initially to have been redundant. After all, as indicated by the below timeline (Graph 6.1), the members of the UNSC had conducted two missions (August 1994; February 1995) and the representatives of Secretary-General another two (March 1994; June 1995). All four deplored the impunity and highlighted the ethnic nature of the civil war in Burundi. They also blamed both Tutsis and Hutus, called for a return to democracy and the punishment of those who assassinated Melchior Ndadaye. At the same time, the peace agreement was tenuous, the presence of Rwandan Hutu refugees and *Interahamwe* members,[77] who had been fleeing Rwanda, led to more ethnic tensions in Burundi, the Tutsi led armed forces of Burundi were not trusted by the Hutu majority, and massacres were continuing.[78] But the UNSC only created another mission of inquiry.

From a rationalist perspective, the actions of the UNSC members appear sensible. Burundi, a small land-locked country in Africa, was beyond the radar of most UNSC members. Only two of the P5, France and the United States, had embassies there.[79] During the massacres, these embassies were functioning with only essential personnel. With the exception of Rwanda,[80] none of the other UNSC members had

[72] S/1995/631 (p. 12).

[73] S/1995/631 (p. 17).

[74] S/PV.3569 (August 23, 2014).

[75] S/RES/1012 (1995).

[76] S/RES/1012 (1995).

[77] The *Interahamwe* (Kinyarwanda, meaning "those who stand/work/fight/attack together") is a Hutu paramilitary organization. The militia enjoyed the backing of the Hutu-led Rwandan government leading up to, during, and after the Rwandan Genocide.

[78] Krueger and Krueger (2007).

[79] Krueger and Krueger (2007).

[80] Rwanda was a member of the UNSC in 1994 and 1995. During the UNSC's debates on Burundi, the Tutsi-led Rwandese government had close ties to the Tutsi factions in Burundi. Rwanda was also actively fighting against the Interahawme elements in Burundi. It, therefore, had no interest in highlighting the plight faced by the residents of Burundi.

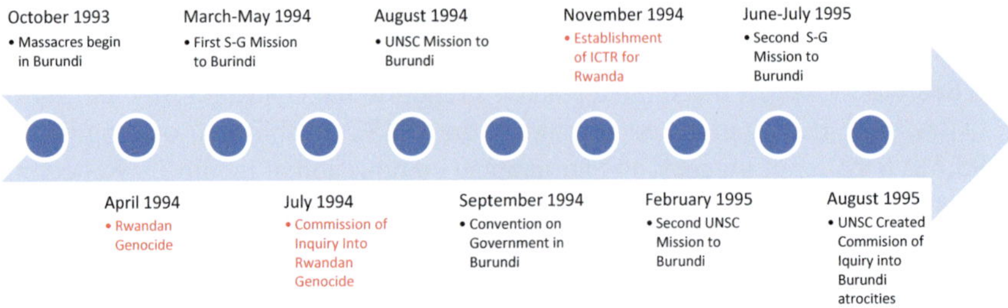

Graph 6.1 Timetable of UNSC's involvement in Burundi

a close connection to Burundi. While all of the UNSC members expressed repeated interests in stopping the massacres, their other international interests often took priority.

While they were dealing with the massacres in Burundi, the UNSC members were also confronted with the Rwandan genocide and the civil war in Bosnia. The latter was politically sensitive, as it had the potential to divide the UNSC again into its Cold War camps. It was also a European conflict, closer to home for many of the UNSC members. The former required an unprecedented humanitarian response, as the Rwandan Hutu refugees kept pouring into Zaire.[81] Additionally, no member of the UNSC appeared interested in sending its own troops to Burundi. To the contrary, even UN peacekeeping missions were hard to create, because after the events in Somalia, they faced criticism from the United States. In light of these facts, the UNSC resorted to verbal condemnations of the atrocities, tried to encourage diplomatic solutions, and created four commissions of inquiry.

Furthermore, the UNSC members also had valid reasons to shy away from creating yet another tribunal. By the end of 1995, the UNSC members had already created two tribunals, one for the former Yugoslavia and one for Rwanda, and understood the bruising diplomatic process needed to create those. Additionally, due to the 'fatigue' from the prior two experiences, the UNSC members realized that a tribunal would require money from the United Nations, costly political cooperation from the local government, and relative safety for witnesses and the investigatory teams. None of these elements existed in the case of Burundi. The United Nations coffers were already struggling to keep up with the refugee crisis in Zaire. The government of Burundi, led by a Tutsi group and backed by a Tutsi army, had expressed considerable opposition to the UNSC's actions in Burundi. Appearing at the UNSC public meetings as an invited party, the delegate from Burundi made the UNSC members aware of these views. While supportive of the idea of an international commission of inquiry in theory, the delegate from Burundi told the UNSC that there was "[a] malicious campaign orchestrated by foes of the Burundian army aim[ed] at poisoning international opinion."[82] In the view of the Burundian government, its military was "far from being perpetrators of or accomplices in the abortive

[81] This chapter uses the name Zaire, as that was the country's official name at the time. It has since changed to the Democratic Republic of Congo.

[82] S/PV.3571 (August 28, 1995).

Table 6.3 UNSC tension between power-politics and legitimacy for Burundi at the UNSC

The gap	Independent commission of inquiry
Focus only on UNSC member	Brings more perspectives
Indifferent with procedural fairness	Adopts fair procedures
Assumes differences with Rwanda	Explains differences
Prioritizes the end of the conflict vs. the justice cascade norm	Minimizes the norm clash
Present oriented	Becomes point of reference in future

coup or in the assassination of President Ndadaye."[83] The UNSC members knew that the similar tactics of the Kagame regime vis-à-vis the ICTR were impeding the operations of that court in Rwanda. Finally, the situation in Burundi remained so volatile that politicians and members of parliament were often assassinated even when they were guarded around the clock. The UN commission of inquiry was also facing security problems.[84] In such circumstances, it would be difficult for a court to collect evidence and find witnesses.

A decision, however, not to proceed with a tribunal risked undermining the UNSC's legitimacy in the eyes of many international actors who were not represented in the UNSC. Following the atrocities in Burundi, these other international actors, such as human rights NGOs and the UN Human Rights Committee, called for the creation of an investigation.[85] Furthermore, the normative understanding prevailing in the international community was in favor of creating atrocities investigations. After the creation of the ICTY and the ICTR, the international human rights community supported the prospect of international atrocities investigations with enthusiasm. It was, furthermore, difficult for other actors to believe that the UNSC's lack of action in Burundi ought to be respected, as there was no substantive fairness in the decision of the UNSC not to create a tribunal in Burundi while it had recently created a court for the same type of atrocities committed in Rwanda. Procedurally, the UNSC also made the decision not to act without including many relevant actors. Tanzania and Zaire, for example, were not parties to the UNSC decision, even though they had received hundreds of thousands of Burundian refugees. Burundi's Hutus were also not heard, as the local government represented exclusively the Tutsi minority.

As Table 6.3 summarizes, the use of the commission of inquiry allowed the UNSC to overcome these problems. First, the commission was well positioned to reflect the interests of all international actors. At the instructions of the UNSC to

[83] S/PV.3571 (August 28, 1995).

[84] S/1996/6 (letter from Secretary-General to UNSC); S/PV.3639 (March 5, 1996) (Statements from the United States, by Ambassador Madeleine Albright, and Honduras, by Ambassador Martínez Blanco).

[85] E.g. Human Rights Commission, Report on Displaced People, E/CN.4/1995/50/Add.2 (November 28, 1994); Human Rights Commission, Report of the Special Rapporteur on Extrajudicial, Summary or Arbitrary Executions on his mission to Burundi, E/CN.4/1996/4/Add.1 (July 24, 1995).

select five impartial and internationally respected, experienced jurists, the Secretary-General selected five such commission members from Madagascar, Morocco, Turkey, Venezuela and Canada.[86] Their stature and diversity allowed the commission to be cognizant of the preferences of the international human rights community and of states beyond those represented at the UNSC. The selection process, with the intervention of the Secretary-General, also dispelled any fears for endogeneity in the UNSC's actions, as it became highly unlikely that the commission's members would have a predetermined view on the creation of an atrocities investigation and to have been selected because of their views.

Additionally, due to their backgrounds in human rights law, the members of the commission understood the normative clash between the need for an end to the conflict and the requirement for proper judicial process. To that end, the commission conducted its work as if it was a judicial investigation, gathered facts from witnesses, conducted visits at the places of the massacres, presented written findings of fact and justified its recommendations.

The commission was well suited to dispensing with the lack of substantive fairness by the UNSC's actions. There was no ICTR for Burundi, but the commission's work highlighted the differences in the situation between Rwanda and Burundi. While the numbers of the victims were disproportionately large in both cases, the genocide in Rwanda was one-sided. In Burundi, the commission established that the Tutsi military killed Hutu civilians and Hutu armed groups targeted Tutsi civilians, who then called upon the Tutsi military, which in turn targeted Hutu civilians. Similar to Rwanda, Tutsis were systematically hunted and were the victims of "acts of genocide."[87] Contrary to Rwanda, however, the commission's findings established that Burundi was in the midst of a cycle of violence, with no clear separation between perpetrator and victim, thus indicating why a tribunal would have a heavier and more complex case-load in Burundi.

Additionally, the commission imbued the UNSC's decisions with some degree of procedural fairness. It justified its findings through a long and detailed report and conducted meetings with numerous individuals. It also developed rules of procedure, weighed the evidence presented to it, and heard testimony both in Bujumbura and at the site of massacres from leaders, soldiers, victims, and foreigners. In doing so, it made sure to respect both the local laws and the constitution of Burundi, as well as international human rights. It therefore acted as an arbiter of fact and law, satisfying the requirement of procedural justice in the work of the UNSC.

At the end of its investigation, the commission recommended that "international jurisdiction should be asserted with respect to" the acts of genocide.[88] But, it believed "that it is not possible to carry out an adequate international investigation

[86] The members of the commission were: Edilbert Razafindralambo (Madagascar) (Chairman), Abdelali El Moumni (Morocco), Mehmet Guney (Turkey), Luis Herrera Marcano (Venezuela), and Michel Maurice (Canada).

[87] S/1996/682 (p. 74).

[88] S/1996/682 (p. 75).

of these acts while the present situation persists in Burundi."[89] The commission, thus, supported the creation of a tribunal, but considered it inappropriate to create one at that time. It also clarified that "making the suppression of impunity a precondition for the solution of the crisis is complete unrealistic and can serve only to give excuses to those who are unwilling to take the necessary actions."[90] The commission thus recommended that the political solution be prioritized and decoupled from the issue of impunity.

The commission's report was transmitted to the UNSC on July 25, 1996. That same day, the government of Burundi that was established under the Convention of Government was overthrown in a coup d'état and Pierre Buyoya ascended to the presidency. The situation once again was explosive and remained so for a few more months. The UNSC took a strong stance against this new coup. After holding a public debate,[91] which is a rare occurrence, the UNSC adopted Resolution 1072 calling for the restoration of the old government and threatening to place economic sanctions and an arms embargo against the Buyoya government. In the preamble to the resolution, the UNSC:

> Recall[ed] that all persons who commit or authorize the commission of serious violations of international humanitarian law are individually responsible for such violations and should be held accountable, and reaffirm[ed] the need to put an end to impunity for such acts and the climate that fosters them.[92]

The creation of a tribunal for the atrocities in Burundi was now only an aspirational goal. Despite their initial preference for the creation of a tribunal, the members of the UNSC could, on the basis of the findings of the commission of inquiry, adopt this other approach without risking the legitimacy of the UNSC.

Finally, the creation of the commission ensured that the UNSC's legitimacy would be shielded from future attacks. The conflict in Burundi gradually ended after the 1996 coup, only to resurface in the mid-2000s. At that point, commentators reasonably wondered if the UN's actions in the mid-1990s were to be blamed for the resurgence of the armed conflict.[93] No one, however, questioned the UNSC's earlier decision to forgo the creation of an international criminal tribunal. Since an independent commission had recommended against creating a tribunal, the UNSC had valid reasons to follow that recommendation.[94]

Apart from supporting the argument of this Chapter, the above facts cannot be explained by the four alternative explanations. First, the UNSC members had the knowledge and competence to assess the situation in Burundi and decide on a tribunal without specialized help from a third-party. As the record demonstrates, in creating the commission, the UNSC members were not seeking outside expertise. UNSC

---

[89] S/1996/682 (p. 75).

[90] S/1996/682 (p. 75).

[91] S/PV.3695 (August 30, 1996).

[92] S/RES/1072 (1996).

[93] Boulden (2013).

[94] Interview 5.

members had undertaken two missions to Burundi, had witnessed the effect of the atrocities first hand, and had expressed a preference for an atrocities investigation.

Additionally, there was no need for an independent decision by an impartial third-party. As indicated by their lack of any meaningful action towards the conflict, none of the UNSC members had an interest in Burundi. They were thus not biased in their perceptions and their reactions to the conflict.

The UNSC members were, furthermore, not concerned with how other international actors would react to the atrocities in Burundi. The UNSC missions to Burundi had included a wide mix of UNSC members, ranging from China, Russia and the United States to Honduras, Indonesia and Nigeria. Their recommendations were thus already indicative of broader support for an atrocities investigation. Additionally, numerous other international actors were already supportive of a tribunal.[95]

Finally, the use of a commission of inquiry was not intended to prolong a decision by the members of the UNSC. While the atrocities were continuing in Burundi, no less than four reports were issued on the need to end impunity and the difficulties of this process. If the UNSC desired to avoid a decision on this issue, it could have stopped at the fourth report. The creation of the commission of inquiry did not so much delay the decision, as it kept a dying issue alive.

As indicated above, however, by relying on a third-party commission of inquiry, the members of the UNSC were able to balance their power preferences with the legitimacy of their action. Precisely, because of the wisdom of this decision, when atrocities reappeared in Burundi in the mid-2000s, the UNSC again requested a recommendation from another third-party on the Burundian request for an international criminal tribunal. The description of those events, however, exceeds the boundaries of this Chapter.[96]

---

[95] See e.g. Human Rights Commission, Initial report of the Special Rapporteur on the situation of human rights in Burundi, E/CN.4/1996/16 (November 14, 1995); Amnesty International Burundi (October 27, 1993).

[96] In summary, the Arusha Peace and Reconciliation Agreement of 2000 stipulated the creation of an international judicial commission of inquiry. After the government of Burundi sought the help of the United Nations, the UNSC requested that the Secretary-General dispatch an assessment mission to Burundi to consider the advisability and feasibility of establishing an international commission. The mission recommended the establishment of "a twin mechanism: a non-judicial accountability mechanism in the form of a truth commission, and a judicial accountability mechanism in the form of a special chamber within the court system of Burundi." Aware of Burundi's recent history, the mission also noted that the "United Nations can no longer engage in establishing commissions of inquiry and disregard their recommendations without seriously undermining the credibility of the Organization in promoting justice and the rule of law." S/2005/158 (March 11, 2005). The UNSC requested the Secretary-General to engage in negotiations with the government of Burundi on the implementation of these two goals. S/RES/1606 (June 20, 2005). These negotiations proved fruitless. In April 2014, the government of Burundi launched a reconciliation commission without the help of the United Nations, which was considered within Burundi as an unfair attempt to shield the ruling party from accountability (see e.g. Nduwimana 2014).

6.5 Conclusion

The commission's negative recommendation against creating an international criminal tribunal influenced not only the decision of the UNSC, but also the views of the Secretary-General. After the publication of the commission's report, the Secretary-General in his subsequent report on the situation in Burundi, on July 15, 1997, declined to recommend the creation of an international tribunal.[97] Yet, the UNSC's decision to follow the advice of the commission seems to clash with the fact that the UNSC wields unlimited power. *Why should UNSC members defer to the findings of a third-party commission? And why should they even seek a commission's advice?*

Despite the capacity of its members to decide on their own, the UNSC routinely outsources parts of its deliberations to an independent third-party. The members of the UNSC resort to the use of independent third-parties in order to balance their rationalist-calculations with their desire to maintain and promote the legitimacy of the UNSC. In the case of Burundi, there were obvious rationalist-calculations that stopped the UNSC from taking any significant action, even though the massacres were continuing. As the Secretary-General stated, however, "if another tragedy befalls the Burundian people…it will cause untold human suffering and gravely damage the credibility of the United Nations."[98] The creation of the commission of inquiry aimed to preserve this credibility. As Table 6.3 summarizes, the commission was able to bridge the gap between materialist and legitimacy concerns at the UNSC.

The explanation of this Chapter is applicable beyond Burundi to all instances the UNSC has deliberated its options on atrocities. But, more interestingly, it is important to pause and briefly consider how the argument of this Chapter is applicable to the outlier case of Libya. For the atrocities in Libya, the UNSC members created an international atrocities investigation without creating an international commission of inquiry. In that case, however, the UNSC did not suffer from a clash between considerations of power-politics and legitimacy.

In brief, several important elements in the UNSC's deliberations over the atrocities in Libya negated the usual imbalance between power-politics and legitimacy. The international community was openly and vociferously against the atrocities committed by the Qaddafi regime. The Arab League, a traditional bastion for Arab states such as Libya, suspended Libya's membership in the League on February 22, 2011, 3 days before the UNSC's decision on the creation of an investigation.[99] On the same day, the 15 UNSC member states held a closed meeting with a representative of the Secretary-General, the Libyan ambassador to the UN and 75(!) other

[97] S/1997/547 (July 15, 1997) ("... that given the circumstances prevailing in Burundi I was not in a position to recommend to the Security Council the establishment of such a tribunal at the present time. It is my intention to remain seized of the matter, however, and to review the question of the establishment of such a tribunal at a later date.").

[98] S/1996/116 (p. 9).

[99] Galla (2011).

countries.[100] The next day, the African Union, another traditional supporter of Libya, strongly condemned the violence of the Qaddafi regime and urged all Libyans to stop fighting.[101]

The opposition of the Arab League and the African Union to the atrocities, combined with the vast participation of other states at the UNSC discussion guaranteed increased procedural fairness in the decision-making process. The right afforded to the Libyan ambassador to address the UNSC and present Qaddafi's perspective further contributed to such fairness. Both facts decreased the reasons for which a commission of inquiry would be necessary to the UNSC's institutional legitimacy.

Additionally, a commission was not required to deal with the normative clash between peace and justice, as this clash was well captured by the debates among the UNSC members. The presence of India, Nigeria and South Africa on the UNSC, coupled with the permanent representation of China and Russia, meant that the traditional normative preference for state sovereignty and peace, rather than the focus on interventions and justice, was well represented in the debates on Libya.[102] This view was counterbalanced by the presence of Bosnia and Herzegovina, Germany, France, Portugal and the United Kingdom, which were state-parties to the ICC and supported a role for justice. A commission of inquiry had nothing to add to this normative clash.

Through the vast international support for an investigation, the procedural safeguards and the lack of normative clash at the UNSC, the UNSC's deliberations did not suffer from the preponderance of power-politics to the detriment of legitimacy. As such, it appears that the outlier status of the UNSC's actions on Libya lends support to the argument of this Chapter on the use of third-parties as a bridge between considerations of power-politics and legitimacy at the UNSC. When there is nothing to bridge, the UNSC forgoes the use of a third-party.

In summary, this Chapter explains that an independent third-party has been used by the UNSC to bridge the gap between materialist interests and legitimacy by (a) reflecting the interests of the international community, (b) using a fair and transparent procedure as well as prioritizing consistency, and (c) engaging with the normative disagreements over a specific course of action. It has the additional benefit of providing the UNSC with a response to potential time-delayed criticisms. By recog-

[100] These 75 states were: Afghanistan, Algeria, Argentina, Austria, Australia, Bahrain, Belgium, the Plurinational State of Bolivia, Botswana, Brunei Darussalam, Bulgaria, Chad, Comoros, Croatia, Cuba, Cyprus, the Czech Republic, Denmark, Djibouti, the Democratic People's Republic of Korea, Ecuador, Egypt, Estonia, Finland, Georgia, Ghana, Greece, Guatemala, Hungary, Iceland, the Islamic Republic of Iran, Iraq, Ireland, Italy, Japan, Jordan, Kuwait, the Libyan Arab Jamahiriya, Liechtenstein, Malaysia, Maldives, Malta, Mexico, Morocco, the Netherlands, New Zealand, Nicaragua, Niger, Norway, Oman, Pakistan, Poland, Qatar, the Republic of Korea, Romania, Saudi Arabia, Serbia, Singapore, Slovakia, Slovenia, Spain, Sweden, Switzerland, Sudan, the Syrian Arab Republic, the United Republic of Tanzania, Tunisia, Turkey, Ukraine, the United Arab Emirates, Uruguay, the Bolivarian Republic of Venezuela, Viet Nam, Yemen and Zimbabwe.

[101] African Union, Communiqué (February 23, 2011).

[102] S/PV. 6490 (February 25, 2011).

nizing that third-parties can play this function, this Chapter also highlights a new way in which such actors can influence international politics.

More importantly for this book, the role that third-parties have in protecting the legitimacy of an international institution also explains the constant demand by UNSC members, across all issues, for recommendations from third-parties. The recommendations of these third-parties allow the UNSC to come to a decision over a specific matter. At that point, the decision has to be codified. The politics behind the codification of the UNSC's decisions form the topic of the following Chapter.

References

Interviews

Interview No. 5; Interview Details: Member of NGO Security Council Report (July 31, 2013).

Books and Articles

Allison, Graham. 1969. Conceptual Models and the Cuban Missile Crisis. *American Political Science Review* 63 (3): 689–718.
Basu, Kaushik. 2003. *Prelude to Political Economy: A Study of the Social and Political Foundations of Economics*. London: Oxford University Press Catalogue.
Bosco, David. 2009. *Five to Rule Them All: The UN Security Council and the Making of the Modern World*. New York: Oxford University Press.
Boulden, Jane, ed. 2013. *Responding to Conflict in Africa: The United Nations and Regional Organizations*. New York: Palgrave.
Bowett, Derek. 1994. The Impact of Security Council Decisions on Dispute Settlement Procedures. *European Journal of International Law* 5: 89–97.
Caron, David D. 1993. The Legitimacy of the Collective Authority of the Security Council. *American Journal of International Law*: 552–588.
Chayes, Abaham, and Antonia Handler Chayes. 1995. *The New Sovereignty: Compliance with International Regulatory Agreements*. Cambridge, MA: Harvard University Press.
Claude, Inis, Jr. 1966. Collective Legitimization as a Political Function of the United Nations. *International Organization* 20 (03): 367–379.
———. 1967. *The Changing United Nations*. New York: Random House.
Doyle, John. 2004. Irish Diplomacy on the UN Security Council 2001-2: Foreign Policy-Making in the Light of Day. *Irish Studies in International Affairs* 15: 73–101.
Doyle, Michael W. 2008. *Striking First, Preemption and Prevention in International Conflict*. Princeton: Princeton University Press.
Forsythe, David P. 1994. Politics and the International Tribunal for the Former Yugoslavia. *Criminal Law Forum.* 5 (2): 401–422.
Franck, Thomas. 1988. Legitimacy in the International System. *American Journal of International Law* 82: 705–759.
Habermas, Jurgen. 1979. *Communication and the Evolution of Society*. Toronto: Beacon Press.
Hooghe, Liesbet. 2005. Several Roads Lead to International Norms, But Few via International Socialization: A Case Study of the European Commission. *International Organization* 59 (04): 861–898.

Hurd, Ian. 2002. Legitimacy, Power, and the Symbolic Life of the UN Security Council. *Global Governance* 8: 35–54.

———. 2005. The Strategic Use of Liberal Internationalism: Libya and the UN Sanctions, 1992–2003. *International Organization* 59 (03): 495–526.

———. 2007. *After Anarchy: Legitimacy and Power in the United Nations Security Council*. Princeton: Princeton University Press.

Johnstone, Ian. 2003a. Security Council Deliberations: The Power of the Better Argument. *European Journal of International Law* 14 (3): 437–480.

———. 2003b. The Role of the UN Secretary-General: The Power of Persuasion Based on Law. *Global Governance*: 441–458.

———. 2008. Legislation and Adjudication in the UN Security Council: Bringing Down the Deliberative Deficit. *American Journal of International Law* 102: 275–308.

Kirgis, Frederic L., Jr. 1995. The Security Council's First Fifty Years. *American Journal of International Law*: 506–539.

Kokott, Juliane, and Christoph Sobotta. 2012. The Kadi Case–Constitutional Core Values and International Law–Finding the Balance? *European Journal of International Law* 23 (4): 1015–1024.

Krueger, Robert, and Kathleen Tobin Krueger. 2007. *From Bloodshed to Hope in Burundi, Our Embassy Years During Genocide*. Austin: University of Texas Press.

March, J.G., and J.P. Olsen. 1989. *Rediscovering Institutions*. New York: Free Press.

Mavroidis, Petros C. 2013. *Trade in Goods*. Oxford: Oxford University Press.

Nordström, Håkan. 2005. The World Trade Organization Secretariat in a Changing World. *Journal of World Trade* 39 (5): 819–853.

Padelford, Norman J. 1948. The Use of the Veto. *International Organization* 2 (2): 227–246.

Prantl, Jochen. 2005. Informal Groups of States and the UN Security Council. *International Organization* 59 (03): 559–592.

Rawls, John. 1993. *Political Liberalism*. New York: Columbia University Press.

Reisman, W. Michael. 1993. The Constitutional Crisis in the United Nations. *The American Journal of International Law* 87: 83–100.

Rousseau, Jean-Jacques. 1762. *The Social Contract*.

Rudzinski, Alexander W. 1951. The So-Called Double Veto. *The American Journal of International Law* 45 (3): 443–461.

Skjelsbæk, Kjell. 1991. The UN Secretary-General and the Mediation of International Disputes. *Journal of Peace Research* 28 (1): 99–115.

Thompson, Alexander. 2006. Coercion Through IOs: The Security Council and the Logic of Information Transmission. *International Organization* 60 (01): 1–34.

Urquhart, Brian. 1995. Selecting the World's CEO: Remembering the Secretaries-General. *Foreign Affairs* 74: 21–26.

Voeten, Erik. 2001. Outside Options and the Logic of Security Council Action. *American Political Science Review* 95 (4): 845–858.

———. 2005. The Political Origins of the UN Security Council's Ability to Legitimize the Use of Force. *International Organization* 59 (03): 527–557.

Weiler, Joseph. 1999. *The Constitution of Europe*. New York: Cambridge University Press.

Young, Oran R. 1967. *The Intermediaries – Third Parties in International Crises*. Princeton: Princeton University Press.

News Sources

Amnesty International

Report on Burundi (October 27, 1993) (http://www.amnesty.org/en/library/asset/NWS11/139/1993/en/3fa57514-ec36-11dd-8d9d-a7825928c0bf/nws111391993en.html).

Human Rights Watch

Off the Radar: Human Rights in the Tindouf Refugee Camps (October 18, 2014) (https://www.hrw.org/report/2014/10/18/radar/human-rights-tindouf-refugee-camps).

Various News Sources

Galla, Ola, Arab League Bars Libya From Meetings, Citing Forces' 'Crimes', Bloomber Business (February 22, 2011) (at http://www.bloomberg.com/news/articles/2011-02-22/arab-league-bars-libya-from-meetings-citing-forces-crimes-).

Ghosts of Rwanda, PBS Frontline (April 1, 2004).

Khator, Neta, *India Deserves Place at UN High Table*, Deccan Herald (March 10, 2010).

Nduwimana, Patrick, *Burundi creates reconciliation body that divides public opinion* (April 18, 2014) (at http://www.reuters.com/article/2014/04/18/us-burundi-politics-idU.S.BREA3H0E020140418).

Court Documents

International Courts

Case C–402/05 P and C–415/05, P. Kadi and Al Barakaat International Foundation v. Council and Commission [2008], Court of Justice of the European Union, ECR I–6351.

International Criminal Court

International Commission of Inquiry on Darfur, Report (January 25, 2005), accessible at http://www.icc-cpi.int/NR/rdonlyres/F87E244D-B27C-4A0A-BE1B-D27CECB5649E/278008/Report to UN on Darfur.pdf.

Government Documents

African Union, Communiqué of the 261st Meeting of the Peace and Security Council (February 23, 2011), at http://www.au.int/en/sites/default/files/PSC%20Communique%20on%20the%20situation%20in%20Libya.pdf.

Chinese Foreign Ministry, Spokesperson Hong Lei's Remarks on the Report of the UN Secretary-General's Panel of Experts on Sri Lanka (April 30, 2011), at http://lk.china-embassy.org/eng/fyrth/t819905.htm.

Convention on Governance, Burundi, S/1995/190 (March 8, 1995).

UN Documents

Reports

S/1994/1039, Report of the UNSC Mission to Burundi on 13 and 14 August 1994 (September 9, 1994).

S/1995/157, Report of the Preparatory Fact-Finding Mission to Burundi to the Secretary-General (February 24, 1995).

S/1995/163, Report of the Security Council mission to Burundi on 10 and 11 February 1995 (February 28, 1995).
S/1996/116, Report of the Secretary-General on the Situation in Burundi (February 15, 1996).
S/1997/547, Report of the Secretary-General on the Situation in Burundi (July 15, 1997).
E/CN.4/1995/50/Add.2, Human Rights Commission, Report on Displaced People (November 28, 1994).
E/CN.4/1996/4/Add.1, Human Rights Commission, Report of the Special Rapporteur on Extrajudicial, Summary or Arbitrary Executions on his mission to Burundi (July 24, 1995).
E/CN.4/1996/16, Human Rights Commission, Initial report of the Special Rapporteur on the situation of human rights in Burundi, (November 14, 1995).
Report of the Secretary-General's Panel of Experts on Accountability in Sri Lanka (March 31, 2011.), at http://www.un.org/News/dh/infocus/Sri_Lanka/POE_Report_Full.pdf.

Records of United Nations Security Council Meetings

S/PV.3506, Burundi (March 9, 1994).
S/PV.3492, Agenda for Peace (January 18, 1995).
S/PV.3569, Rwanda (August 23, 1995).
S/PV.3571, Burundi (August 28, 1995).
S/PV.3695, Burundi (August 30, 1996).
S/PV.6490, Peace and security in Africa – Libya (February 25, 2011).

Letters

S/1994/1039, Letter dated 7 September 1994 from the members of the Security Council Mission to Burundi addressed to the President of the Security Council (September 9, 1994).
S/1995/631, Letter dated 28 July 1995 from the Secretary-General addressed to the President of the Security Council (July 28, 1995).
S/1996/6, Letter dated 29 December 1995 from the Secretary-General addressed to the President of the Security Council (January 5, 1996).
S/1996/682, Letter dated 25 July 1996 from the Secretary-General addressed to the President of the Security Council (August 22, 1996).

Presidential Statements

S/26631, Burundi (October 25, 1993).
S/PRST/1995/13, Burundi (March 29, 1995).

Resolutions

S/RES/691, Western Sahara (April 29, 1991).
S/RES/935, Rwanda (July 1, 1994).
S/RES/1012, Burundi (1995).
S/RES/1072, Burundi (1996).

Chapter 7
The Third Step: Issuance of the Decision: The Use of Precedent

Now, the language of this resolution is virtually identical with language which has been used before, notably in the action under Article 29 of the Charter, in the Spanish case in 1946. In that case the vote in the Security Council was 10 for, none against, and 1 abstention; and the member who abstained was the then representative of the Soviet Union, Mr. Gromyko, who is now the Foreign Minister of the Soviet Union. This resolution is squarely within the provisions of Article 29 of the Charter. It is a step which is necessary for the Council in the performance of its functions in this case. It is a subsidiary organ—that is, when it is created it will be a subsidiary organ—which will in effect provide for the continuation of the Council's consideration on this subject.

Henry Cabot Lodge, Jr., U.S. Ambassador to the UNSC, supporting the creation of an investigation in the situation in Laos (September 7, 1959).
(S/PV.847, Laos (September 7, 1959))

Abstract In the third step of the UNSC decision-making process, the creation of an atrocities investigation by the UNSC requires that the UNSC members draft one resolution committing their agreement into words. Beyond political bargaining, the UNSC members routinely use precedent to convince other states to vote in favor of their draft resolutions. As presented in this chapter, the UNSC resorts to precedent, contrary to prior explanations, to not only (i) safeguard the interests of the affected parties, (ii) ensure consistent outcomes to similar issues, and (iii) render the decision-making process more efficient. Instead, the members of the UNSC use precedent as a bargaining tool to overcome the uncertainty inherent in UNSC deliberations. Five short case studies from the UNSC's deliberations over atrocities investigations lend support to the bargaining use of precedent.

C. Kaoutzanis, *The UN Security Council and International Criminal Tribunals: Procedure Matters*, Studies in Global Justice 20,
https://doi.org/10.1007/978-3-030-23777-6_7

Once the attention of the UNSC members has been seized on specific atrocities by a patron diplomat and the UNSC members have received the support of a commission of inquiry for the creation of an atrocities investigation, the UNSC members consider their options. At that moment, as outlined in Chap. 4, the states leading the deliberations put forth draft resolutions with their proposals and try to convince other UNSC members to support these drafts.

As expected, a myriad of political tactics are used to convince, or even coerce, other UNSC members on accepting specific proposals. *Quid pro quos*, alliances, economic aid, and all the other tools of traditional diplomacy come into play in the drafting process. For example, as detailed below, the United States and France both used such methods to convince other UNSC members to support their respective proposal for an investigation into the atrocities of Darfur. Similar to the prior two decision-making steps discussed in the previous two Chapters, the use of such diplomatic tools in the drafting process defies a neat classification or understanding.[1]

Apart from the traditional diplomatic tools, the drafting phase also gives rise to textual arguments amongst the participants. The syntax and grammar of the operative clauses are of central importance to the decision, as they set the legal parameters of all subsequent actions. In dealing with peacekeeping missions, for example, it is important to distinguish if these missions can use force, arrest belligerents, or receive weapons from specific countries. As this Chapter illustrates, in addition to the traditional diplomatic tools highlighted above, some states try to persuade other states of the viability of specific text by pointing to properties of the text itself. Interestingly enough, during the drafting phase across all topics, the UNSC members constantly rely on precedent UNSC decisions. But, *why would the UNSC members rely on precedent in forming their decisions?*

This Chapter argues that, when decision-makers are divided over a specific issue, some of them convince their other colleagues through the use of precedent. Precedent thus becomes a *bargaining* tool.

This argument is developed in six parts. Section 7.1 sets the stage by explaining why the use of precedent by the members of the UNSC is surprising. Then, Sect. 7.2 presents the three accepted explanations on the use of precedent. Section 7.3 presents an alternative fourth explanation, while Sect. 7.4 explains the expectations of each explanation. Section 7.5 includes five short case studies and, Sect. 7.6 presents the discussion. The chapter concludes by summarizing its main argument and extending the findings to decision-making bodies other than the UNSC.

7.1 Precedent at the UNSC

The UNSC's decisions rarely innovate. As detailed in the Chap. 2, the UNSC has always resorted to diplomatic initiatives, sanctions, peacekeeping missions, international courts or the use of force in dealing with international problems since 1945.

[1] Interviews: 1, 2, 7, 9, 11, 14, 18, 20; see also previous Chapters.

These tools have been consistently applied across international problems with little variation. In 1997, for example, the UNSC authorized a peacekeeping mission in Angola that was very similar to the one it had created for that country 9 years earlier, in 1988.[2] Despite its unrestricted freedom to use its great powers, the UNSC generally elects to follow its prior decisions in subsequent cases.

Precedent can be defined as a prior decision taken in response to a situation reasonably analogous to the situation at hand.[3] In the setting of the UNSC, precedent consists of prior UNSC resolutions for reasonably similar facts. As such, use of, or reliance on, precedent refers to the UNSC's decision to copy the text of a previous resolution for a present situation.

For several reasons, it is surprising that the UNSC most often decides by reference to a past decision. Theoretically, the UNSC, as the top decision-making body at the UN, is unrestrained in the exercise of its powers. From a legal point of view, as long as it acts within the boundaries of *jus cogens*, i.e. the peremptory norms of international law, the UNSC can take any decision it desires on issues of peace and security.[4] In the task of maintaining international peace and security, the UNSC has legal power to go so far as abrogating a state's sovereignty.[5] Even more, the UNSC has the unfettered freedom to deploy such powers as it sees fit, since it enjoys supremacy over other international institutions and individual states.[6] It is also unlikely that its decisions will, or even can, be reviewed by the UN General Assembly or the International Court of Justice.[7] Finally, precedent does not exist in the field of international law.[8] In so far as the UNSC is acting as an international legal body, it is not bound by its own precedent and does not have to worry about "set[ting] general legal precedents."[9]

There are also practical reasons for which the UNSC should not constantly rely on its precedent. To begin with, the insistence on following precedent stifles innovation. When certain UNSC actions do not eradicate or even mitigate international threats to peace and security, one would expect deviations from precedent in dealing with similar situations at a later time.[10] After, for example, 10 consecutive renewals of the peacekeeping mission in the former Yugoslavia had failed to stem the violence in 1992 and 1993, it is puzzling that the main elements of the 11th renewal

---

[2] S/RES/626 (1988); S/RES/1118 (1997).

[3] Deutsch (1974).

[4] See e.g. Orakhelashvili (2005).

[5] UN Charter, Chapter VII.

[6] UN Charter, Article 2(2) and Article 103.

[7] Johnstone (2003a); Alvarez (1996).

[8] See Article 59 of the International Court of Justice.

[9] Doyle (2015, p. 114).

[10] This assumes that the UNSC members care about the outcome. In a more cynical take, the UNSC members may be relying on precedent for efficiency (see below), which is less puzzling.

followed those of the 10 prior renewals rather than including any changes.[11] Furthermore, crises in international affairs are multivariate products. A solution for an older crisis will rarely, if ever, work for a present crisis without being tailored to meet specific demands. It is thus difficult to understand why the UNSC developed a sanctions regime against the Central African Republic in 2014 that mimicked the one put in place against Iraq in 2003.[12] Additionally, prior studies on decision-making highlight that precedent should be less prominent in situations where the relevant decision-makers interact repeatedly.[13] Since the most-relevant decision-makers at the UNSC are the P5, who enjoy perpetual tenure on the UNSC (i.e. they do not discount the future), ruling by historical analogy is not necessary to overcome decision-making problems. The P5's long-term outlook should have led the UNSC to effectively use the ICC in Libya, rather than repeat the—highly criticized and ineffective—manner in which the ICC had been used in Darfur.[14]

Despite the issues outlined above, the UNSC's insistence on following its own precedent mirrors the practice of highest courts in all domestic and international legal systems. Courts such as the U.S. Supreme Court, the French Cour de Cassation, the Inter-American Court of Human Rights and the European Court of Justice have the wherewithal to decide each dispute as they see fit, despite their prior decisions. Yet, these courts routinely adhere to their own precedent and make only gradual departures from their past rulings. Past studies have highlighted three reasons for which these highest courts adhere to their own precedent, namely the need for consistency, predictability and efficiency. The following Section presents these explanations.

7.2 Three Existing Explanations

As the use of precedent forms a building block for most legal systems, the present question has received significant attention from legal scholars, who have attempted to understand why the highest court of any legal system would consistently, both historically and across many different issues, abide by its prior jurisprudence. Overall, these past studies suggest three answers to the present question. Namely, precedent allows a court to (i) consistently treat an issue,[15] (ii) respect the reliance

[11] UNPROFOR was established under S/RES/743 (1992). It was renewed and extended by a series of UNSC resolutions, see e.g. S/RES/749 (1992); S/RES/758 (1992); S/RES/761 (1992); S/RES/762 (1992); S/RES/770 (1992); S/RES/779 (1992); S/RES/786 (1992); S/RES/787 (1992); S/RES/802 (1993); S/RES/842 (1993).

[12] The sanctions regime against the Central African Republic was instituted under S/RES/2127 (2013). The latest sanctions regime against Iraq was created under S/RES/1518 (2003).

[13] Maggi and Staiger (2011).

[14] The referral for Darfur was authorized under RES/2005/1593 (2005). The Libya referral was authorized under RES/2011/1970 (2011).

[15] As explained below, this encompasses the court's desire to be impartial.

of parties on the court's past decisions, and (iii) optimally allocate its decision-making resources.

The following section presents these three approaches. It also examines the applicability of these three approaches to the UNSC, in order to evaluate if and how these three uses of precedent can explain the drafting decisions of the UNSC members. Finally, it derives testable explanations from each of the three approaches.

Before proceeding, however, in thinking about the role precedent, it is useful to consider an example of ordinary individuals who use precedent in their daily decisions. The favorite example of past studies involves parental decision-making in a family of two parents and two children of different ages.[16] Each child in this example wants to attend a concert when it reaches age 15. The parents' decision whether to allow the first child to attend the concert becomes a critical factor when making the decision with regards to their second child. While it is obviously simplistic to compare the UNSC's decisions on maintaining peace and security or the legal decisions of a highest court to parents' decisions with regards to their concert-going children, this Chapter will use this analogy to provide some color and levity in the subsequent discussion.

7.2.1 *Present Issue*

Decision-makers have a strong preference for consistent decisions on similar matters, as consistency ensures the *legitimacy* and *fairness* of their decisions. The use of precedent allows them to achieve this goal.

Consistency ensures that all decisions made by a decision-making body on a specific issue are substantively similar. Over time, assuming that prior decisions have been otherwise correct,[17] the attribute of consistency strengthens the credibility of the decision-making institution and the *legitimacy* of its decisions. Blackstone, for example, considered that the legitimacy of the common law judicial system came from its "custom" and "immemorial usage."[18] More recently, Spriggs and Hansford documented how the U.S. Supreme Court uses precedent as a way to bolster the credibility of its decision, when the Justices are trying to "increase the likelihood that their opinions will be efficacious [in lower courts]."[19]

The value of consistency in decision-making is also closely related to theoretical discussions on legal equality, which is a foundational element of the rule of law.[20] Postema, for example, argues that consistency and equality are closely related manifestations of impartiality and *fairness*.[21] While these considerations appear abstract,

[16] E.g. Schauer (2008).

[17] This assumption reflects the need to avoid being consistently wrong.

[18] Blackstone (1765–1769).

[19] Spriggs and Hansford (2002).

[20] Barzun (2013) Similar concepts are also found in the writings of Aristotle, Kant, and Rawls.

[21] Postema (1991).

they influence the decision-making process through the normative pull that consistency exerts on decision-makers.[22]

The use of precedent is an ideal way to maintain consistency in the decision-making process. Through the use of precedent, decision-makers not only ensure that past decisions are respected, but also that these past decisions are strengthened. Examples of such use of precedent abound. In the U.S. legal system, courts have consistently relied on precedent in holding that the President has to respect the powers of Congress when conducting foreign relations, even though such powers are limited.[23] While aspects of this doctrine have been clarified over time, the consistent opinion of the U.S. Supreme Court on the distribution of foreign policy powers has ensured that lower courts and other branches of the U.S. government perceive the U.S. Supreme Court to be a legitimate judicial institution and respect its decisions on this point. It has also ensured the appearance of fairness as all Presidents are treated the same with regards to their foreign policy powers. In the case of the children who wanted to go to the concert, the parents' decision to consistently follow the rule established for their first child with their second child has the same effects.

Returning to the focus of this book, the UNSC could attempt to deal with each threat to international peace and security on a case-by-case basis. Doing so, however, would risk creating an inconsistent record, which would likely delegitimize its actions in the eyes of other international organizations and individual states. Inconsistent decisions by the UNSC would also give rise to criticism and complaints by parties, who might feel that they were being discriminated against. When compared to the referral of the atrocities in Libya to the ICC, the absence of any action on the atrocities in Syria has engendered such criticisms. A consistent approach across similar issues most easily avoids these two problems. Such consistency can be achieved by the UNSC through the repetition of its precedent.

7.2.2 *The Interested Parties*

Every decision made by a decision-making body affects a series of actors, who internalize the decisions and structure their behavior in light of them. Decision-makers can set third-party expectations through the use of precedent.

The use of precedent allows a decision-maker to accomplish two goals that are crucial to the functioning of the decision-maker's community. First, precedent can act as an *informational device* for a wide variety of actors.[24] It allows various parties to predict future rules and to structure their actions accordingly.[25] When domestic

---

[22] Knight and Epstein (1996).

[23] E.g. *Youngstown Sheet & Tube Company,* et al. *v. Charles Sawyer, Secretary of Commerce,* 343 U.S. 579; *United States v. Belmont*, 301 U.S. 324–32; *Goldwater v. Carter*, 444 U.S. 996, 996–1007; *Kucinich v. Bush*, 236 F.Supp.2d 1, 2–18 (D.D.C. 2002).

[24] Schotter (1978).

[25] Deutsch (1974).

courts, for example, reaffirm their precedent in an age discrimination lawsuit, they send a strong signal to all employers and employees, who are the future's potential plaintiffs and defendants, about the scope of permissible conduct. Precedent also informs the two opposing sides of their probabilities to succeed in a dispute and determines their settlement target.[26]

Additionally, the use of precedent bolsters the integrity of the decision-maker's community, as it ensures *stability* of societal practices. As Postema notes on this topic, "[p]eople tend to rely on past decisions."[27] The use of precedent rewards the parties that relied on these prior decisions and ensures the continuity and stability of communal practices. By extension, precedent is a tool through which decision-makers minimize future uncertainty within their community. Anderson notes that precedent can be seen as "the basis for sustaining desired expectations."[28] If, for example, after having granted permission to their elder child in the past, the parents of the family in the concert example deny their younger child permission to go to the same or a similar concert, the family dynamics will be awkward, if not hostile, with both children incapable of ex-ante structuring their behavior towards any issue requiring parental approval.

The informational and stabilizing role of precedent may explain why the UNSC most often repeats its prior decisions. As the UNSC is at the top of the UN system, other UN bodies, international organizations and individual countries structure their behavior according to the decisions of the UNSC. By relying on its prior decisions, the UNSC sends a clear and coherent informational message to all these interested parties. The UNSC can also use precedent to ensure that its decisions promote international peace and stability, while rewarding those actors who structured their behavior according to the UNSC's precedent and have contributed towards that goal.

7.2.3 The Decision-Making Process

It is usually difficult for different actors to agree on one decision especially in situations in which there is no easy solution. Scholars have highlighted how the use of precedent can facilitate the decision-making process in at least two ways—by relying on the collective logic of the past and by safeguarding an efficient use of resources.

The use of precedent can simplify the decision-making process by allowing decision-makers to *avoid mistakes*. By relying on precedent, the decision-maker is not only relying on a decision that has already been formulated, but is also drawing on the collective logic of prior decision-makers.[29] Writing on legal precedent, in

[26] Che and Yi (1993).

[27] Postema (1990).

[28] Anderson (1981).

[29] Oliphant (1928).

1881, Justice Holmes held that "the life of the law has not been logic; it has been experience….the law embodies the story of a nation's development through many centuries."[30] By relying on the experience and knowledge learned through the trials and errors of prior times, a decision-maker can use precedent to avoid pitfalls.

The use of precedent can also simplify the decision-making process through its *efficiency* implications. As each decision takes time and effort, a decision-maker can save resources and cut costs by relying on prior decisions.[31] In such use of precedent, efficiency considerations have to be balanced against the risk of error, as prior decisions may not always match the present facts. When two issues, however, are very similar, and assuming the first decision is considered to be correct, there is less risk of error in using precedent. Decision-makers can thus rely on precedent without fearing errors, and turn their attention to more pressing novel matters.

These two functions of precedent may explain why the UNSC sometimes resorts to the use of precedent rather than innovating. The majority of threats to international peace and security, such as civil wars, are repeatedly in front of the UNSC. By relying on prior decisions, the UNSC may be acting with humility and risk-aversion, as collective knowledge is likely to outweigh the benefits of innovation. At the same time, the UNSC is regularly faced with multiple crises at once. Currently, a list of the problems at the UNSC includes the conflicts in South Sudan, Democratic Republic of the Congo, Central African Republic, Syria, Iraq, Afghanistan, Pakistan, Yemen, and the nuclear programs of Iran and North Korea. Reliance on precedent allows the UNSC to rapidly dispense with another topic of its agenda without having to reinvent the proverbial wheel.

7.3 Precedent in Decision-Makers' Bargaining

When the decision-making body is comprised of more than one individual, decisions are only made after an agreement among the various decision-makers. At the U.S. Supreme Court, for example, five of the Justices have to agree to a common position to have a majority when deciding a case. Such agreements, however, are fraught with coordination and cooperation problems. The use of precedent can overcome these problems, by enabling decision-makers to reach agreements on issues over which they disagree. Precedent becomes a *bargaining* tool.

The use of precedent as a bargaining tool presupposes that precedent can be applied strategically for the benefit of a decision-maker's ulterior goals. So far, the strategic application of precedent by decision-makers has received some attention in the literature on domestic courts. Landes and Posner, who considered that precedent is a form of legal investment, argued that a judge strategically adheres to precedent to avoid undermining his own prior decisions and increase the value of his

[30] Holmes (1881).

[31] Baker and Mezzetti (2012).

investment.[32] Rasmusen, through the use of a different formal model, reached a similar conclusion.[33] Other commentators have found that lower court judges selectively use precedent to signal their willingness to be promoted.[34] Appellate judges have also been found to use precedent as a way to guide trial judges towards their own preferred outcomes.[35] Finally, the strategic use of precedent can be seen in the fact that justices of the U.S. Supreme Court are more likely to follow the court's precedent when they are less experienced, and thus less confident about their own views.[36]

Since precedent can be applied strategically, the use of precedent can improve decision-making through a two-step bargaining process. It is assumed that a decision involves two players, who both have symmetric bargaining power and who cannot act unilaterally (i.e. no outside option). Both of these assumptions are well suited to describing the interaction of UNSC members when it comes to the creation of an international investigation into the commission of atrocities.

First, decision-maker A suggests the use of precedent to convince his or her colleague B to follow a specific course of action that is in line with A's goals. In selecting precedent, A is departing from his or her preferred course of action in favor of a choice that is acceptable, but not ideal. A does so because a decision can only materialize if B agrees. To convince B, A suggests the use of precedent, because B has already accepted it in the past and is likely to feel more comfortable with its implications rather than those of a different, non-precedential, course of action. This is a fairly uncontroversial suggestion. Such use of precedent has been found to exist in opinions of the U.S. Supreme Court, where the writer of the majority opinion is more likely to use precedent when attempting to stave off criticism from other judges.[37] This step of the process is an attempt by decision-maker A to take a conservative course of action towards accomplishing his or her own preferences.

In the second step of the decision-making sequence, there are three ways in which decision-maker B may respond. First, B may be a priori opposed to the use of the suggested precedent for reasons unrelated to precedent itself. In Syria, for example, Russia does not support an ICC referral, not because it opposes the ICC and the previous UNSC referrals to the ICC, but because it supports the Assad regime. In this case bargaining fails. Second, B may be again a priori supportive of the use of the suggested precedent for reasons that are again unrelated to precedent itself. In this case, B's preferences happen to be independently centered around the course of action that was previously applied in a different situation. When, for example, the UNSC condemned the terrorist attacks in London, it acted in line with several previous actions, not because of their precedential value, but because the UNSC members independently came to the same conclusion. Neither of the two above mechanisms is controversial or counterintuitive, as they are based on the

[32] Landes and Posner (1976).

[33] Rasmusen (1994).

[34] Morriss et al. (2005).

[35] Bueno de Mesquita and Stephenson (2002).

[36] Hurwitz and Stefko (2004).

[37] Lupu and Fowler (2013).

assumption that B assigns a higher value to items other than the UNSC's precedent.

Apart from the above two possibilities, there is a third way in which B may react to A's proposal, one which allows for an independent role for precedent. In this case, the precedent action is not B's top preference. After receiving A's offer to follow precedent, B is also uncertain about the actions that decision-maker A may be willing to take in order to advance A's own preferences. More importantly, A's potential preferred actions may be further away from B's preferences than the use of precedent. The use of precedent can independently be instrumental in solving this uncertainty, with decision-maker B accepting the suggested use of precedent as a way to contain the more eager decision-maker A, even though precedent is a second-best option for B. The use of precedent as a mechanism to remove uncertainty has previously been recognized by Crawford and Haller, who present a formal model in which precedent is a focal point for the coordination of decision-makers with divergent preferences.[38] The second step of the decision-making process indicates that decision-makers can tackle uncertainty through the use of precedent.

An illustration can clarify the above. In the family from the earlier example, the second child, who is otherwise shy and anti-social, has received three invitations for Thursday night, one to a friend's house for dinner, another to a concert with his music class, and a third to his high school's basketball game in the neighboring town. The mother thinks that the friend's house would be more appropriate for a school night. The father prefers that his shy child get exposure to loud public events, and hopes that his child would attend the basketball game that night. Both parents agree that there is no single optimal event for their child, as each of the three events has certain benefits and certain drawbacks. The father also remembers that, a few years ago, the mother had acquiesced to the first child's request to attend a concert with his music class. To convince the mother to forget about the friend's invitation in favor of a public event, the father suggests to the mother that they allow their second child to attend the concert with class. The mother not only remembers her experience with her first child, but is also afraid of the rowdiness of the basketball game. She also suspects that the father prefers the basketball game, but does not trust that her husband would admit his preference if she asked, as they constantly disagree over the shyness of their second child. As she is faced with uncertainty and desires to avoid the basketball game, the mother acquiesces to precedent, agrees on the concert and remains closer to her comfort zone.

Such strategic use of precedent may take place at the UNSC. As the epigraph of this Chapter illustrates, a precedent of the UNSC indicates a solution that was acceptable to the P5 in a prior setting and can act as a focal point for negotiations. During the intra-council bargaining, the leading states can resort to precedent as a way of building winning majorities. At the UNSC, however, the P5 can veto any decision over which they have low preferences. The presence of the veto changes the range of available options. Because the consent of both players is required in a two-player interaction, it is unreasonable to expect that any option that falls within

[38] Crawford and Haller (1990).

Table 7.1 Questions and goals

Explanation focuses on:	Main question of this explanation:	Use of precedent for:
1. Present issue	How will a decision affect the present issue?	Legitimacy
		Fairness
2. The interested parties	How will a decision affect the interested parties?	Information
		Communal stability
3. Decision-making process	How will the decision-making body arrive at an optimal decision?	Avoid mistakes
		Efficiency
4. Decision-makers' bargain	How will the decision-makers arrive at a decision?	One proposes
		Other accepts

one player's veto zone would be a viable option. Outside of their veto zones, however, players A and B will be indifferent towards some options and will seek all options that are preferable to both. These zones of preferences are not set in stone, but fluctuate overtime and over different issues. They capture, however, the preferences of the P5 in a particular negotiation, where some options are unacceptable, others are ideal and some are merely acceptable. In essence, for bargaining to succeed at the UNSC, A has to propose an acceptable precedent that will bring B outside its veto zone.

The five short case studies presented in Sect. 7.5 of this Chapter illustrate the full potential of this explanation. Before proceeding to these, the next Section outlines the testable expectations of each explanation presented in this Chapter.

7.4 Comparing All Explanations

The scope and conditions of the above explanations is markedly different. They have different focus, different ambit and different expectations. Apart from the resort to precedent, their sole similarity is that they all arise within the decision-making process. Chapter 4 explained how the use of case studies allows for a proper evaluation of this step in the UNSC's decision-making process. This Section delineates the ambit, and presents the testable expectations, of each explanation, which will be tested through the case studies in the subsequent Section.

It is sometimes hard to distinguish the effect of the explanations set forth above, as their rationales coalesce into a single decision to use precedent.[39] Yet, as summarized in Table 7.1, these explanations play out in very different ways vis-à-vis the actions of the UNSC. The first explanation predicts that the UNSC will resort to precedent in an attempt to treat all issues in a consistent manner out of concerns for its legitimacy and fairness. The second explanation expects that the UNSC will use

[39] Schauer (1987) (on the first three explanations coming together).

precedent to safeguard the reliance of all interested parties and to signal its position on a given issue. According to the third explanation, the UNSC will follow precedent to streamline the decision-making process, either because it believes in the wisdom of its past actions or is concerned with the efficiency of its decision-making process. Finally, the fourth explanation presents a two-stage interaction, in the first stage of which one UNSC member suggests the use of precedent, which a second UNSC member accepts in the second-stage as a way to deal with uncertainty even though it is a second-best option. Because the explanations have a different focus, the predictions derived from these explanations have different ambit and conditions.

In the case of the first set of explanations, decision-makers are expected to have a strong interest in resolving the issue at hand in a manner consistent with prior decisions, so as to improve the legitimacy or fairness of the decision. These explanations can be valid only if decision-makers have an a priori interest in the legitimacy or fairness of a UNSC decision (i.e. an interest not influenced by precedent) by the UNSC.

In the second set of explanations, rather than focusing on the present issue, decision-makers are expected to focus on the affected parties. In this instance, decision-makers are expected to consider if and how their decision to use precedent will affect others. The use of precedent is thus predicated on an external orientation by decision-makers. For these explanations to be valid, decision-makers should (i) agree on the message sent by using precedent and (ii) demonstrate an interest in how that message will be understood by the interested parties.

The third set of explanations turns the focus to the decision-making process itself. There, decision-makers are expected to shed considerations for the present issue and the affected parties and focus, instead, on how they arrive at a decision. Contrary to the scope of the prior explanations, decision-makers are expected to consider precedent as the appropriate tool to accomplish markedly self-centered reasons (avoiding mistakes or remaining efficient). These explanations can be valid only if (i) the decision-makers agree on a specific outcome but (ii) disagree on how to best reach that outcome.

The fourth explanation focuses on different preferences among decision-makers. Contrary to the prior explanations, in this instance decision-makers are not seen as a collective unit with clearly defined goals and priorities. Amidst their different preferences, decision-makers are expected to use precedent as a focal point. In doing so, there are two important conditions for the use of precedent. First, the independent power of precedent arises only in those situations where decision-makers do not know, and cannot control for, the preferences of their opposing state. Second, the negotiating member states have to disagree about their preferred outcome. Outside the boundaries of these two conditions, the bargaining role of precedent is curtailed. As a result, if the fourth explanation is valid, the case studies should demonstrate that decision-makers use precedent in cases they face (i) uncertainty and (ii) competing preferences.

The ambit and conditions of each explanation is summarized in Table 7.2. Because of the different orientation behind each set of explanations, the task of process tracing appears, at first, to be relatively straightforward. If the facts of a case study indicate that the actions of the UNSC members fulfilled the conditions rele-

Table 7.2 Questions, goals and conditions

Explanation focuses on:	Main question of this explanation:	Use of precedent for:	Under what conditions:
1. Present issue	How will a decision affect the present issue?	Legitimacy	A priori interest in fairness or legitimacy of a decision
		Fairness	
2. The interested parties	How will a decision affect the interested parties?	Information	Agreement on message sent by precedent
		Communal stability	Interest in the reaction of outside parties
3. Decision-making process	How will the decision-making body arrive at an optimal decision?	Avoid mistakes	Agreement on outcome
		Efficiency	Disagreement on process
4. Decision-makers' bargain	How will the decision-makers arrive at a decision?	One proposes	Uncertainty
		Other accepts	Competing preferences

vant to each explanation, then it is possible that the UNSC members resorted to the use of precedent because of the reason suggested by such explanation.

Yet, as past studies on precedent argue, multiple explanations may be valid simultaneously.[40] This complicates the task of process tracing, as it is possible that several of the above conditions will co-exist. Decision-makers may, for example, agree on the message sent by precedent and have an interest in how that message will be understood by the interested parties, while they may simultaneously also agree on the outcome but disagree on the process of their decision. To account for this possibility, the next Section only presents the facts surrounding each of the five case studies, without attempting to present the facts through the prism of the above conditions. Then, Sect. 7.6 examines which of the above explanations (i.e. their conditions and reasons) are supported by the facts of each case-study.

The next Section presents five brief case studies that revolve around five instances in which the UNSC created an international criminal investigation. The role of precedent in each of these case studies is significant. Overall, these five case studies demonstrate that, out of the above explanations, most commonly precedent is used at the UNSC as a bargaining tool.

7.5 Case Studies

7.5.1 UNSC Deliberations on Rwanda: 1994

On April 6, 1994, almost 11 months after the UNSC created the ICTY, the plane carrying the Hutu Presidents of Rwanda and Burundi was shot down as it was approaching Kigali airport. Soon after the shooting, an organized massacre of Tutsi civilians began in Rwanda. We now know that the massacre was well-planned. It

[40] Schauer (1987) (on the first three explanations coming together).

amounted to the genocide of Tutsis and systematic killings of moderate Hutus. In what turned into the most horrific collective crime since the Holocaust, more than 800,000 people died in the course of 30 days.

As the international condemnation of the genocide increased and at the prodding of Colin Keating, Ambassador from New Zealand, and Karel Kovanda, Ambassador from the Czech Republic, the UNSC decided on July 1, 1994 to establish a Commission of Experts to investigate serious violations of international humanitarian law in Rwanda.[41] Three months later, on October 4, 1994, the Commission of Experts issued its report.[42] This report determined that what occurred in Rwanda amounted to genocide of the Tutsis. It also stated that:

> The Commission of Experts wishes to register its strong support for the creation of an international criminal tribunal (or perhaps expansion in the jurisdiction of an existing one) to undertake prosecutions of individuals on the basis of international law. It considers that prosecution of individuals for having committed crimes under international law during the armed conflict in Rwanda would be better undertaken by an international, rather than by a municipal, tribunal….

The Secretary-General endorsed this recommendation on October 6, 1994.[43] The following week, on October 13, the UN Human Rights Commission's Special Rapporteur on Rwanda René Degni-Ségui added his endorsement.[44]

While the commission had been investigating, the members of the UNSC had been deliberating on whether to initiate an atrocities investigation. There were two factors motivating their desire to create an investigation. To begin with, most delegates felt frustrated and angry that, during their watch, the UNSC had failed to act to prevent and stop the genocide. At the same time, and more central to this Chapter, the shadow of the newly created ICTY loomed large over their deliberations. Feeling a need to demonstrate that they would handle the various crises consistently, the UNSC members insisted on the need for a legal investigation.

ICTY precedent guided much of the debate among the members of the UNSC. In early August 1994, the United States proposed expanding the jurisdiction of the ICTY to include the events in Rwanda, thereby having the same court investigate both sets of atrocities. A Russian-French proposal suggested the creation of a new court that would investigate only the events in Rwanda with all other features of the second court, such as jurisdictional scope, modeled after that of the ICTY.[45] At the end, a solution was brokered through the indefatigable efforts of Colin Keating, the Ambassador from New Zealand.[46] Keating, even in 2013 (19 years later), felt that there was a need for consistency in dealing with the atrocities in the former

[41] S/RES/935 (1994).

[42] S/1994/1125 (October 4, 1994).

[43] S/1994/1133 (October 6, 1994).

[44] S/1994/1157 (October 13, 1994).

[45] Scheffer (2013, p. 74–78); Kovanda (2010, p. 213).

[46] Kovanda (2010, p. 206).

Yugoslavia and in Rwanda.[47] With the majority of UNSC members having decided that the atrocities in Rwanda constituted genocide and favoring an investigation, Keating took charge. He proposed a compromise between the U.S. and Russian-French positions, according to which the ICTY and the ICTR would share a prosecutor and an appellate chamber, but otherwise act as separate institutions. For their separate branches (e.g. the defense teams, trial judges, court facilities), the ICTY precedent would be duplicated for the ICTR. This proposal received significant support from the other members of the UNSC.

The government of Rwanda, however, was a non-permanent member of the UNSC during 1994. While it had only one vote in the UNSC, the Rwandan delegation carried significant weight in the negotiations over the ICTR. After all, it represented the victims of the genocide. It could also play the sovereignty card, which carried special weight with the so far non-committal, and veto-wielding, Chinese delegation. Dealing with Rwanda in these negotiations was not easy,[48] because the Tutsi RPF government had its own preferences when it came to establishing an international court. The Rwandans and the New Zealand-led western alliance reached a compromise only after trading on numerous points.[49]

After long negotiations, the Rwandans dropped their insistence on having Rwandan judges at the ICTR, the primacy of the ICTR over domestic Rwandan courts, the criminalization of group membership (i.e. collective culpability) and the right to pardon or commute sentences. The criminal jurisdiction of the ICTR thus followed that of the ICTY. The Rwandans, however, managed to limit the temporal jurisdiction of the court to 1 year (January 1, 1994 to December 31, 1994), effectively barring the investigation from looking into many Tutsi committed atrocities that fell outside these dates. They also convinced the other UNSC members to authorize the ICTR to look into crimes committed by Rwandan citizens outside Rwanda, which necessarily led to an investigation of actions committed by Hutu militias in the Democratic Republic of the Congo. As a result, the temporal and geographical boundaries of the ICTR differed from those of the ICTY precedent.

Ultimately, despite these compromises from other UNSC members, the Rwandan government still voted against Resolution 955 establishing the ICTR.[50] Its insistence on the use of the death penalty could not be squared with the strong feelings of western countries against the use of this punishment by an international court. The RPF's negative vote foreshadowed many problems the ICTR would face with the Kagame regime.

[47] Interview: 7.

[48] Interview: 7.

[49] Scheffer (2013, p. 80–84).

[50] S/RES/955 (1994).

7.5.2 UNSC Deliberations on Sierra Leone: 2000

As Chap. 5 describes, a major turning point for the use of international criminal justice in the civil war in Sierra Leone was the inclusion of the amnesty provision in the Lomé Peace Accords. Yet, after the Lomé Peace Accords, peace was not restored in Sierra Leone. The RUF rebels continued fighting. Among others, on May 2, 2000, they notoriously disarmed approximately 500 UN peacekeepers and held them hostages. In the midst of more atrocities, the UNSC, on August 14, 2000, unanimously voted in favor of Resolution 1315. Through this resolution, the UNSC "[r]equest[ed] the Secretary-General to negotiate an agreement with the Government of Sierra Leone to create an independent special court consistent with this resolution." The subject matter of this special court would include crimes against humanity, war crimes and "other serious violations of international humanitarian law," and—since it would be a Sierra Leonean creation—would also include crimes under the laws of Sierra Leone. The court would have jurisdiction over those "who bear the greatest responsibility" for these crimes.[51] The UNSC thus took actions that led to the creation of a court.

> [Yet,] unlike either the International Tribunals for the Former Yugoslavia and for Rwanda, which were established by resolutions of the Security Council and constituted as subsidiary organs of the United Nations, or national courts established by law, the Special Court, as foreseen, is established by an Agreement between the United Nations and the Government of Sierra Leone and is therefore a treaty-based sui generis court of mixed jurisdiction and composition.[52]

A court was created, albeit one that diverged greatly from the precedent of the ICTY, ICTR or the blueprint for the ICC.

The negotiations for the creation of the SCSL started 2 months before the ratification of Resolution 1315, in early June of 2000. At that point, Richard Holbrooke, the U.S. Ambassador at the UNSC, presented a draft resolution to the UNSC in favor of an international criminal tribunal. The U.S. proposal envisioned the creation of an ad hoc tribunal, similar to the ICTY and ICTR. The United Kingdom, as well as France and Russia, opposed this proposal. As, however, Russia, France and China had secondary roles in the UNSC's negotiations over Sierra Leone, the main negotiations took place between the United States and the United Kingdom.

In the years following the creation of the ICTR, the United Kingdom's relationship with international criminal justice was a troubled one. On the one hand, the United Kingdom was, domestically, at the forefront of accountability, as the House of Lords, the United Kingdom's highest court, in March 1999, verified that the former Chilean dictator Augusto Pinochet could not use his official immunity as a bar to atrocity prosecution. On the other hand, the United Kingdom's experience with the prosecutor of the ICTY dampened its desire to create another international tribunal.

---

[51] S/RES/1315 (2000).

[52] S/2000/915 (October 4, 2000).

Following the 1998 military campaign into Kosovo, the ICTY Prosecutor Louise Arbour received requests to investigate the actions of the NATO aerial bombings. In her last months in office, during the Spring of 1999, Arbour notified all NATO countries of the preliminary investigation that she was conducting, but did not indicate that she would investigate their actions.[53] Her successor, however, Carla del Ponte, known for her more brash and aggressive style, fanned the flames of tribunal-resentment in all NATO capitals. In December 1999, in an interview published in *The Observer*, Del Ponte informed the NATO governments that once the preliminary report was ready, she was going to "read it very attentively and decide what to do."[54] Washington and London were extremely concerned about the possibility of a prosecutor targeting their governments' military actions. Yet, they cooperated with the ICTY investigation, which turned out to be the end of the matter. In June 2000, Prosecutor Del Ponte found insufficient evidence to open a proper investigation into the NATO crimes.[55]

Despite the outcome of this investigation, the Blair government worried over the possibility of any independent prosecutor backed by UNSC powers reviewing the actions of its own troops. With active combat troops on the ground in Sierra Leone, the stakes were high for the United Kingdom, higher than for any other UNSC member. When, in June of 2000, U.S. Secretary of State Albright called U.K. Foreign Secretary Cook about the creation of a court in Sierra Leone, "[s]till smarting from the Yugoslav Tribunal prosecutor's review of NATO bombing decisions during the Kosovo campaign, Cook did not want another Carla Del Ponte in charge as a prosecutor."[56]

In addition to their fear of an overly zealous prosecutor, the United Kingdom was also concerned about the financing and operational difficulties of an international criminal tribunal. It had been experiencing 'tribunal fatigue'. For the past 6 years, the United Kingdom—through the UNSC—had financed and supported the ICTY and the ICTR in the face of consistent Russian criticism. As neither of these courts seemed to be producing concrete results—and with the Rome Statute for the creation of the permanent International Criminal Court having been agreed upon in 1998—the United Kingdom did not want another UNSC court.[57] They preferred that, with international assistance, a domestic court in Sierra Leone be tasked with handling these atrocities.

To overcome their disagreements, the United States and the United Kingdom engaged in bilateral negotiations over a Sierra Leonean court for 2 months in the summer of 2000. At various times, these talks implicated the UN Office of Legal Affairs and the government of President Kabbah in Sierra Leone.

Realizing that the ad hoc precedent was not convincing the United Kingdom, the United States changed its proposal during their bilateral talks. Instead of a purely

[53] Scheffer (2013, p. 292).

[54] The Observer (December 26, 1999).

[55] Prosecutor's Press Release (June 13, 2000).

[56] Scheffer (2013, p. 331).

[57] Scheffer (2013, p. 327–328).

international or purely domestic court, the United States proposed to create a mixed tribunal following the precedent of the Cambodian tribunal. While travelling to Phnom Penh in April 1999, in an effort to overcome serious opposition within the Cambodian government towards an atrocities investigation, Senator John Kerry had proposed the creation of a mixed tribunal for the trial of Khmer Rouge leaders.[58] By July 1999, the creation of such a tribunal had become the official position of the United States for Cambodia. Understanding that the benefits of a court modeled after the Cambodian example could satisfy the United Kingdom demands, the United States changed its proposal for Sierra Leone in July 2000. The court would be national and international. It would also remain outside the control of the UNSC, both administratively and financially. The United States also proposed that the UNSC instruct the Secretary-General to create a court with a treaty between his office and the government of Sierra Leone, rather than create the court through UNSC resolution.

By the end of July, the United Kingdom informed the United States that it would support this U.S. innovation.[59] While the United Kingdom was reluctant to establish any court, the United Kingdom was also uncertain over the U.S. position in Sierra Leone. As described in Chap. 5 of this book, the United Kingdom had troops on the ground and had conducted its diplomacy through high level government officials, such as Secretary of State for International Development, Clare Short, and its Permanent Representative to the United Nations, Jeremy Greenstock. To the contrary, the United States had been conducting its diplomacy there through envoys such as Jesse Jackson, who had attempted to appease RUF leader Foday Sankoh and in his last visit to Sierra Leone had even compared Sankoh to Nelson Mandela, earning the ire of the local government and stirring resentment towards his interventions. As a result, in the eyes of the United Kingdom, it was not clear what (if any) actions the United States would take towards the Sierra Leonean conflict and whether such actions would stabilize or weaken a very volatile environment. Uncertain about the U.S. position, and generally hesitant towards any idea that could threaten reconciliation in Sierra Leone,[60] the United Kingdom was satisfied with a mixed tribunal, which would target those few individuals most responsible for the atrocities rather than another time consuming and all-encompassing ad hoc tribunal.

In order to accommodate the concerns of the United Kingdom, the United States undertook extensive revisions to the court's design on the basis of the Cambodian precedent. Then, on July 27, 2000, Holbrooke presented to the UNSC a proposal for an idiosyncratic international criminal tribunal for Sierra Leone. This proposal was met by the immediate support of the United Kingdom. The other UNSC members, who continued to have a passive role on the events in Sierra Leone, were also supportive.[61]

[58] Scheffer (2013, p. 383).

[59] Scheffer (2013, p. 331).

[60] Interview: 18.

[61] Châtaignier (2005, p. 120).

Subsequently, after many important discussions between the Secretary-General and the UNSC over the budgetary allocations towards this Court,[62] and after important deliberations between the Office of Legal Affairs and the Government of Sierra Leone,[63] on January 16, 2002, an agreement was signed between "the Government of Sierra Leone and the United Nations on the Establishment of a Special Court for Sierra Leone."[64]

7.5.3 UNSC Deliberations on Darfur: 2005

The referral of the atrocities committed in Darfur to the ICC in March of 2005 signaled the beginning of a new era in international criminal law. The UNSC had found a way to use the referral powers bestowed upon it by the Rome Statute. Instead of creating another ad hoc or mixed tribunal, such as the ICTY, the ICTR, the SCSL or the ECCC, Resolution 1593 outsourced the investigation to the ICC.[65] The decision to break with precedent was hardly surprising, as the ICC had been active since 2002 and the international human rights community was largely supportive of its mission. The ad hoc model had also been heavily criticized in the prior decade. Yet, the break with precedent was not easy. Since 2000, the United States had consistently and actively opposed the ICC. It became comfortable with the idea of referring the atrocities in Darfur to the ICC only after France agreed to exempt non-ICC nationals from the scope of the referral. This was a difficult compromise for France. To convince its negotiating partner to make this shift, the United States relied on language from UNSC resolution 1497 relating to peacekeeping in Liberia,[66] which had established limits on the ICC's investigative powers. This section illustrates why this added text, which has since been copied in all future ICC referrals, became part of Resolution 1593.

Since 2003, the UNSC continued receiving negative news on Darfur.[67] Yet, even after it created a commission of inquiry that, in turn, suggested a referral of the atrocities to the ICC, the UNSC did not act. As has been well-documented elsewhere,[68] the United States had championed the creation of ad hoc and mixed tribunals, but felt uncomfortable with the creation and existence of the ICC. To stem the likelihood of an ICC investigation into U.S. actions, the first George W. Bush

---

[62] Interviews: 2, 3, 6, 15, 16.

[63] For all the deliberations, see S/2000/915, S/2000/1234, S/2001/40, S/2001/95, S/RES/1346 (2001), S/2000/693, S/2000/722, S/RES/1370 (2001), S/2001/1320, S/2002/246, S/2002/267, S/2002/246/Corr.2, S/2002/246/Corr.3.

[64] S/RES/1400 (2000).

[65] S/RES/1593 (2005).

[66] S/RES/1497 (2003).

[67] S/2005/68 (February 4, 2005).

[68] Scheffer (1999); Schabas (2004).

administration signed bilateral Article 98 agreements with a series of countries.[69] The U.S. Congress also passed the American Service-Members' Protection Act, which apart from authorizing an invasion of the Hague if a U.S. citizen was brought there for trial at the ICC, prohibited the U.S. government from funding or assisting the ICC.[70] As a result, the United States supported an international criminal investigation into Darfur, but opposed a referral to the ICC.

On the other side of the spectrum, France had championed the ICC from early on. Satisfied with its French civil law elements, and following France's desire for only one permanent international criminal tribunal, the French government signed and ratified the Rome Statute, and undertook a consistent effort to promote the court through its foreign policy.[71] The prior 10 years of UNSC practice had also exhausted many states' patience with the ad hoc tribunals as the UNSC had to decide everyday items, such as their budget and the appointment of judges. The situation was worse for the ICTY, because of Russia's opposition to that court. But, even for the ICTR, budgeting and personnel decisions took up a significant part of the UNSC's time. The creation of the SCSL had also faced considerable funding obstacles.[72] Additionally, France felt emboldened to focus its attempts for justice on an ICC referral because, that year, 9 of the UNSC's 15 members happened to be state-parties to the ICC.[73] This group of nine states, nicknamed by the U.S. Foreign Service "the ICC-9," unofficially formed a working group to promote the referral of the atrocities in Darfur to the ICC.[74]

To understand the nature of the diplomatic bargain on this issue between the United States and France, it is necessary to recall the larger context of the UNSC at that time period. After the 2003 invasion of Iraq, cooperation at the UNSC had reached an all-time low. The main clash at the UNSC was based on a U.S.-French axis. The UNSC was in institutional paralysis, with very little being accomplished. In this environment, the U.S. opposition to the ICC took a different dimension. For France, and for several other UNSC members, this opposition was yet another manifestation of unreasonable policy from the United States. Despite their beliefs, these countries realized that a referral to the ICC could face a U.S. veto.

The United States fought hard to avoid a referral to the ICC. Afraid that such a referral would set a precedent,[75] the United States worried that referring the situation in Darfur was inconsistent with its agenda to undermine the ICC.[76] It initially proposed expanding the jurisdiction of the ICTR to include the events in Darfur.[77] The

[69] E.g. Kelley (2007).

[70] The American Service-Members' Protection Act (2002).

[71] Interview: 10.

[72] Interview: 2.

[73] The ICC-9 were: Argentina, Brazil, Denmark, France, Greece, Benin, Romania, Tanzania, and the United Kingdom.

[74] Hamilton (2011, p. 59); Interview: 12.

[75] Fake and Funk (2009).

[76] Amnesty International Report (2007).

[77] Interview: 12.

African states on the UNSC were supportive of this idea, but later changed their mind in light of European pressure. Understanding that the idea of expanding the ICTR's jurisdiction was not gaining any traction, Ambassador-at-Large for War Crimes, Pierre Prosper met in New York with representatives from Tanzania, Benin, and the United Kingdom to convince them of referring the case to an ad hoc tribunal, which would be jointly administered by the UN and the African Union, and would use the infrastructure of the ICTR in Tanzania.[78]

This diplomatic effort, however, was thwarted by extensive European resistance. With the guidance of French Ambassador at the UN, Jean-Marie de la Sablière, the ICC-9 states held together in the face of U.S. pressure.[79] The French had understood that the U.S. administration would have a hard time vetoing a proposal on an international criminal investigation to actions it had already labeled genocide.[80] De la Sablière was convinced of this after meeting with a group of conservative U.S. lawmakers, who opposed the ICC, but at the same time were horrified by the atrocities in Darfur.[81] France thus circulated a draft resolution that referred the Darfur atrocities to the ICC, breaking with the precedent of ad hoc or mixed tribunals. France was also ready to put this proposal up for a vote when the U.S. delegation asked for an extra day.

During that day, March 29, 2004, the United States countered with a proposal that agreed to the referral to the ICC, but at the same time, attempted to undermine the ICC's powers. To do so, the United States relied on UNSC resolution 1497, which in 2003 had approved a UN peacekeeping mission to Liberia. In that resolution, the UNSC had exempted citizens of non-ICC member states from the jurisdiction of the ICC, as it:

> [d]ecid[ed] that current or former officials or personnel from a contributing State, which is not a party to the Rome Statute of the International Criminal Court, shall be subject to the exclusive jurisdiction of that contributing State for all alleged acts or omissions arising out of or related to the Multinational Force or United Nations stabilization force in Liberia, unless such exclusive jurisdiction has been expressly waived by that contributing State;[82]

France had abstained from Resolution 1497, because it did:

> not believe that the scope of the jurisdictional immunity thus created is compatible with the provisions of the Rome Statute of the International Criminal Court, the norms of French law or the principles of international law. Furthermore, it causes a problem of consistency at a time when the Security Council has the intention of spearheading the movement to reject impunity in all its forms.[83]

[78] Hamilton (2011, p. 58); Interview: 12.

[79] Hamilton (2011, p. 58).

[80] Hamilton (2011, p. 62).

[81] Hamilton (2011, p. 65).

[82] S/RES/1497 (2003).

[83] S/PV.4803 (August 1, 2003).

As France continued to feel uncomfortable with this jurisdictional exception, it was in a bind. On March 30, 2005, it adjourned the UNSC meeting on the Darfur atrocities for another 24 h.

During these 24 h, France turned to the United Kingdom for help with the negotiations. If the United Kingdom would sponsor the resolution, France was willing to compromise and to accept the text proposed by the United States.[84] This tactic would allow France to vote in favor of a Darfur referral without openly endorsing its controversial jurisdictional exceptions. It also allowed France to pin the United States in support of the ICC, a position that was theretofore highly uncertain.

The United Kingdom, which was one of the ICC-9, had so far taken a back-seat in this debate. Interested in having an international criminal investigation take place in Sudan and believing that another ad hoc tribunal was not a good idea, it agreed to take the lead from France. Yet, in a surprising move that day, U.S. Secretary of State Rice personally called her counterparts in some of the ICC-9 to explain that the United States still felt uncomfortable with the ICC.[85] Even though the counterproposal had originated in Washington, no one was sure if it would escape the U.S. veto when it came up for a vote.

The next day, going into the UNSC meeting on Darfur, the same uncertainty about the U.S. position remained.[86] At 9:30 pm, on March 31, 2005, the UNSC members gathered for an informal private meeting. The U.K. Ambassador, Emyr Jones Parry, informed the UNSC members that he had a prepared resolution. He explained that "[i]f the President were informally to invite me to share it with the other council members, and if the Chair were to ascertain if there are nine votes in favor and no veto, then I would, for the U.K., be prepared to sponsor it."[87] When it was clear that the conditions set by Jones Parry were met, the UNSC's deliberations opened to the public at 10:30 p.m. on March 31, 2005. In a meeting that ended at 11:55 p.m., right before the end of the Brazilian Presidency of the UNSC, the referral of the Darfur atrocities to the ICC was adopted. By a vote of 11 in favor and four abstaining (China, Russia, the United States, and Brazil), the UNSC referred the investigation of atrocities in Darfur to the Prosecutor of the ICC.[88]

After the adoption of Resolution 1593, the mood at the UNSC was best captured by a story narrated in the early hours of April Fools' Day, April 1, 2005, by the representative of the Philippines. According to the story:

> [t]here was a middle-aged couple who had two stunningly beautiful teenage daughters, but who decided to try one last time for the son they had always wanted. After months of trying, the wife became pregnant, and, sure enough, delivered a healthy baby boy nine months later. The happy father rushed to the nursery to see his new son. He took one look at him, but was horrified to find that he was the ugliest child he had ever seen. He went to his wife and said that there was no way that he could have fathered the child. "Look at the two beau-

[84] Hamilton (2011, p. 67).

[85] Interview: 19.

[86] Interview: 19.

[87] Hamilton (2011, p. 66–67).

[88] S/RES/1593 (2005).

tiful daughters I fathered", he cried. Then he gave her a stern look, and asked, "Have you been fooling around?" The wife smiled sweetly and said, "Not this time…."

Similar to the parents, France and the United States were in the aftermath of the Iraq war cooperating again. Yet, similar to the newborn son, the referral of the Darfur atrocities to the ICC was, in comparison to the previous ad hoc or mixed tribunals, rather ugly. The break from previous tribunals did not, however, occur in a vacuum. It was agreed on the basis of a prior UNSC decision that limited the jurisdiction of the ICC, reflecting both the incremental progress of the UNSC towards issues of justice and the manner in which prior decisions can be used to coordinate actors with different preferences.

7.5.4 UNSC Deliberations on Libya: 2011

The response of the UNSC with regards to the civil war in Libya was swift. The unrest in Libya began in Benghazi on February 15, 2011 and, by February 22, had spread throughout the country and escalated into civil conflict.[89] On February 26, 2011, at night, the UNSC imposed sanctions and an arms embargo on Libya, and referred the investigation of atrocities to the ICC.[90] The need for efficient solutions to complicated problems was never more at play.

The protests in Libya were an offshot of the Arab Spring, which had already taken root in Tunisia and Egypt. The response of the Qaddafi regime was heavy handed. On February 22, in a closed doors discussion on the events on Libya, the members of the UNSC and a great number of invited states were concerned that Qaddafi would violently suppress the revolution, as he had amassed a long rap sheet of, domestic and international, atrocities in his more than 30 years in power.[91] Aside from extensive media coverage, the UNSC members were aware of the public defection, on Monday, February 21, of a number of high officials of the Libyan mission to the United Nations in New York. The highest defector, Ibrahim Dabbashi, deputy chief of the mission, gave a detailed media presentation regarding the situation in Libya and, among his many comments, called Qaddafi a "genocidal war criminal" and requested an ICC investigation into the Libyan atrocities.[92] At approximately the same time as the UNSC was holding its closed doors meeting, on February 22, 2011, a defiant Qaddafi, in a televised address to the Libyan people, called for the perpetuation of his regime. Standing in front of his Tripoli compound, which had been bombed by the United States in 1986, Qaddafi waved his green

[89] Libya profile, BBC, 2014.

[90] S/RES/1970 (2011).

[91] S/PV.6486 (February 22, 2011).

[92] Moynihan, New York Times (February 21, 2011).

book and vowed to "die as a martyr" fighting against the "greasy rats" of the insurgency.[93]

Four days later, on February 26, when the UNSC passed Resolution 1970 authorizing—among others—the ICC referral, the situation in Libya had worsened. Rumors of atrocities continued to circulate, the fighting had intensified and was moving towards Tripoli, and Qaddafi appeared intransigent. The UNSC members needed a fast and substantive response. Yet, the negotiations at the UNSC, which had been continuing for several days, were not as straightforward as one would imagine.[94] The United Kingdom and France were eager to intervene and topple the Qaddafi regime, even if it required a military intervention on behalf of the rebels. They clearly supported the use of the ICC in the conflict.[95] Russia, while not outright hostile to the idea of an ICC intervention, was more skeptical of this option than its European counterparts. It was also not in favor of a NATO-led military intervention and seemed to prefer an incremental approach to solving the crisis. China's public stance remained opposed to the ICC or any other violation of sovereignty (e.g. sanctions). Yet, China had also grown skeptical of the Qaddafi regime, which regularly attacked Chinese policies in Africa. Additionally, Chinese investments in Libya had become imperiled by Qaddafi's actions and more than 30,000 Chinese workers were stranded in Libya in the wake of the revolution.[96] The United States, which had transitioned from the George W. Bush to the Obama administration and was finalizing its exit from Iraq, was also ambivalent. Not wanting to enter into another war, Obama and some of his advisers wanted no military involvement in the Libya crisis. However, three members of the Obama administration, Ambassador to the UN, Susan Rice, Senior Director for Multilateral Affairs and Human Rights at the National Security Council, Samantha Power, and Secretary of State, Hillary Clinton, advocated for a U.S. intervention.[97] As the later view gradually prevailed within the U.S. administration, the chances of an ICC referral in Libya increased.

The P5 were frantically debating the UNSC's reaction to the crisis in Libya, which included a travel ban, asset freeze, arms embargo, sanctions committee, a no-fly zone, military intervention and an ICC referral. As certain members of the P5 remained ambivalent about the value of an ICC referral, the members of the UNSC debated if the referral to the ICC should be used as a threat.[98] Or, did a direct referral make more sense in order to prevent any further atrocities? While debating these options, the delegates of the UNSC received a jolt from a letter sent by the Libyan permanent representative at the United Nations, who had not defected earlier with the rest of his staff. In his letter, dated and delivered on February 25, 2011, Libya's permanent representative to the UN compared Qaddafi to infamous dictators such as

[93] Black, The Guardian (February 22, 2011).

[94] For an overview, see Moreno-Ocampo (2013a).

[95] Moreno-Ocampo (2013a).

[96] Washington Post (August 27, 2011).

[97] See e.g., The Nation (March 19, 2011).

[98] Interview: 4.

Cambodia's Pol Pot "who were willing to sacrifice large portions of their population for their own glory."[99] The call to the UNSC members was clear. An international criminal tribunal was investigating the actions of the Khmer Rouge. Similar tools were warranted for the actions of the Qaddafi regime.

At that moment, the U.K. and French delegations suggested that a referral of Libya to the ICC be based on the Darfur referral from 2005. This was a very efficient decision, as the text would be copied and pasted, with no substantive discussion on its provisions. Yet, at the same time, the use of this text was controversial. The Darfur resolution had been repeatedly criticized as being ineffective and unfair.[100] It shielded all people who were not citizens of Sudan from an ICC investigation, restricted the scope of the investigation to Darfur and exempted the UNSC from any duty to fund the investigation. It had also failed to stop the regime in Khartoum from committing atrocities and did not lead to the arrest of those Sudanese officials who had been indicted by the ICC.[101] The human rights community, academics and members of the UNSC had repeatedly criticized this resolution. Despite these problems, the same precedent was proposed for Libya.

Apart from the apparent need for an efficient solution, the hasty reliance on the Darfur precedent was also predicated on the need to secure the ambivalent votes of the United States, Russia and China. The sponsors of the resolution had to ensure that the reluctant countries would come on board.

It was not hard to convince the United States. Couched among other provisions authorizing sanctions and an arms embargo, the U.S. agreement on the Libya referral was easily accomplished for two reasons. First, there was significant pressure from within the U.S. administration to act against Qaddafi. Second, since the Darfur referral in 2005, the United States had gradually changed its attitude towards the ICC. Starting with the second George W. Bush administration and continuing into the Obama presidency, the United States did not oppose the ICC as long as the court did not threaten U.S. interests. Paramount among the U.S. concerns on the ICC stood the possibility that the court would investigate U.S. troops, a particularly strong fear since a military intervention in Libya was still being debated. The text of the Darfur referral, which was being replicated word-for-word, included protections for these U.S. concerns.

The use of the Darfur precedent was also important for the Russian and Chinese delegations. Despite its reluctance towards the use of the ICC in Libya, the Russian delegation had voted in favor of the Darfur referral, which signaled its comfort with the scope of the previous referral. After the U.K. and French proposal to replicate the Darfur resolution, a decision was taken at the highest levels of the Russian government in Moscow,[102] which—at the time under the Medvedev presidency—affirmed Russia's continued comfort with the Darfur precedent. The information on

[99] SC/10185 (February 25, 2011); for similar statements by Ambassador Shalgam (Libya's representative at the UNSC) on the same day, see S/PV.6490 (February 25, 2011).

[100] Cassese (2006); Cryer (2006).

[101] For more on this, see Gosnell (2008).

[102] Interview: 13.

China's reaction to the Darfur precedent is not as clear. Towards the end of the negotiations, Mr. Li Baodong, the Chinese diplomat at the UNSC, received new instructions from Beijing to support the resolution.[103] Perhaps China's comfort with the text of the Darfur resolution, on which China had abstained in 2005, was one reason for which it supported the resolution. At the end, by copying and pasting the text of the Darfur referral, the UNSC, in the span of a handful of days, authorized its second referral to the ICC.

7.5.5 UNSC Deliberations on Syria: 2014

As of the writing of this Chapter, the UNSC has, thus far, remained in a gridlock over the civil war in Syria. In this context of institutional paralysis,[104] there have been attempts from some UNSC members to achieve a referral of the atrocities to the ICC. These attempts have failed repeatedly, culminating in a Russian and Chinese veto in June 2014. Despite the scant record of action with regards to Syria, the record of the UNSC's deliberations on an ICC referral reveals that the Darfur/Libya precedent was very important. As the facts below illustrate,[105] this precedent was geared towards collecting votes among the P5 rather than ensuring consistency, efficiency and predictability of the UNSC's actions.

Since the earliest massacres, in late 2011, the main state behind an ICC referral has been France. A strong supporter of the ICC, France was also represented at the UN by a team that includes former-ICC employees.[106] For the first stage of their efforts, the French were supported by the United Kingdom and a number of states that were not part of the P5. The most notable support came from 57 other states, under the leadership of Switzerland, which, on January 13, 2013, authored a letter to the UNSC calling for a referral.[107]

These initial French attempts were, however, mired with problems. First, some commentators thought that an outright referral would be misplaced. For example, Moreno-Ocampo, the former ICC Prosecutor, argued that, to stop the killings, the UNSC should use the ICC as the sword of Damocles.[108] An immediate referral could lead to more violence. The threat of a referral would be more likely to deter atrocities and stem the war. Additionally, the French actions and the Swiss letter failed to corral the support of some states that strongly supported the ICC. Guatemala—a non-permanent member of the UNSC at the time—and a vocal

[103] Interviews: 1, 9, 13.

[104] For a critical explanation of the paralysis and its comparison to the UNSC's actions in Libya, see Weiss (2016).

[105] Some of these facts are reprinted in Chap. 3, but are also added here for convenience.

[106] E.g. The French legal adviser at the UN was a former advisor to ICC Prosecutor Moreno-Ocampo.

[107] S/2014/361 (May 19, 2014).

[108] Moreno-Ocampo (2013b).

supporter of international criminal law was perhaps the most surprising absence. For these states, another referral that lacked provisions on financing of the investigation and cooperation with the ICC was—again like Darfur and Libya—doomed to fail.[109] Then, the proposal for an ICC referral also faced the hurdles of Russia and China, which had been opposed to any action on Syria. In private consultations with the other P5, Russia clarified its intent to use its veto against such a resolution.[110] Before, however, even reaching a Russian veto, the ICC referral faced the opposition of the United States.

The U.S. government supported the use of a justice mechanism for Syria. But, it did not think that this mechanism should be the ICC.[111] Afraid that any ICC investigation in Syria could look into the status of the Golan Heights, the United States was skeptical about authorizing an investigation that could implicate Israel.[112] Additionally, many in the Obama administration were not convinced that an international court could be of any help. Having seen the constant failures of the Darfur and Libya investigations, as well as the inability of the Special Tribunal for Lebanon to arrest any of those charged by its prosecutor, the United States preferred to support a Syrian justice mechanism as part of a future domestic transitional justice system. A court, together with a truth and reconciliation commission similar to those set up in Sierra Leone would provide the best option for U.S. preferences.[113]

Admittedly, the United States was not alone in its suggestion of a domestic judicial mechanism. Guatemala's negative reaction to another ICC referral reflected some of the same concerns.[114] Additionally, a few influential individuals in the field of human rights supported the regionalization of the justice mechanism. The Middle East, as a geographical region, would be better served with a permanent human rights court rather than a one-off ICC referral.[115]

The position of the United States, however, changed significantly over the ensuing months. In January and February 2014, talks among the Syrian parties and the international community ended with little success. At the UNSC, Russia was holding out for the Assad regime's survival. After months of debate, in February 2014, Russia accepted an innocuous UNSC resolution for humanitarian aid.[116] Then, in the beginning of April 2014, the Ukrainian crisis became the focal point of the relationship between the United States and Russia, which had continued to stray in the course of the prior years.

At approximately the same time, the French rejuvenated their efforts for an ICC referral on Syria. On April 3, 2014, France circulated to the UNSC members a report on the atrocities perpetrated by the Assad regime, which included 55,000

[109] Interview: 20.

[110] Interviews: 10, 13, 14, 20.

[111] Interview: 14.

[112] Interview: 20.

[113] Interview: 14.

[114] Interview: 20.

[115] The New York Times (April 4, 2012).

[116] S/RES/2139 (2014).

photos from Assad's secret prisons provided by a defector code-named Caesar.[117] The chilling report was accompanied by an interview with France's ambassador to the UN regarding the need for accountability.[118] Because the United States was generally comfortable with the language used in the Darfur and Libya referrals, the French included the most important provisions from this language in the Syria resolution. U.S. personnel would, for example, be exempted from investigation.[119] The temporal scope of the investigation was, similar to resolution 1970 for Libya, limited to the events of the Arab Spring. The draft resolution for Syria—like the Darfur and Libya referrals—clarified that none of the expenses of the Syria referral would be paid for by the United Nations. It was thus clear that the text of the resolution was not predicated on the facts in Syria, where—for example—the ICC would have trouble investigating without UN funds, but was created to accommodate the U.S. interest in a referral.

Despite the apparent problems with such a resolution, problems that have been known since the Darfur resolution in 2005, the French initiative was welcomed by various states. Again under Swiss leadership, on May 21, 2014, 58 countries co-sponsored the French resolution.[120] By the time France submitted the resolution to the UNSC for a vote, on May 22, 2014, 64 states were listed as co-sponsors.[121] Satisfied with all the provisions,[122] the United States was among them.

When draft resolution S/2014/348 was put to the UNSC for a vote, it was quickly vetoed by Russia and China, who remained opposed to any intervention in Syria. The trajectory of the draft resolution, however, underscores how precedent was used to pull the United States into the ICC camp before the resolution was presented for a vote.

7.6 Discussion

Table 7.3 indicates how more than one explanation is generally at play whenever the UNSC decides to use precedent. This Section explains why bargaining carries more explanatory power than the other explanations for the use of precedent by the UNSC.

117 France, Press Release (April 15, 2014).
118 The New York Times (April 4, 2014).
119 The New York Times (May 21, 2014).
120 S/2014/361 (May 19, 2014).
121 S/2014/348 (May 22, 2014).
122 The New York Times (May 21, 2014).

Table 7.3 Summary of findings

Explanation	Rationale	Conditions	Rwanda	Sierra Leone	Darfur	Libya	Syria
Consistency	Legitimacy of decision	A priori interest in fairness or legitimacy	✓	X	X	X	✓
	Fairness of actions		✓	X	X	X	✓
Reliance	Informational device	Agreement on message sent by precedent	–	–	–	–	–
	Stability for community	Interest in the reaction by outside parties	–	–	–	–	–
Decision-making	Avoid mistakes	Agreement on outcome	X	X	X	X	X
	Efficiency	Disagreement on process	✓	X	X	✓	X
Bargaining among decision-makers	One proposes	Uncertainty	X	✓	✓	✓	✓
	Other accepts	Competing preferences	X	✓	✓	✓	✓

7.6.1 *Consistency*

According to the consistency category, the UNSC is expected to rely on precedent in order to (i) safeguard and promote its legitimacy as an international institution or (ii) ensure the fairness of its decisions. The above case studies indicate that the members of the UNSC relied on these reasons for the use of precedent in the creation of the ICTR and the failed attempt to refer the Syrian atrocities to the ICC.

As the events in Rwanda clearly amounted to genocide, the 'crime of crimes,' the members of the UNSC considered the resort to an international atrocities investigation a fair and legitimate reaction.[123] In line with the increasing power of the "justice cascade," the UNSC members expressed similar preferences in all other cases of atrocities examined above. As a result, the condition for the existence of the legitimacy and fairness explanations, namely the a priori belief in the legitimacy or fairness of an international atrocities investigation beyond the role of precedent, was satisfied in the above case studies.

Yet, while the pre-existing condition for these two explanations was present, these explanations came into play only in the debates on Rwanda and Syria. In the case of Rwanda, the UNSC's need for fairness offers the most likely reason for the use of the ICTY precedent in the creation of the ICTR. The ICTY had been created only months before the Rwandan genocide, so the issue of fairness arose from the first moments of the UNSC's debates on these atrocities. At that time, the UNSC

[123] S/PV.3453 (November 8, 1994).

was consistently—even from within[124]—criticized for not responding to an African crisis in the same way with the one engulfing the Balkans. In the case of Syria, the fairness consideration has also consistently been at the forefront. The obvious perception of unfairness of the UNSC's actions in Syria as compared to Libya, and the consequences of this unfairness for the credibility of the UNSC, is one of the many reasons for which some UNSC members supported an ICC referral for Syria.

The UNSC's desire for a legitimate outcome was a driving force in the use of precedent in Rwanda and Syria. For Rwanda, the concerns over consistency with the ICTY were accentuated because of the UNSC's failure to prevent or stop the Rwandan genocide. Not only did the UNSC's failure challenge the positive tone of post-Cold War international cooperation, it also questioned the UNSC's legitimacy. Reliance on the ICTY was a first step in recovering this lost legitimacy. Similar to Rwanda, the ongoing atrocities in Syria and the paralysis at the UNSC tarnish the UNSC's legitimacy today. Involving the ICC in that conflict can be a legitimizing step for the otherwise sidelined UNSC.

Beyond Rwanda and Syria, however, and even though the conditions for their existence were satisfied, the legitimacy and fairness explanations were not at play in the debates over Sierra Leone, Darfur and Libya. Despite the theoretical predictions, the decision-makers relied on precedent, but did not do so in order to satisfy the UNSC's desire for legitimacy and fairness, highlighting thereby that other reasons should exist behind the reliance on precedent.

7.6.2 *Reliance*

According to the reliance category, the UNSC is likely to use precedent in order to (i) transmit credible information or (ii) ensure the stability of the international community. As explained in Sect. 7.4, both prongs of the reliance category of explanations presuppose that the UNSC members have a (i) common understanding on the role of precedent and (ii) are concerned about how their decisions will affect the interested actors. The case studies indicate that these conditions were never fulfilled during the UNSC's debates on the creation of an atrocities investigation.

The case studies, first, indicate that all UNSC members do not view precedent the same way, mainly because there is no common understanding among the UNSC members on the use of international criminal investigations.[125] The members of the UNSC, particularly the P5, disagree over the role that international criminal investigations should have in an international system of sovereign entities. As a result, and similar to most other actions of the UNSC, investigations are ad hoc and carry limited informational value for subsequent debates at the UNSC.

---

[124] E.g. statement by Nigeria to the UNSC, S/PV.3377 (May 16, 1994) ("we are not entirely satisfied with the manner in which African issues that come before the Council tend generally to be treated").

[125] See e.g. S/2012/731 (October 1, 2012).

In addition to the above, it is not clear that the UNSC members had a clear preference about the effects of an investigation on the affected parties. The absence of this condition does not mean that the UNSC members did not care about the affected parties. But, in all of the examined conflicts, the UNSC members never had a clearly preferred interlocutor who could benefit from an atrocities investigation. During the UNSC debates on each case of atrocities, there were significant allegations that the Hutus and Tutsis in Rwanda, the RUF, the AFRC and the CDF in Sierra Leone, the Sudanese government, the Janjaweed and the rebels in Darfur, the Qaddafi forces and the opposition in Libya, as well as the military and the opposition in Syria had all committed atrocities that violated the UNSC precedent, international law and common ideas of universal morality. An atrocities investigation would target all sides in each of these conflicts. While an investigation would benefit the victims, it could also increase the resentment of those holding the guns on both sides of each conflict against the UNSC. The message sent by using precedent had no value in such circumstances.

As a result, it is not that reliance does not matter for the use of precedent, but that the present study does not capture its causal power because its two main conditions were never met. Since the UNSC has no information to share with the outside world on the value and role of international atrocities investigations, it could not use precedent to signal its expectations. Additionally, since very few actors obeyed the laws of war, the UNSC was not interested in using precedent to stabilize the local communities. For these two reasons, the present case studies cannot confirm or reject the applicability of the reliance based explanations.

7.6.3 Decision-Making

According to the decision-making explanations, the UNSC is likely to use precedent to (i) avoid mistakes or (ii) efficiently arrive at decisions. These possibilities are predicated on the condition that the UNSC members (i) agree on the desirability of having an atrocities investigation, but (ii) do not agree on how to optimally create this investigation.

With the exception of Syria, where Russia and China oppose the use of an investigation, these conditions are satisfied in the other case studies of this Chapter. In Rwanda, all UNSC member states agreed that an investigation into the genocide was appropriate. Their debate focused around the properties of this investigation. Similarly, in Sierra Leone, the negotiations focused on the characteristics of the investigation more than the creation of the investigation itself. In Darfur, the debates between the United States and the ICC-9 centered on the use of the ICC or an ad hoc investigation, with both sides accepting the need for an investigation. Again, in Libya, the minimal debate on the investigation focused on its jurisdictional scope, notably on how to protect western military members from being the targets of an investigation.

Within these conditions, however, the case studies indicate that the UNSC members use precedent to efficiently arrive at decisions, rather than avoiding past mistakes. The first explanation of the decision-making category never appeared in these case studies, as the UNSC did not use precedent to avoid its past mistakes. If the applicability of the bargaining explanation is discounted, this realization should be surprising. After all, the UNSC's attempts to create international criminal tribunals have been highly criticized. Even those UNSC members who most support them have acknowledged their problems.[126] Yet, in using precedent, the UNSC has never sought to avoid these problems by tweaking the precedent.[127]

Despite the above, the UNSC has used precedent to streamline its decision-making process, per the second prong of the decision-making explanation. This was demonstrated in the UNSC's debates on Libya. Overwhelmed by the rapid escalation of Qaddafi's response to the uprising of the Arab spring, the western UNSC member states desired a quick solution. By copying and pasting the Darfur precedent, and having no substantive debate on its provisions, the UNSC used precedent for decision-making efficiency. This rationale was also present in the negotiations over the creation of the ICTR, where the UNSC members agreed that the ICTR would share the Prosecutor and Appeals Chamber of the ICTY precisely to avoid re-inventing the wheel.

Despite its applicability, the efficient rationale was absent in the debates over Sierra Leone and Darfur. In those instances, the UNSC members' preference for efficiency was outweighed by their concerns for the substantive consequences of an investigation. In Sierra Leone, for example, both the United Kingdom and the United States were in favor for a tribunal, yet disagreed on its jurisdictional scope, financing plans, and general administration. Because of these disagreements, the two sides spent a few months deliberating on the details of a tribunal. Similar substantive disagreements also overshadowed the applicability of the efficiency explanation in the debates on Darfur.

Overall, the decision-making explanation for the use of precedent is not as applicable at the UNSC as expected. The UNSC members have resorted to precedent for efficiency only in the cases of Rwanda and Libya. And, they have never used precedent to avoid past mistakes, despite the numerous critiques with their past actions in this field. This trend counters findings of past legal studies on the use of precedent,[128] and points to the need for a different explanation on the use of precedent by the UNSC.

[126] Interviews: 10, 20.

[127] Interview: 4.

[128] See e.g. Holmes (1881); Oliphant (1928).

7.6.4 Bargaining

Despite their applicability, the explanatory power of the consistency and the decision-making explanations is limited. First, these explanations do not account for the use of precedent in most of the case studies. For example, both are absent with regards to the use of precedent in Sierra Leone and Darfur. Additionally, even for the case studies in which they are present, these two explanations are of secondary importance. The revolt, for example, that some states feel towards the atrocities in Syria would have been sufficient for them to support a referral even if there had been no referral for Libya. Similarly, it is highly likely that the investigation in Libya would have mirrored the one in Darfur even if the UNSC did not need a fast solution, since the United States has strong preferences for the jurisdictional exceptions of the Darfur referral.

A better explanation for the use of precedent by the UNSC is provided by the two-step bargaining explanation. In all of the above case studies, the debates have been characterized by competing preferences and uncertainty among UNSC members. While these conditions exist in all case studies, the example of Libya is the most telling. In that case, as illustrated in the previous Section, western states were in favor of an ICC investigation as part of their efforts to transition to a post-Qaddafi era. They never, however, openly discussed the possibility of regime change. Other UNSC members, such as Russia and China, could see behind the smoke screen, but were not sure if the western states were fully determined to remove Qaddafi. They were also not sure if they wanted to support Qaddafi that much, as he had impinged on their own interests and both Arab and African states were distancing themselves from him. The bargaining potential for precedent arose in light of the competing preferences and the underlying uncertainty.

In most of the above case studies, one member of the UNSC who desired to take action proposed the use of precedent to the other members of the UNSC in order to nudge them towards that action. In the case of Sierra Leone, the United States suggested a mixed tribunal as a way to overcome the United Kingdom's hesitation with regards to another ad hoc investigation. For Darfur, the United States put forth the exemption from the ICC jurisdiction for nationals of non-ICC state parties to overcome France's insistence on an unlimited ICC investigation. In the case of Libya, the United Kingdom and France supported the use of the Darfur precedent as a way to ensure that the other P5 would support an ICC investigation. Finally, for Syria, France included the Libya/Darfur precedent in its draft resolution as a way to accommodate U.S. concerns.

In the second step of the bargaining, the receiving states agreed to the proposal to use precedent, even though precedent was a second-best option, in order to contain other possible actions of the proposing UNSC state. The receiving state thus limited its uncertainty over the actions of their counterparty. In the case of Sierra Leone, the United Kingdom agreed with the idea of a mixed tribunal as a way to both placate its own preferences for justice and to stop the United States from destabilizing the Sierra Leonean conflict. In the case of Darfur, France accepted the U.S.

proposal in order to get an ICC investigation for Darfur and also undermine the U.S. efforts to create an African criminal court, which would compete with the ICC. The United States agreed with the ICC referral in Libya, not only because it wanted the ICC to investigate the atrocities, but also because it was eager to protect U.S. service-members from an investigation, which would have happened if (at France's prodding) the Libyan government would refer the case to the ICC on its own.

It therefore appears that the fourth explanation has significant explanatory power. The historical facts of the five case studies indicate that the UNSC members used precedent as a way to coordinate their different preferences over the text of a resolution. Nonetheless, the use of precedent cannot be seen as the silver bullet of bargaining. Instead, the case studies illustrate the limitations that precedent has as a coordination tool at the UNSC. As demonstrated in the above Sections above, precedent can only work if it falls outside the veto zone of the other P5. The Syria case aptly demonstrates this limitation, as the precedent of an ICC referral falls within Russia's veto zone. In essence, the bargaining explanation confirms that the use of precedent cannot move mountains. It is more likely to tilt those undecided rather than change the mind of those opposed to a specific course of action.

By underscoring the role that precedent has in the bargaining stage, this Section can also shed some light on the use of precedent for the creation of the ICTR and the Syria referral. As described in Sect. 7.3 above, A has no benefit from bargaining if all points acceptable to A fall within B's veto zone. As a result, if the veto zones block out the decision-making space, there should be no negotiations at the UNSC. This may explain the lack of UNSC negotiations over issues such as Taiwan, Palestine and Chechnya. It also explains why, despite the New Zealand compromise, Rwanda still voted against the creation of the ICTR. The Tutsi RPF government of Rwanda considered that the ICTR's inability to impose death sentences was unacceptable. For the western UNSC members, the death penalty was a non-starter. As a result, the area outside Rwanda's veto zone fell entirely within the veto zone of the western UNSC members, and there was no room for an agreement.

Apart from the Rwanda case, the attempt to refer the Syrian atrocities to the ICC takes on a new character in light of the significance of precedent. It appears likely that the western states did not put forth the Darfur/Libya precedent in order to convince Russia and China to ratify the resolution. Russia and China had repeatedly informed them of their opposition to any action on Syria, including an ICC referral.[129] The western states knew that the precedent set by the Darfur/Libya atrocities investigations fell within Russia's and China's veto zones. It thus appears more likely that the western states decided on the Syria referral in order to name and shame the veto-wielding countries. These two UNSC members now appear to be acting inconsistently, in violation of expectations, and against justice. As France, the United Kingdom and the United States knew that precedent remained in Russia's and China's veto zones, this resolution appears to, in the words of the former ICTY

[129] Interviews: 1, 4, 10, 13, 20.

Prosecutor Louise Arbour, belong more in the "museum of political scoring"[130] than in the attempts to use precedent to reach an agreement.

7.7 Conclusion

The use of precedent is the third and final necessary step through which the UNSC members create an international atrocities investigation. This Chapter has presented that decision-makers resort to precedent for reasons that center not only on (i) the debated issue, (ii) the interested parties or (iii) decision-making, but also (iv) bargaining. This Chapter has explored the use of precedent at the UNSC through the UNSC's decisions on the creation of international criminal investigations into atrocities committed in Rwanda, Sierra Leone, Libya, Darfur, and Syria. As the five case studies indicate, the bargaining explanation carries significant explanatory power. Yet, as Schauer recognized for the prior three explanations,[131] the fourth one also does not act alone. In most occasions, more than one explanation accounts for the use of precedent.

By distinguishing the applicability of the bargaining explanation, this Chapter clarifies why the UNSC remains tied to its prior decisions rather than using its unrestricted powers in new ways. It suggests that instead of hoping that the UNSC may suddenly innovate, it is more appropriate to examine how the UNSC members become comfortable with gradual departures from their prior actions. For the children of our paradigmatic family, this means that, after being allowed to attend a concert, their parents are more likely to accept a theatre outing or a museum visit rather than vacations in a foreign country.

While precedent cannot change a state's veto zone, it allows for coordination among the UNSC members over those issues that fall outside their veto zone. In essence, *but for* the use of precedent, the UNSC members would not have coordinated their actions to result in a UNSC Resolution on atrocities investigations. The value of the bargaining explanation is that it captures how this coordination on the basis of precedent takes place at the UNSC. By doing so, it sheds light into why the UNSC members routinely resort to precedent in drafting new resolutions.

As this Chapter presented how the UNSC completes the third and final step in its deliberations through the use of precedent, the following Chapter returns to the main question posed by this book and concludes by bringing together the findings of the previous three Chapters.

[130] The New York Times (May 21, 2014).

[131] Schauer (1987).

References

Interviews

Interview No. 1; Interview Details: Diplomat from United Kingdom, New York (June 13, 2013).
Interview No. 2; Interview Details: Member of UN Office of Legal Affairs, on Skype (June 24, 2013).
Interview No. 3; Interview Details: Diplomat from the United Kingdom, New York (July 11, 2013).
Interview No. 4; Interview Details: Diplomat from United States, New York (July 12, 2013).
Interview No. 6; Interview Details: Member of UN Office of Legal Affairs, New York (August 6, 2013).
Interview No. 7; Interview Details: Diplomat from New Zealand, New York (August 23, 2013).
Interview No. 9; Interview Details: Official from the International Criminal Court, New York (September 9, 2013).
Interview No. 10; Interview Details: Diplomat from France, New York (October 7, 2013).
Interview No. 11; Interview Details: Cherif Bassiouni, telephone call (October 15, 2013).
Interview No. 12; Interview Details: Diplomat from United States, telephone call (November 6, 2013).
Interview No. 13; Interview Details: Diplomat from Russia, New York (November 26, 2013).
Interview No. 14; Interview Details: Diplomat from United States, Washington, D.C. (December 4, 2013).
Interview No. 15; Interview Details: Member of UN Office of Legal Affairs, New York (December 6, 2013).
Interview No. 16; Interview Details: Member of UN Office of Legal Affairs, New York (December 6, 2013).
Interview No. 18; Interview Details: Diplomat from United Kingdom, London (January 7, 2014).
Interview No. 19; Interview Details: Diplomat from Greece, on Skype (January 19, 2014).
Interview No. 20; Interview Details: Diplomat from Guatemala, New York (January 21, 2014).

Books and Articles

Alvarez, Jose E. 1996. Judging the Security Council. *American Journal of International Law* 90 (1): 1–39.
Anderson, Paul A. 1981. Justifications and Precedents as Constraints in Foreign Policy Decision-Making. *American Journal of Political Science* 25: 738–761.
Baker, Scott, and Claudio Mezzetti. 2012. A Theory of Rational Jurisprudence. *Journal of Political Economy* 120 (3): 513–551.
Barzun, Charles L. 2013. Impeaching Precedent. *The University of Chicago Law Review* 80: 1625–1681.
Blackstone. Section the Third: Of the Laws of England (1765–1769).
Cassese, Antonio. 2006. Is the ICC Still Having Teething Problems? *Journal of International Criminal Justice* 4 (3): 434–441.
Châtaignier, Jean-Marc. 2005. *L'ONU dans la crise en Sierra Leone*. Paris: Éditions KARTHALA.
Che, Yeon-Koo, and Jong Goo Yi. 1993. The Role of Precedents in Repeated Litigation. *Journal of Law, Economics, and Organization* 9 (2): 399–424.
Crawford, Vincent, and Hans Haller. 1990. Learning How to Cooperate: Optimal play in Repeated Coordination Games. *Econometrica* 58: 571–595.
Cryer, Robert. 2006. Sudan, Resolution 1593, and International Criminal Justice. *Leiden Journal of International Law* 19 (1): 195–222.

de Mesquita, Ethan Bueno, and Matthew Stephenson. 2002. Informative Precedent and Intrajudicial Communication. *American Political Science Review* 96 (4): 755–766.
Deutsch, Jan G. 1974. Precedent and Adjudication. *Yale Law Journal* 83: 1553–1584.
Doyle, Michael W. 2015. *The Question of Intervention, John Stuart Mill & the Responsibility to Protect*. New Haven: Yale University Press.
Funk, Kevin, and Steven Fake. 2009. *Scramble for Africa: Darfur-intervention and the U.S.A.* Black Rose Books Ltd.
Gosnell, Christopher. 2008. The Request for an Arrest Warrant in Al Bashir Idealistic Posturing or Calculated Plan? *Journal of International Criminal Justice* 6 (5): 841–851.
Hamilton, Rebecca. 2011. *Fighting for Darfur*. New York: Palgrave Macmillan.
Holmes, Oliver Wendell. 1881. In *The Common Law*, ed. M. De Wolfe Howe. Boston: Little, Brown and Co., 1963.
Hurwitz, Mark S., and Oseph V. Stefko. 2004. Acclimation and Attitudes: 'Newcomer' Justices and Precedent Conformance on the Supreme Court. *Political Research Quarterly* 57 (1): 121–129.
Johnstone, Ian. 2003a. Security Council Deliberations: The Power of the Better Argument. *European Journal of International Law* 14 (3): 437–480.
———. 2003b. The Role of the UN Secretary-General: The Power of Persuasion Based on Law. *Global Governance*: 441–458.
Kelley, Judith. 2007. Who Keeps International Commitments and Why? The International Criminal Court and Bilateral Nonsurrender Agreements. *American Political Science Review* 101 (03): 573–589.
Knight, Jack, and Lee Epstein. 1996. The Norm of Stare Decisis. *American Journal of Political Science* 40: 1018–1035.
Kovanda, Karel. 2010. The Czech Republic on the UN Security Council: The Rwandan Genocide. *Genocide Studies and Prevention* 5 (2): 192–218.
Landes, William M., and Richard Posner. 1976. *Legal Precedent: A Theoretical and Empirical Analysis, NBER Working Paper No. 146*.
Lupu, Yonatan, and James H. Fowler. 2013. Strategic Citations to Precedent on the U.S. Supreme Court. *The Journal of Legal Studies* 42 (1): 151–186.
Maggi, Giovanni, and Robert W. Staiger. 2011. The Role of Dispute Settlement Procedures in International Trade Agreements. *The Quarterly Journal of Economics* 126 (1): 475–515.
Moreno-Ocampo, Luis. 2013a. The Gaddafi Case (Draft Paper). *NYU School of Law's Hauser Colloquium on International Law* (September 2013).
Morriss, Andrew P., Michael Heise, and Gregory C. Sisk. 2005. Signaling and Precedent in Federal District Court Opinions. *Supreme Court Economic Review* 13: 63–97.
Oliphant, Herman. 1928. A Return to Stare Decisis. *American Bar Association Journal* 14: 71–76.
Orakhelashvili, Alexander. 2005. The Impact of Peremptory Norms on the Interpretation and Application of United Nations Security Council Resolutions. *European Journal of International Law* 16 (1): 59–88.
Postema, Gerald J. 1990. On the Moral Presence of Our Past. *McGill Law Journal* 36: 1153.
Rasmusen, Eric. 1994. Judicial Legitimacy as a Repeated Game. *Journal of Law, Economics, & Organization* 10: 63–83.
Schabas, William A. 2004. United States Hostility to the International Criminal Court: It's All About the Security Council. *European Journal of International Law* 15 (4): 701–720.
Schauer, Frederick. 1987. Precedent. *Stanford Law Review* 39 (3): 571–605.
———. 2008. Why Precedent in Law (and Elsewhere) Is Not Totally (or Even Substantially) About Analogy. *Perspectives on Psychological Science* 3 (6): 454–460.
Scheffer, David J. 1999. The United States and the International Criminal Court. *American Journal of International Law* 93: 12–22.
———. 2013. *All the Missing Souls: A Personal History of the War Crimes Tribunals*. Princeton: Princeton University Press.

Schotter, Andrew. 1978. The Effects of Precedent on Arbitration. *Journal of Conflict Resolution* 22 (4): 659–678.
Spriggs, James F., and Thomas G. Hansford. 2002. The U.S. Supreme Court's Incorporation and Interpretation of Precedent. *Law and Society Review* 36: 139–160.
Weiss, Thomas G. 2016. *Humanitarian Intervention: Ideas in Action*. 3rd ed. Cambridge, UK: Polity Press.

News Sources

New York Times

Moynihan, Colin, *Libya's UN Diplomats Break with Qaddafi*, The New York Times (February 21, 2011).
Neier, Aryeh, *An Arab War-Crimes Court for Syria*, The New York Times (April 4, 2012).
Sengupta, Somini, *UN Will Weigh Asking Court to Investigate Ware Crimes in Syria*, The New York Times (May 21, 2014).

The Guardian

Black, Ian, *Gaddafi Urges Violent Showdown and Tells Libya 'I'll Die a Martyr.'* The Guardian (February 22, 2011).

Amnesty International

The U.S.A. and the International Criminal Court (November 11, 2007) (http://www.amnesty.org/en/international-justice/issues/international-criminal-court/usa-icc).

Various News Sources

[anonymous], *15 April 2014 – Security Council Meeting on the "Caesar" Report Concerning Mass Torture Perpetrated by the Syrian Government*, French Mission to the United Nations, Press Release (April 15, 2014) (at http://www.franceonu.org/france-at-the-united-nations/press-room/speaking-to-the-media/remarks-to-the-press/article/15-april-2014-security-council).
[anonymous], *Libya Profile*, BBC, 2014 (at http://www.bbc.com/news/world-africa-13755445).
Daly, Emma, *Dossier of 'NATO' Crimes Lands in Prosecutor's Lap*, The Observer (December 26, 1999).
Dreyfuss, Bob, *Obama's Women Advisers Pushed War Against Libya*, The Nation (March 19, 2011).
Higgins, Andrew, *Libya policy a balancing act for China as Moammar Gaddafi's rule collapses*, Washington Post (August 27, 2011).
Moreno-Ocampo, Luis, *The ICC as the Sword of Damocles* (September 23, 2013b) (at http://justsecurity.org/914/icc-sword-damocles/).

Court Documents

Domestic Courts

Goldwater v. Carter, 444 U.S. 996, 996-1007.
Kucinich v. Bush, 236 F.Supp.2d 1, 2-18 (D.D.C. 2002).
United States v. Belmont, 301 U.S. 324-32.
Youngstown Sheet & Tube Company, et al. v. Charles Sawyer, Secretary of Commerce, 343 U.S. 579.

International Criminal Tribunal for the Former Yugoslavia

Prosecutor's Report on Nato Bombing Campaign, Press Release, ICTY, The Hague (June 13, 2000).

Government Documents

The American Service-Members' Protection Act (ASPA, Title 2 of Pub.L. 107–206, H.R. 4775, 116 Stat. 820, enacted August 2, 2002).

UN Documents

Foundational Documents

Charter of the United Nations.
Statute of the International Court of Justice.

Reports

S/1994/1125, Preliminary Report of the Independent Commission of Experts established in accordance with Security Council resolution 935 (October 4, 1994).
S/1994/1133, Progress Report of the Secretary-General on the United Nations Assistance Mission for Rwanda (October 6, 1994).
S/2000/915, Report of the Secretary-General on the Establishment of a Special Court for Sierra Leone (October 4, 2000).
S/2002/267, Thirteenth report of the Secretary-General on UNAMSIL (March 14, 2002).
S/2005/68, Report of the Secretary-General on the Sudan pursuant to paragraphs 6, 13 and 16 of Security Council resolution 1556 (2004), paragraph 15 of Security Council resolution 1564 (2004) and paragraph 17 of Security Council resolution 1574 (2004) (February 4, 2005).
S/1994/1157, Situation of human rights in Rwanda (October 13, 1994).

Records of United Nations Security Council Meetings

S/PV.847, Laos (September 7, 1959).
S/PV.3377, Rwanda (May 16, 1994).
S/PV.3453, The situation concerning Rwanda (November 8, 1994).
S/PV.4803, Liberia (August 1, 2003).
SC/10185, Peace and security in Africa – Libya (February 25, 2011).
S/PV.6486, Peace and security in Africa – Libya (February 22, 2011).
S/PV.6490, Peace and security in Africa – Libya (February 25, 2011).

Letters

S/2000/693, Letter dated 12 July 2001 from the Secretary-General addressed to the President of the Security Council regarding revised budget estimates for operation of the Court (July 13, 2001).
S/2000/722, Letter dated 23 July 2001 from the President of the Security Council to the Secretary-General referring to plans to move forward with establishment of a Special Court (July 23, 2001).
S/2001/1320, Letter dated 26 December 2001 from the Secretary-General to the President of the Security Council regarding contributions to commence the establishment and operation of the Special Court (December 28, 2001).
S/2001/40, Letter from the Secretary-General addressed to the President of the Security Council on the Secretary-General's understanding of the meaning, scope and legal effect of proposals made by members of the Council (January 12, 2001).
S/2001/95, Letter dated 31 January 2001 from the President of the Security Council addressed to the Secretary-General referring to the Secretary-General's letter to the President of 12 January 2001 (S/2001/40) (January 31, 2001).
S/2002/246, Letter dated 6 March 2002 from the Secretary-General addressed to the President of the Security Council (March 8, 2002).
S/2014/361, Letter dated 19 May 2014 from the Permanent Representative of Switzerland to the United Nations addressed to the Secretary-General, (May 19, 2014).
S/2000/1234, Letter from the President of the Security Council addressed to the Secretary-General reaffirming the Council's support for resolution 1315 (2000) and suggesting amendments to the draft Agreement between the United Nations and the Government of Sierra Leone (December 22, 2000).
S/2012/731, Letter from the Permanent Representative of Guatemala to the United Nations addressed to the Secretary-General (October 1, 2012).

Resolutions

S/RES/626, Angola (December 20, 1988).
S/RES/743, Socialist Federal Republic of Yugoslavia (February 21, 1992).
S/RES/749, Socialist Federal Republic of Yugoslavia (April 7, 1992).
S/RES/758, Bosnia and Herzegovina (June 8, 1992).
S/RES/761, Bosnia and Herzegovina (June 29, 1992).
S/RES/762, Former Yugoslavia (June 30, 1992).
S/RES/770, Bosnia and Herzegovina (August 13, 1992).
S/RES/779, Croatia (October 6, 1992).
S/RES/786, Bosnia and Herzegovina (November 10, 1992).
S/RES/787, Bosnia and Herzegovina (November 16, 1992).
S/RES/802, Croatia (January 25, 1993).
S/RES/842, Former Yugoslav Republic of Macedonia (June 18, 1993).

S/RES/935, Rwanda (July 1, 1994).
S/RES/955, International Tribunal – Rwanda (November 8, 1994).
S/RES/1181, Sierra Leone (July 13, 1998).
S/RES/1315, Sierra Leone (August 14, 2000).
S/RES/1346, Sierra Leone (March 30, 2001).
S/RES/1370, Sierra Leone (September 18, 2001).
S/RES/1400, Sierra Leone (March 28, 2002).
S/RES/1497, Liberia (August 1, 2003).
S/RES/1518, Iraq – Kuwait (November 24, 2003).
S/RES/1593, Sudan (March 19, 2005).
S/RES/1970, Peace and security (February 26, 2011).
S/RES/2139, Middle East situation – Syria (February 22, 2014).
S/RES/2127, Central African Republic (December 5, 2014).
S/2014/348, Draft Resolution referring the situation in the Syrian Arab Republic to the International Criminal Court (May 22, 2014).

Chapter 8
Conclusion

The United States is obliged by international law to investigate its citizens suspected of engaging in torture, but even if it does not, Americans who ordered or carried out torture can be prosecuted abroad, by legal bodies including the International Criminal Court, legal experts say.

Whether they will be is another question. That's largely a political determination.

Somini Sengupta, New York Times, December 10, 2014.
(Sengupta, New York Times (December 10, 2014))

Abstract The Conclusion summarizes the question, the methodology, the main argument and the contributions of this book. It presents a short case study of the UNSC's response to the atrocities in Darfur to illustrate how the three step argument of this book comes together into one UNSC decision. Finally, it develops theoretical and policy implications of the findings of this book.

As mentioned in the Introduction of this book, the ICC Prosecutor, Louis Moreno-Ocampo, charged the President of Sudan, Omar al Bashir, for war crimes, crimes against humanity and genocide. Moreno-Ocampo's power to investigate atrocities committed in a state that was not a party to the ICC stemmed from UNSC Resolution 1593, whereby the UNSC members authorized an investigation into atrocities committed in Darfur. This book explains the UNSC's decisions to initiate such international atrocities investigations.

This conclusion first summarizes the research question, the methodology, the main argument and the contributions of this book. It then presents a short case study of the UNSC's response to the atrocities in Darfur to illustrate how the three step argument of this book comes together into one UNSC decision. Finally, it develops theoretical and policy implications of the findings of this book.

C. Kaoutzanis, *The UN Security Council and International Criminal Tribunals: Procedure Matters*, Studies in Global Justice 20,
https://doi.org/10.1007/978-3-030-23777-6_8

8.1 Summary of the Argument

The UNSC has authorized atrocities investigations in only 11 of the 92 states that have experienced atrocities since the end of the Cold War. As Chap. 3 illustrates, however, past explanations on the creation of atrocities investigations do not sufficiently explain the work of the UNSC in this field, as they focus on individual states and omit the coordination difficulties that occur when it comes to having 15 UNSC members agree on one course of action. Additionally, past studies on the UNSC offer explanations that do not capture the UNSC's work on the creation of atrocities investigations. The main shortcoming of these studies is that they rarely apply to facts beyond their specific case studies. Because the political calculations of a 15-member body are ever changing, this book suggests that it will never be easy or feasible to theoretically generalize as to how the UNSC functions by focusing on the preferences of the UNSC members.

To avoid this difficulty, this book looks at the one constant feature of the UNSC, its decision-making process. To examine the role of the decision-making process on the actions of the UNSC members, this book relies on the historical records of the UNSC's actions on atrocities. Apart from the written archives, this record was supplemented by a series of original interviews with individuals who participated in the UNSC's deliberations and decisions on atrocities.

This book's main argument is that, while the UNSC's decision-making process is not solely responsible for any specific decision taken by the UNSC, it has a central influence on the UNSC's decisions by aggregating individual state preferences, controlling the process through which states respond to crises and guiding undecided states towards a single outcome. Because a UNSC decision is a committee process, each step of the committee's procedures is a step necessary for a final outcome. In essence, the UNSC members decided to investigate only certain atrocities because they were able to successfully complete each of the three steps in the UNSC's decision-making process only for those certain atrocities. As a result, and since an explanation focusing on state preferences cannot explain the actions of the UNSC, the institutional procedures of the UNSC deserve independent study. To accomplish this task, this book looks at the three steps of the UNSC's institutional procedures (i.e. preliminary steps, deliberation and issuance of decision) and identifies the central feature of each step (i.e. patron diplomat, use of third-party, reliance on precedent). It then explains why and how these features have become part of the UNSC's procedure.

Through its analysis, this book asserts that the creation of an atrocities investigation depends on three factors. First, it requires that a diplomat of a UNSC member state brings the atrocities to the attention of the UNSC. It is commonly accepted that diplomats do so (i) at the instruction of their states, (ii) at the discretion afforded to them by their states, and (iii) rarely, against the instructions of their states. Chapter 5 advances the understanding of the role diplomats play in the UNSC's decision-making process by examining how atrocities often come to the attention of the UNSC as the outcome of a disagreement between the diplomats at the UNSC and their superiors. It also highlights, through its case studies, how the work of diplomats is far from mechanical.

Second, the creation of an atrocities investigation by the UNSC requires that the UNSC members collectively believe that the investigation will benefit their states and the UNSC. The UNSC members are capable of weighing the material benefits of the investigation. They are, however, also concerned about the legitimacy of their actions. As discussed in Chap. 5, UNSC members resort to the use of an independent third-party to bridge the gap between these two competing concerns. Under this explanation, it makes sense that the UNSC consistently relies on the recommendations of an independent fact-finding mission prior to authorizing an international atrocities investigation.

Finally, the creation of an atrocities investigation by the UNSC requires that the UNSC members draft one resolution committing their agreement into words. Similar to the two above steps, many different reasons influence the negotiations that continue to take place in this drafting phase. But beyond political bargaining, the UNSC members routinely use precedent to convince other states to vote in favor of their draft resolutions. As presented in Chap. 7, the UNSC resorts to precedent, contrary to prior explanations, to not only (i) safeguard the interests of the affected parties, (ii) ensure consistent outcomes to similar issues, and (iii) render the decision-making process more efficient. Instead, the members of the UNSC also use precedent as a bargaining tool to overcome the uncertainty inherent in UNSC deliberations.

The argument of this book is innovative in two ways. On the one hand, it explains the work of the UNSC in a way that applies not only to atrocities investigations, but also to the other issues in front of this institution. As a result, the same three step explanation presented here can be applied to other examples of the UNSC's activities, such as the creation of peacekeeping missions or imposition of economic sanctions. On the other hand, through the focus on the historical records and interviews, this book was able to uncover how the UNSC works beyond limiting its focus on the role of state preferences. While these preferences always exist in the background, the UNSC is able to take important actions within their limits. To do so, however, requires the coordination of the 15 UNSC members, a topic that has so far been assumed away in prior studies, despite its central significance in arriving at decisions.

Standard political reasons, such as alliances and national interests, carry some weight, but do not explain why the UNSC decided not to investigate the atrocities, for example, of Burundi in 1994 and Chad in 2005. The lack of investigations can be explained, however, by the diminishing likelihood of the UNSC undertaking an investigation as it progresses along its three step decision making process. Even though they had a patron diplomat, the atrocities in Chad, for example, never caught the attention of the entire UNSC, as it was dealing with the much more pressing issue of Darfur. An independent commission of inquiry suggested that the UNSC not authorize an investigation into the atrocities in Burundi. As indicated by Map 4.3, it appears that the UNSC rarely manages to complete all these three steps, which is why so few atrocities investigations exist.

8.2 The UNSC's Referral of Darfur to the ICC

Returning to the example presented in the Introduction, the UNSC investigation into the atrocities committed in Darfur resulted from (i) the decision of the United States Permanent Representative at the UNSC to place the atrocities on the UNSC's agenda, (ii) the recommendation of an independent commission of inquiry to refer the atrocities to the ICC, and (iii) the French compromise to the use of text from a prior resolution, which allowed the United States to get comfortable with the jurisdictional obligations of Resolution 1593. It is interesting, however, to see how these three steps came together in practice.

The impetus for the UNSC's actions came from the United States, where political actors had begun referring to the atrocities in Darfur as genocide. In the early summer of 2004, Secretary of State Powell—who had hereto considered genocide a legal determination[1]—in collaboration with the U.S. Agency for International Development, created the Darfur Atrocities Documentation Team and sent a team of investigators to various points along the Chad-Sudan border. There, in the months of July and August 2004, investigators interviewed more than 1100 refugees.[2] Even before their report was ready, the U.S. Congress unanimously—and concurrently in both House and Senate—passed a resolution on July 22, 2004, urging the administration "to seriously consider multilateral or even unilateral intervention to stop genocide in Darfur, Sudan, should the United Nations Security Council fail to act."[3]

Six weeks later, on September 9, 2014, with the results of the investigation in hand, Secretary Powell informed the Senate's Foreign Relations Committee that the U.S. government had determined that the acts in Darfur constituted genocide against the non-Arab Sudanese. Yet, at the same time, instead of pressing for action, Secretary Powell invoked Article VIII of the Genocide Convention and referred the matter to the UNSC.[4] This was the first time this article had ever been invoked.[5] At the instructions of the State Department, the U.S. permanent representative to the UNSC placed the topic of the Darfur atrocities on the UNSC's agenda (Step 1).

The UNSC greeted Colin Powell's announcement that the atrocities in Darfur constituted genocide with concern. The U.S. declaration and the referral to the UNSC were unprecedented actions, which grabbed the attention of the international community. China and some African and Arab countries were hesitant to get the ICC involved. The United States and other western states were, however, appalled at the magnitude of the atrocities. Since the United States had reached the conclusion that the events constituted genocide only after a detailed investigation into the

[1] See e.g. Powell's interview on June 30th, 2004, in Totten and Markusen (2006, p.113).

[2] Totten and Markusen (2006, p. xiii).

[3] H.Con. R. 467—S.Con.R. 124 (July 22, 2004).

[4] Article VIII reads: "Any Contracting Party may call upon the competent organs of the United Nations to take such action under the Charter of the United Nations as they consider appropriate for the prevention and suppression of acts of genocide or any of the other acts enumerated in article III."

[5] Totten and Markusen (2006, p.123).

facts, it made sense for the UNSC to do the same before proceeding with further action on the atrocities. As a result, on September 18, 2004, with Secretary-General Annan in attendance, the UNSC passed resolution 1564,[6] which requested that the Secretary-General "rapidly establish an international commission of inquiry" to (i) investigate violations of international humanitarian law and human rights, (ii) determine if acts of genocide occurred, and (iii) identify alleged perpetrators of these violations.

On October 4, the Secretary-General announced the establishment of the International Commission on Inquiry into Darfur.[7] Several months later, on February 1, 2005, with the atrocities continuing, the International Commission of Inquiry into Sudan issued its report.[8] The five-person committee included Antonio Cassese (Chairperson), Mohamed Fayek, Hina Jilani, Dumisa Ntsebeza and Therese Striggner-Scott. Their stature in the field of human rights added to the significance of the commission's findings. The report:

> established that the Government of the Sudan and the Janjaweed are responsible for serious violations of international human rights and humanitarian law amounting to crimes under international law. In particular, the Commission found that Government forces and militias conducted indiscriminate attacks, including killing of civilians, torture, enforced disappearances, destruction of villages, rape and other forms of sexual violence, pillaging and forced displacement, throughout Darfur. These acts were conducted on a widespread and systematic basis, and therefore may amount to crimes against humanity.[9]

Despite these findings, the commission determined that the crime of genocide had not been committed. While genocidal acts occurred, the commission found that genocidal intent was missing.[10] The possible genocidal intent of certain individual perpetrators was "a determination that only a competent court can make on a case-by-case basis."[11]

For this reason, and because the crimes committed in Darfur were of upmost importance, the commission "strongly recommend[ed] that the Security Council immediately refer the situation of Darfur to the International Criminal Court, pursuant to article 13(b) of the Statute of the Court."[12] To that end, the commission compiled a list of people who it considered responsible for the perpetration of these atrocities. The commission sealed the list and gave it to Secretary-General Annan

---

[6] S/RES/1564 (September 18, 2004).

[7] S/2004/812 (October 4, 2004).

[8] Report on Darfur (2005).

[9] Report on Darfur (2005, p. 3).

[10] Report on Darfur (2005, p. 132). The commission concluded that the Government's policy: does not evince a specific intent to annihilate, in whole or in part, a group distinguished on racial, ethnic, national or religious grounds. Rather, it would seem that those who planned and organized attacks on villages pursued the intent to drive the victims from their homes, primarily for purposes of counter-insurgency warfare.

[11] Report on Darfur (2005, p. 161).

[12] Report on Darfur (2005, p. 162).

with the hope that it would be given to a prosecutor. Finally, the commission considered that a referral to the ICC would not only end impunity but also contribute "to the restoration of peace in the region."[13] (Step 2).

The UNSC continued receiving negative news on Darfur.[14] Yet, it did not act on the referral to the ICC suggested by the Commission of Inquiry. Because of this inaction, the UNSC was prodded towards a referral during its public deliberations on two occasions. Mr. Baba Gana Kingibe, the Special Representative of the Chairperson of the Commission of the African Union in the Sudan, speaking on February 8, 2005 on behalf of the African Union, warned the international community to stop "allowing the guilty to escape punishment simply because there is no consensus on the appropriate forum in which to prosecute the crimes."[15] Then, on February 16, 2005, the UNSC heard a presentation from Ms. Louise Arbour, UN High Commissioner for Human Rights. Ms. Arbour—the former Prosecutor of the ICTY—summarized to the UNSC the recommendations made by the report International Commission of Inquiry. Similar to Mr. Kingibe, Ms. Arbour also focused on the fact that the commission had ruled out the establishment of a mixed or of an *ad hoc* tribunal.[16] In effect, Ms. Arbour was pushing the UNSC towards referring the situation in Darfur to the ICC.

The statements of both Mr. Kingibe and Ms. Arbour only make sense against the diplomatic backdrop at the UNSC. As has been documented in Chap. 7 and elsewhere,[17] the United States had championed the creation of *ad hoc* and mixed tribunals, but felt uncomfortable with the creation and existence of the ICC. To stem the likelihood of an ICC investigation into U.S. actions, the first George W. Bush administration signed bilateral Article 98 agreements with a series of countries.[18] The U.S. Congress also passed the American Service-Members' Protection Act, which prohibited the U.S. government from funding or assisting the ICC.[19] As a result, the United States supported an international criminal investigation into Darfur, but opposed a referral to the ICC. On the other side of the spectrum, France championed a referral to the ICC. As a result, the debates between the French and the U.S. sides started on February 1, 2005, when the Commission of Inquiry issued its report, and lasted until the end of March 2005.

Meanwhile, on March 4, 2005, the Secretary-General issued to the UNSC his monthly report on Sudan of February 2005. In this report, the Secretary-General again determined that the security situation was fragile. The 9,000 humanitarian workers could not cope with the magnitude of the crisis, while the African Mission in Sudan ('AMIS') had a hard time amassing its target of 3,300 troops. Confronted

[13] Report on Darfur (2005, p. 148).
[14] S/2005/68 (February 4, 2005).
[15] S.PV/5120 (February 8, 2005).
[16] S.PV/5125 (February 16, 2005).
[17] Scheffer (1999); Schabas (2004).
[18] E.g. Kelley (2007).
[19] The American Service-Members' Protection Act (2002).

with more negative news, the UNSC undertook two actions on Darfur that were not related to an atrocities investigation.

First, on March 29, 2005, the UNSC imposed a system of military and financial sanctions against those responsible for the violence in Sudan.[20] Acting under Chapter VII of the UN Charter, the UNSC decided to establish a Committee that would approve the government's movement of military equipment and supplies into Darfur and designate people or entities responsible for the violence in Darfur. Then, the UNSC decided that "[a]ll States shall freeze all funds, financial assets and economic resources that are on their territories on the date of adoption of this resolution or at any time thereafter, that are owned or controlled, directly or indirectly, by such persons...." In the presence of Secretary-General Annan, 12 UNSC members voted in favor of this step, with Algeria, Russia, and China abstaining.

In the background, diplomats continued to work relentlessly on the issue of atrocities. As set forth in Chap. 7, the United States overcame its opposition towards the ICC only after France accepted jurisdictional restrictions on the ambit of the investigation, which were based on the UNSC's precedent in peacekeeping missions in Liberia (Step 3).

Hence, on March 31, 2005, 2 days after it imposed sanctions on the government of Sudan, the UNSC also authorized the ICC to investigate the atrocities committed in Darfur. As a consequence of this decision, which was taken through the three step institutional process and the explanations presented in this book, ICC Prosecutor Moreno-Ocampo could investigate and request an arrest warrant for the President of Sudan, even though Sudan was not a party to the Rome Statute.

8.3 Theoretical Implications

The conclusions of this book may be disappointing. Not only does the book deal with the dark topic of atrocities, but the research behind the book points to an entrenched inability of the UNSC to create more investigations or to prevent mass atrocities. After all, victims of atrocities and the international community cannot reasonably rely on a three step procedure, which has so far worked in 11 out of 92 instances. However, the book offers four theoretical observations that can hopefully improve the general understanding of international institutions and of the UNSC system on atrocities investigations, thereby concluding on a more positive note.

As explained in Chap. 4, the three step procedural sequence of the UNSC's decision-making process lends itself to specialized expertise. The role of diplomats, the reliance of third-party commissions and the use of precedent all indicate how such expertise has an important role in international affairs and within the UNCS, which is considered one of the toughest real-politik international institutions. In dealing with atrocities, the UNSC members lack a clear definition of atrocities, access to reliable information, and the capacity to effectively deal with such events. The

[20] S/RES/1591 (2005).

UNSC members also care about the UNSC's reputation and try to avoid the negative externalities associated with false positives (i.e. create an investigation for facts that are later proven not to be atrocities) and false negatives (i.e. fail to create an investigation for true atrocities). As illustrated through the previous Chapters, to navigate through these perilous decision-making straits, the UNSC members rely on specialized expertise in each of the three steps of the process.

The observation that specialized expertise matters should give us pause. It illustrates that the main question posed by this book can be reversed. Instead of asking why the UNSC created an investigation into 11 of the 92 states that have experienced atrocities, one can also ask why the UNSC did not avoid creating an investigation into these 11 instances of atrocities. As the case studies in prior Chapters indicate, many UNSC member states were lukewarm towards some of these atrocities investigations (e.g. the United States in Darfur). Yet, in these cases the political preferences of the UNSC member states caved in when faced with opposing views from diplomats, third parties and precedent. In Darfur, the recommendations of the commission of inquiry and the precedent in favor of an investigation shifted the preferences of the United States, thereby adding Darfur to the list of 11 investigations. Per the predictions of this analysis, the UNSC members relied on and were influenced by the three forms of professional expertise. It thus appears that the UNSC does not avoid an investigation when the professional expertise of diplomats, third party commissions and precedent points towards an investigation.

The reliance on professional expertise further indicates that such expertise within international institutions matters. In doing so, it follows the lead of the literature on epistemic communities, which argues that uncertainty over complex or technical issues often leads to the rise of expert groups with important political power.[21] This book thus illustrates that knowledgeable individuals may carry disproportionate influence to the power of their state within an institution. Colin Keating's example is instructive. While the permanent representative of New Zealand, Keating used his legal skills and training to steer the UNSC towards the creation of the ICTR, which should not have been the case if it relied on New Zealand's influence within the UNSC in any other terms. It further describes how choices of institutional design, such as the use of procedural rules, the mandate of a third party and the reliance on precedent, can also influence the decision-making process. This can be illustrated again through the creation of the ICTR. In that case, as explained in Chap. 7, the effect of the ICTY's precedent on the creation of the ICTR exceeded the influence exerted by many UNSC member states. By introducing the role of professional expertise at the UNSC, this book provides one more building block to understanding international organizations.

Beyond the role of professional experience, this book illustrates why all studies on the UNSC can benefit from turning to the micro-dynamics of the UNSC's work. Instead of, for example, focusing on peacekeeping by looking at the target state and other variables unrelated to the UNSC, peacekeeping studies may benefit from an appreciation of the decision-making patterns at the UNSC. The answer, for example,

[21] Haas (1992); Adler and Haas (1992).

to why a 45,000 force rather than a 90,000 force is authorized for a particular mission may have as much to do with intra-UNSC bargaining, as it does with concrete needs on the ground. Similar observations can be made for those studies that examine the UNSC's practice on sanctions, diplomatic missions, humanitarian aid or authorizations for the use of force.

This book, furthermore, indicates that commentators evaluating the success of an international investigation have to take into consideration the political dynamics at the UNSC at the moment the decision to begin an investigation is made. The significance of these dynamics on the success of the investigation has, thus far, been overlooked. Snyder and Vinjamuri, for example, measure the use of international trials in an empirical study of 32 civil wars.[22] They find that international trials (i.e. the former Yugoslavia and Rwanda) had no effect on reducing worldwide atrocities or imposing any form of deterrence, but that they have caused a domestic backlash in Serbia and Croatia. Contrary to the spirit of these findings, Akhavan presents three case studies (Cote d'Ivoire, Uganda, Darfur) in which the presence of an international tribunal has improved—rather than impeded—peace and stability.[23] In a similarly positive examination of international trials, Nettelfield demonstrates that the creation of the international court for the former Yugoslavia was strongly related to the growth and success of the political order in Bosnia.[24] The above evaluations, however, miss the influence that the dynamics behind the UNSC political decision to create an investigation have on the success of an investigation. One should not, for example, comment on the ICC's investigation into Sudan without appreciating that the political dynamics at the moment it was initiated could not have supported a stronger, more powerful investigation. The President of Sudan, Omar al Bashir, remains at large not because of the ICC's failure, but because the UNSC members could only agree on a toothless investigation.

The past Chapters have, furthermore, underscored the deep divergence between the reasons for (a) why investigations ought to be created and (b) how they are actually created.

As of now, there have been a large number of writings on *why* and *when* there *ought* to be international atrocities investigations. Some argue that international criminal courts are particularly adept at dealing with perpetrators of atrocities, they deter future conflict and they promote the rule of law.[25] Others argue that such trials may be successful as a tool for peace building.[26] A third group contends that these trials help the healing process of those that survived the atrocities and contribute to the reconciliation of the affected communities.[27] Additionally, trials are seen as fundamental to the promotion of the rule of law. Trials should thus take place after any atrocity has been committed, and particularly, when local authorities are unwilling

[22] Snyder and Vinjamuri (2003).

[23] Akhavan (2009).

[24] Nettelfield (2010).

[25] Akhavan (2001); Roth (1998); Orentlicher (1991).

[26] Snyder and Vinjamuri (2003); Elster (1998); Nino (1996).

[27] Minow (1998); van Zyl (2002).

or unable to conduct proper domestic investigations in line with international legal standards.[28] Others, however, tend to be more cautionary. They contend that politicians rather than lawyers should conduct these investigations, and that the investigations should take place after peace has been secured, when they do not risk upsetting the domestic balance of power and when there are no parties likely to disrupt the peace (i.e. spoilers). They also expect the international community to have a strategic engagement with these courts, trying to use them to its benefit and not for the promotion of abstract values such as accountability.[29]

The UNSC's political decisions behind the creation of international investigations cannot be squared with these answers. Deterrence, for example, does not come into play during the decision-making bargains at the UNSC, as the UNSC reacts to atrocities already committed. There is little evidence that the UNSC considers these investigations as part of the peace building process, since they usually created after at least a tenuous peace has been accomplished. While some diplomats and countries at the UNSC have a keen interest on the victims of the conflicts, the debates on the creation of an atrocities investigation generally focus more on the power of the perpetrators than justice for the victims. Similarly, there is no reason to believe that the UNSC's stance towards investigations is influenced by the ability or determination of governments to conduct their own investigations or local balances of power among the warring factions. Of course, there is evidence that all of the above reasons influence the decisions of the UNSC. But, they are not dispositive or even central for the UNSC when it comes to making its final decision.

The disconnect between the aspirational goals of international criminal justice and the realities at the UNSC remains significant. Perhaps, because there is a lack of appreciation for the difficulty of creating an UNSC investigation, international atrocities investigations are constantly criticized as falling short of aspirational standards. Hopefully, this book contributes to changing this perception by aligning normative expectations with the facts on the ground.

8.4 Policy Implications

Ever since the Libya referral to the ICC, in 2011, the field of international atrocities investigations has been in retreat. The attempts of the international community to create accountability mechanisms have failed in Syria, Sri Lanka, and South Sudan. The ICC's attempts to prosecute cases in Kenya, the Democratic Republic of the Congo, and the Central African Republic have had, at best, mediocre results. Even civil society has started doubting the role of justice in the area of conflict resolution. Conflicts, however, remain ever active. Yet, many UNSC members have adopted foreign policies that leave little room for justice initiatives. Recent events in Syria are especially telling. After years of civil war, very few UNSC members (e.g.

[28] Bassiouni (1996); Minow (2000).

[29] Abbott (2009); Kissinger (2001); Snyder and Vinjamuri (2003).

France, Guatemala) have a foreign policy that includes an immediate resort to justice.[30] Few other states (e.g. the United States, the United Kingdom) have debated the resort to justice as a reconstruction tool, after the conflict settles.[31] At the same time, several states, such as Russia and China, remain openly hostile to the idea of justice ever being used.[32]

Yet, despite all these bad facts, the UNSC's reliance on a three step decision-making process allows ample room for human rights practitioners and proponents of international criminal justice to improve the prospects of international criminal justice in previously untested ways. In the first step of the UNSC deliberations, the human rights community can rally diplomats to the cause of specific atrocities. By providing information on the atrocities and ideas on the role that justice can play in a local conflict, human rights practitioners can influence the thoughts of UNSC diplomats. This potential is particularly true for the diplomats of the smaller non-permanent members, who usually have more discretion towards atrocities unrelated to their home state and are also less informed about these atrocities.[33]

When the UNSC members start their deliberation, the human rights community can further support the cause of justice by providing the UNSC with evidence of atrocities and proposals to use justice in flexible ways that address the reluctance of certain UNSC members. Additionally, the human rights community can support the work of the commissions of inquiry. For example, invaluable help can be given to the evidence collection work of these missions through data management programs and liaisons with victims and witnesses on the ground.

Finally, when the UNSC is debating a resolution for investigations, the human rights community can also supply drafting arguments to the states that are working on such resolutions. So far, the human rights community has only criticized the drafts produced at the UNSC, whereas constructive engagement would likely produce better resolutions.

It is noteworthy that all of the atrocity investigations authorized by the UNSC and discussed in previous Chapters of this book were undertaken after some prescient individuals or groups from the human rights community took initiatives such as those described above. Cherif Bassiouni, for example, created a data collection system for the commission of inquiry into the former Yugoslavia. Humanitarian workers were instrumental in collecting testimony for the commission of inquiry into Darfur. Human rights NGOs kept the western countries appraised of the atrocities in Sierra Leone, even as the Kosovo campaign had captivated the UNSC's attention. This book indicates that, rather than allowing such support to take place on an *ad hoc* basis, the human rights movement would increase the prospects of success

[30] Interviews: 1, 3, 10, 14, 20.

[31] Interviews: 1, 2, 3, 4, 9, 14.

[32] Interviews: 1, 2, 3, 10, 14, 20.

[33] In dealing, for example, with the 1994 atrocities in Rwanda, Colin Keating, Ambassador from New Zealand, and Karel Kovanda, Ambassador from the Czech Republic, had more discretion than their P5 colleagues. See Interview 7; Kovanda (2010).

for international atrocities investigations by systematically helping the UNSC members in its three step decision-making steps.

Finally, it is worth considering if and how these three steps of the decision-making process can be improved. In the first step, diplomats may become more effective in dealing with issues of international criminal justice if they have substantive knowledge of international criminal law. Keating and Shaffer, for example, who were instrumental in the creation of the ICTY and the SCSL, respectively, were both lawyers with a focus on human rights. Such training is likely to be helpful in differentiating the instances in which an atrocities investigation is legally feasible. It may also be helpful in getting other states and actors within a state to defer to the diplomat's judgment.

In the second step, third party commissions may be more useful if they are created faster and more frequently. In the current scheme, the UNSC members have to deliberate on atrocities and then agree to create a commission of inquiry. This takes time and carries the risk that evidence gets destroyed or altered and perpetrators flee. To minimize such delays, the UNSC may consider relying on the more frequent investigations of the UN Human Rights Committee. Alternatively, and more realistic due to the politicized nature of the latter committee, the UNSC may rely on investigations created by the Secretary-General, if he or she were to create such investigations soon after an allegation of atrocities. While maintaining their legitimizing role, such investigations would cut the delays in the UNSC decision-making process, potentially rendering investigations a more effective tool for justice.

Finally, the third-step of the decision-making process can be improved if UNSC members expand the ambit of precedent they consider. So far, the case studies indicate that UNSC members look to prior UNCS precedent. But, these same states are members to a multitude of other international organizations and conventions, such as International Court of Justice, the WTO, the Convention on the Law of the Sea and the New York Convention on Recognition and Enforcement of Arbitral Awards. By looking at the work of these international bodies, rather than focusing only on the previous work of the UNSC, the UNSC members are more likely to find precedent that allows them to bargain towards a common outcome.

8.5 Conclusion

Despite the above potential improvements, this book makes clear that, as in all aspects of human life, there is no absolute justice. By design, the UNSC is unable to engage with every conflict. As all those who were interviewed for this book acknowledged, the UNSC is not going to create investigations into numerous atrocities. However, short of creating a replacement, the human rights community and supporters of international justice have to work with the UNSC to promote their causes. By clarifying how the UNSC works, this book seeks to help in this important step.

References

Interviews

Interview No. 1; Interview Details: Diplomat from United Kingdom, New York (June 13, 2013).
Interview No. 2; Interview Details: Member of UN Office of Legal Affairs, on Skype (June 24, 2013).
Interview No. 3; Interview Details: Diplomat from the United Kingdom, New York (July 11, 2013).
Interview No. 4; Interview Details: Diplomat from United States, New York (July 12, 2013).
Interview No. 7; Interview Details: Diplomat from New Zealand, New York (August 23, 2013).
Interview No. 9; Interview Details: Diplomat from United Kingdom, New York (June 13, 2013).
Interview No. 10; Interview Details: Diplomat from France, New York (October 7, 2013).
Interview No. 14; Interview Details: Diplomat from United States, Washington, D.C. (December 4, 2013).
Interview No. 20; Interview Details: Diplomat from Guatemala, New York (January 21, 2014).

Books and Articles

Abbott, Kenneth. 2009. International Relations, International Law and the Regime Governing Atrocities in Internal Conflicts. *American Journal of International Law* 93 (2): 361–379.
Adler, Emanuel, and Peter M. Haas. 1992. Conclusion: Epistemic Communities, World Order, and the Creation of a Reflective Research Program. *International Organization* 46 (1): 367–390.
Akhavan, Payam. 2001. Beyond Impunity: Can International Criminal Justice Prevent Future Atrocities? *American Journal of International Law* 95 (1): 7–31.
———. 2009. Are International Criminal Tribunals a Disincentive to Peace? Reconciling Judicial Romanticism with Political Realism. *Human Rights Quarterly* 31 (3): 624–654.
Bassiouni, M.Cherif. 1996. Searching for Peace and Achieving Justice: The Need for Accountability. *Law and Contemporary Problems*: 9–28.
Elster, Jon. 1998. Coming to Terms With the Past: A Framework for the Study of Justice in the Transition to Democracy. *Archives of European Society* 39 (1): 7–48.
Haas, Peter M. 1992. Introduction: Epistemic Communities and International Policy Coordination. *International Organization* 46 (1): 1–35.
Kelley, Judith. 2007. Who Keeps International Commitments and Why? The International Criminal Court and Bilateral Nonsurrender Agreements. *American Political Science Review* 101 (03): 573–589.
Kissinger, Henry A. 2001. The Pitfalls of Universal Jurisdiction. *Foreign Affairs* 80: 86.
Kovanda, Karel. 2010, August. The Czech Republic on the UN Security Council: The Rwandan Genocide. *Genocide Studies and Prevention* 5 (2): 192–218.
Minow, Martha. 1998. *Between Vengeance and Forgiveness: Facing History After Genocide and Mass Violence*. Boston: Beacon Press.
———. 2000. The Hope for Healing: What Can Truth Commissions Do? *Truth v. justice: The morality of truth commissions* 235: 241.
Nettelfield, Lara J. 2010. *Courting Democracy in Bosnia and Herzegovina*. Cambridge: Cambridge University Press.
Orentlicher, Diane. 1991. Settling Accounts: The Duty to Prosecute Human Rights Violations of a Prior Regime. *The Yale Law Journal.* 100: 2537.
Roth, Kenneth. 1998. The Court the U.S. Doesn't Want. *NY Review of Books* 45 (18): 45–47.
Santiago, Nino Carlos. 1996. *Radical Evil on Trial*. New Haven: Yale University Press.

Schabas, William A. 2004. United States Hostility to the International Criminal Court: It's All About the Security Council. *European Journal of International Law* 15 (4): 701–720.
Scheffer, David J. 1999. The United States and the International Criminal Court. *American Journal of International Law*: 12–22.
Snyder, Jack, and Leslie Vinjamuri. 2003–2004. Trials and Errors: Principle and Pragmatism in International Justice. *International Security* 28(3, Winter): 5–44.
Totten, Samuel, and Eric Markusen, eds. 2006. *Genocide in Darfur: Investigating the Atrocities in the Sudan*. New York: Routledge.
van Zyl, Paul. 2002. Unfinished Business: The Truth and Reconciliation Commission's Contribution to Justice in Post-Apartheid South Africa. In *Post-conflict Justice*, ed. M. Cherif Bassiouni. Ardsley: Transitional.

News Sources

New York Times

Sengupta, Somini. *Americans Involved in Torture Can Be Prosecuted Abroad, Analysts Say*. The New York Times (December 10, 2014).

Government Documents

H.Con. R. 467—S.Con.R. 124 (July 22, 2004).
The American Service-Members' Protection Act (ASPA, Title 2 of Pub.L. 107–206, H.R. 4775, 116 Stat. 820, enacted August 2, 2002).

UN Documents

Reports

Report of the International Commission on Inquiry on Darfur to the United Nations Secretary-General pursuant to Security Council Resolution 1564 of 18 September 2004 (January 25, 2005).
S/2005/68, Report of the Secretary-General on the Sudan pursuant to paragraphs 6, 13 and 16 of Security Council resolution 1556 (2004), paragraph 15 of Security Council resolution 1564 (2004) and paragraph 17 of Security Council resolution 1574 (2004) (February 4, 2005).

Records of United Nations Security Council Meetings

S/PV.5120, Sudan (8 February 2005).
S.PV/5125, Sudan (16 February 2005).

Letters

S/2004/812, Letter from the Secretary-General to the President of the Security Council regarding the establishment of an International Commission of Inquiry for Darfur (October 4, 2004).

Resolutions

S/RES/1564, Sudan (September 18, 2004).
S/RES/1591, Sudan (March 29, 2005).

Index

C. Kaoutzanis, *The UN Security Council and International Criminal Tribunals: Procedure Matters*, Studies in Global Justice 20,
https://doi.org/10.1007/978-3-030-23777-6

MIX
Papier aus verantwortungsvollen Quellen
Paper from responsible sources
FSC® C105338
FSC
www.fsc.org

If you have any concerns about our products,
you can contact us on
ProductSafety@springernature.com

In case Publisher is established outside the EU,
the EU authorized representative is:
Springer Nature Customer Service Center GmbH
Europaplatz 3, 69115 Heidelberg, Germany

Printed by Libri Plureos GmbH
in Hamburg, Germany